Professional
Lighting
Handbook

Professional Lighting Handbook

Second Edition

Verne Carlson
Sylvia E. Carlson

Foreword by

David Quaid

Focal Press
Boston   London

Focal Press is an imprint of Butterworth–Heinemann.

Recognizing the importance of preserving what has been written, it is the ∞ policy of Butterworth–Heinemann to have the books it publishes printed on acid-free paper, and we exert our best efforts to that end.

Library of Congress Cataloging-in-Publication Data

Carlson, Verne.
    Professional lighting handbook / by Verne Carlson and Sylvia E.
Carlson ; with a foreword by David Quaid. – 2nd ed.
    p.   cm.
    Includes index.
    ISBN 0-240-80020-6
    1. Cinematography – Lighting.   2. Television – Lighting.
    I. Carlson, Sylvia.   II. Title.
    TR891.C37   1991
    778.5′2343 – dc20   91-16854
                                                 CIP

British Library Cataloging-in-Publication Data

Carlson, Verne.
    Professional lighting handbook – 2nd ed.
    I. Title II. Carlson, Sylvia E.
    778.5343

    ISBN 0-240-80020-6

Butterworth–Heinemann
80 Montvale Avenue
Stoneham, MA 02180

10 9 8 7 6 5 4 3 2 1

Printed in the United States of America

Contents

Manufacturers of Lighting Fixtures and Related Equipment

FIXTURES AND/OR BALLASTS

Arnold & Richter, K.G.
89 Turkenstrasse, 8 Munich, 13, FRG

Arriflex Corporation of America
500 Route 303, Blauvelt, NY 10913

Clairmont Camera, Inc.
4040 Vineland Ave., Studio City, CA 91604

Colortran, USA
1015 Chestnut St., Burbank, CA 91506-9983

Dedo Weigert Film GMBH
5 Rottmanstrasse, D-8000 Munich 2, FRG

Dedotech USA, Inc.
210 Westlake Dr., Valhalla, NY 10595

DN Labs, Inc.
2048 Midvale Dr., San Diego, CA 92105

(The) Great American Market
826 Cole Ave., Hollywood, CA 90038

Ianiro S.P.A.
Via Cermenati, 80, 00137 Roma, Italia

Lightmaker Company
(A Division of Camera Platforms International, Inc.)
28145 Avenue Crocker, Valencia, CA 91355

Lowel-Light Manufacturing, Inc.
140 58th St., Brooklyn, NY 11220-2552

Note: The above addresses are corporate and United States headquarters. Many companies have national and international branches and distribution centers too numerous to mention here.

LTM Corporation of America
11646 Pendleton St., Sun Valley, CA 91352

LTM France
102–104 Blvd. St., Denis 92400, Courbevois, France

Mole-Richardson Co.
937 North Sycamore, Hollywood, CA 90038

Panavision, Inc.
18618 Oxnard St., Tarzana, CA 91356

Strand Lighting, Inc.
1811 South Santa Fe Ave., Rancho Dominguez, CA 90221

Strand Lighting, LTD
Grant Way (off Syon Lane), Isleworth, Middlesex TW7 5QD, England

Strong Electric Corp.
87 City Park Ave., Toledo, Ohio 43697

Unilux, Inc.
290 Lodi St., Hackensack, NJ 07601

LAMPS

Duro-Test Corp.
2321 Kennedy Blvd., North Bergen, NJ 07047

General Electric Co.
Nela Park, Cleveland, OH 44112

GTE Sylvania
100 Endicott St., Danvers, MA 01923

ILC Technology
399 Java Dr., Sunnyvale, CA 94086

North American Philips Lighting Corp.
One Westinghouse Plaza, Bloomfield, NJ 07003

Osram Corp.
R. D. #3 Jeanne Rd., Newburgh, NY 12550

FILTERS

Eastman Kodak Co.
343 State St., Rochester, NY 14650

Gamcolor
The Great American Market
826 Cole Ave., Hollywood, CA 90038

Harrison & Harrison
677 North Plano St., Porterville, CA 93258-1797

Lee Filters LTD
Central Way, Andover Hampshire SP10 5AN, England

Lee Filters USA
1015 Chestnut St., Burbank, CA 91506-9983

Oleson
1535 Ivar, Hollywood, CA 90028

Rosco Labs
36 Bush Ave., Port Chester, NY 10573

Tiffen Filter Co
90 Oser Ave., Hauppage, NY 11788

GRIPS

Arnold & Richter K.G.
89 Turkenstrasse, 8 Munich, 13, FRG

Arriflex Corporation of America
500 Route 303, Blauvelt, NY 10913

Mathews Studio, Equipment, Inc.
2405 Empire Ave., Burbank, CA 91504

GENERATORS

Media Project
2029 Hill St., Santa Monica, CA 90405 (solar generators)

Foreword

When I was a young cameraman color film was slow (ASA 12), and lighting units, constructed of cast iron, were enormously heavy. The company I worked for traveled to location in a tractor-trailer truck that housed our normal complement of light: twenty 5000W spots; twenty 2000W spots; four 750's for close-ups; and literally thousands of feet of electric cable, plugging boxes, grip stands, and so on. Generators with a capacity of 1500 amps at 110 volts were rarely available at that time, so we got our power from banks of huge oil-filled transformers that followed us around by means of forklift trucks. The transformers were then hooked up to the main electrical yard outside the plant, and finally, to our plugging boxes — set-up after set-up. And the procedure was for modest industrial films. We never had enough light to cover true long shots. When we filmed in an ordinary house we had to contact the local electric company to have a transformer installed at the base of the nearest pole to our location, and wire into the house from that point. Selection of a lighting crew was based on muscles rather than aesthetics.

Today I could make the same films with a stationwagon load of equipment. Tape and film cameras are now lightweight, portable; films are both extremely fast and offer excellent reproduction; and there is a plethora of good lighting equipment. Today children in the elementary grades are completing sophisticated, high-quality film and tape projects and a person's physique or sex is no longer a barrier to participation in our industry — or our art. And it is an art, for it is still the control of light that delivers the shades and nuances of dramatic story and performance.

My own philosophy of lighting is simple: There is no such thing as film lighting or TV lighting, as some would have you believe. There is only good lighting and bad lighting.

Those who practice film lighting have always studied and tried to emulate the great masters of their craft. It was those masters who set the standard for producing three dimensions in a flat medium. The masters did not use formulas for backlighting. Often they separated their subjects from the background by what I refer to as *glowlight,* subtly painting an area of a slightly higher order behind their subjects to create separation. This method is analogous to the black-line lighting we use when photographing a beautiful piece of glassware.

Backlight is the one false note in any frame, unless it is motivated by a window behind the subject, a fire, the sun, etc. A blonde subject would automatically separate from a dark background and a brunette from a light one; there is no need for backlight in these situations. In my own case, the most frequent decision I make in lighting any setup is the use of backlight. I use it in the way I would take arsenic — hardly at all! Naturally, it is a given that the star of the show merits all the glamour that fine lighting can produce. I try to craft action that has the star move in a continuous shot, or turn from glowlight into a motivated, backlighted frame. The effect is like the sun emerging from behind a cloud.

I believe that television has been bogged down by formula, or three-point, lighting. In the early days of TV, the medium was so slow and contrasty that it was necessary to flood the set with illumination just to get an image; in addition, three-camera production makes clean, crisp lighting close to impossible. Unfortunately, this method has survived over the years, so today much of what is seen by the home viewer is merely a bright picture. I feel that formula lighting has robbed this marvelous medium of much of its aesthetic promise.

After screening a film, people often ask my opinion of the camerawork or the lighting. More often than not, I have nothing to say. I am not a critic, I'm a fan! Once the film has caught me, I am totally immersed in the story, characters, and ambiance of the production, and I am unaware of anything else. (However, with a bad film, I am excruciatingly aware of the work of all departments.)

With the above in mind, when I am called on to give lighting seminars at universities, professional film/video associations, and the like, I use only one teaching method: A film that was shot by me, or others, is transferred to video tape, preferably 3/4 inch. This tape is run on a suitable tape deck having the capability to start, stop, and pause. The sound is *turned off* to eliminate the distraction of the story line. Each and every scene is run, stopped, scrutinized, and assessed. It is best if the cinematographer, or videographer, who did the production is present to describe the thought process that produced the aesthetic result.

The advent of the VCR and the availability of thousands of feature films shot over the last century gives an unparalleled opportunity for the student or professional utilizing this method, to study the work of the masters of film and video.

By and large it is not where the lights are placed, but where they are not placed that is important. Black areas and shadows matter just as much as bright areas. I believe that if a set can be lit with one light, then one light it is — assuming, of course, that the one light meets all the requirements of the scene. And if two lights are what do it, then use two — keeping in mind that each additional light should enhance the purity of the single source, not degrade it with double shadows. I still use a truck full of lights when I deem it necessary, but the prime consideration of a lighting cameraperson is still to "keep it simple" no matter how many units are used. When I turn the set over to the director for shooting, and see units standing unused, I feel I have done my best — but if I find every single unit in use I get a sinking feeling that the lighting is complicated and somehow impure. Verne and Sylvia's *Professional Lighting Handbook* deals with the control of light. They tell in exquisite detail just how lighting equipment works and which piece of equipment is available to mold, to soften, to enhance, and, with colored gelatines, to tint the beam of light. Their latest handbook will aid both the beginners and the amateurs, still photographers, video lighting directors, theatrical lighting designers, film directors of photography, and their gaffers as well.

After reading the manuscript I have already put to work many "nuggets" of information that eluded me in the past.

David L. Quaid, ASC

Preface

The excellence of the technical apparatus in use for lighting today has been reached after many experiments — and failures — by innumerable scientists, technicians, and engineers. While it is true that the technologist and the builder hones and refines the tools and materials for the artist, the value of the instruments is only realized when an imaginative mind utilizes all the tools with skill and finesse.

The technique of effective lighting for film and video cameras requires a blend of science and art. Just as Michelangelo, Rembrandt, Picasso, and other masters needed knowledge of the materials they mixed, and of the tools they used in order to define line, texture, shape, and color, so indeed the lighting person of today must acquire a thorough familiarity with the instruments available when he or she is called on to "paint with light."

The authors wish to reemphasize the view that one's range of creativity is greatly expanded through knowledge of the tools and materials at one's disposal: The greater the command of the instruments, the broader the freedom to create. Mastering the equipment will enable an imaginative, artistic person to be creative — the resultant art will be more than apparent to the eye of the beholder, as well as to the creator, when the finished product is viewed on the screen or tube.

Acknowledgments

A note of thanks to the following people for their cooperation and assistance in providing information and technical data for this book: *Grant Loucks,* Alan Gordon Enterprises; *John Gresch,* Arriflex Corporation; *Denny Clairmont* and *Alan Albert,* Clairmont Camera Company; *David Maki,* Colortran USA; *Daniel Naum,* DN Labs, Inc.; *Dick Stockton,* Duro-Test Corp; *Don Adams,* Eastman Kodak Co.; *Jerry Linblad,* General Electric Co.; *Dedo Weigert,* Dedo Weigert Film, GMBH; *Joe Tawil* and *Andrea Tawil,* The Great American Market; *John Brennan,* GTE Sylvania Products Corp.; *H.K. Harrison,* Harrison & Harrison; *Andrea Molinari,* IANIRO S.P.A.; *Lynn Reiter* and *Richard Shaffner,* ILC Technology; *Ed Carlin* and *Ron Dahlquist,* Keylite PSI Rentals, Inc.; *David Holmes,* Lee Filters Ltd.; *Ross Lowell,* Lowel-Light Manufacturing, Inc.; *Gille Galerne* and *Herb Breitling,* LTM Corporation of America; *Ed Philips* and *Fred Farish,* Mathews Studio Equipment, Inc.; *Ty Braswell,* Media Project; *Warren K. Parker,* Mole-Richardson Co.; *Barry Stubblefield,* Oleson; *R.D. Liddle, Jr.,* Osram Corp.; *Jac Holzman,* Panavision, Inc.; *R.D. Anderson,* Philips Lighting Co.; *Stan Miller,* ROSCO Labs; *William Collier,* Strand Century, Inc.; *Gene Shaefer* and *John J. Burlinson,* Strong Electric Corp.; *Nat Tiffen,* Tiffen Filter Co.; *William M. Blethen,* Unilux, Inc.; and *Frank Valert, Larry Roberts, Lawrence Goldberg,* and, *Bruce Davidson.*

Introduction

The increasing—and heartwarming—acceptance of the *Professional Cameraman's Handbook* encouraged the decision to offer you another book. It covers professional video and motion picture lights and how to use them— how to set up lights, accessories and lighting equipment to realize their greatest potential. The more time and study spent on becoming familiar with lights and lighting equipment, the closer one will come to achieving the desired result.

This book is a practical "how to" guide, and is designed to be of value to both professionals and students. It can be consulted on the job for immediate assistance, and it can be studied at leisure as time is available. It is not our intention, as with the *Professional Cameraman's Handbook,* to favor or "sell" any item mentioned. Your comments and suggestions are, as always, more than welcome. It's great to hear from you.

Sylvia E. Carlson

PART I

Light Characteristics
and Lighting Fixtures

chapter 1

Elements of Light

Light is radiant energy, and our knowledge of it existed long before film and video were invented. Today, understanding the basics of radiant energy allows a lighting person to know when to use specific types of light sources, when to employ certain filters, when to select the proper type of film for the job, and how to read certain types of meters.

What we know about light and its related elements is the result of the collective efforts of international scientists and engineers. Science has settled on two complementary theories to explain the phenomenon of light. James C. Maxwell (1831–1879, Scotland) initiated the *electromagnetic theory*, while Albert Einstein (1875–1955, Germany) evolved the *photon theory*.

Briefly, the electromagnetic theory presents the view that *all* radiant energy travels as electric *and* magnetic waveforms and that our eyes register the impact of a small part of this radiation as light. On both sides of the visible spectrum are the invisible spectra. These comprise cosmic rays, gamma rays, x-rays, radar, FM, television, radio, power transmission, and the like. The photon theory of radiation sets forth the premise that "energy clumps" travel in straight lines and that our eyes register the impact of such radiation as light.

Both theories are valid. Maxwell's is effective when applied to the science of lamps, filters, and film, while Einstein's theory works when applied to such phenomena as photocells in light meters and radiation in x-ray tubes. However, it is Maxwell's electromagnetic theory that is most often used by those involved in lighting for motion picture *emulsion* and/or the video *target*.

1.1 EMULSION AND TARGET

In this text there will be continual reference to two base terms, *emulsion* and *target,* both of which are the prime surfaces of concern to the lighting person.

1.1a Emulsion

Emulsion is the term employed in the context of motion pictures. In a motion-picture camera, light rays enter the lens and are focused and registered on the film emulsion. Beyond this (after exposure and removal of film from the camera), other than for aesthetic recommendations and suggestions, the lighting person has no control over the emulsion's development at the laboratory, the making of prints, or the projection of the film on the screen.

1.1b Target

Target refers to the video medium. In a video camera, light rays enter the lens and are focused and registered on the face of the pickup tube, also called the *target*. (In the case of a color camera, the rays are divided and focused on two or more tubes.) Beyond this, the lighting person has no control over the image being converted to an electronic signal, which is then carried by wire to a monitor and/or recorded on tape. At either one of these two points, aesthetic recommendations and suggestions may be possible before the signal is transmitted over the air to home receivers, where it is then reconverted to picture.

1.2 THE ELECTROMAGNETIC SPECTRUM

Maxwell explains that there are many types of electric and magnetic waveforms, with frequencies varying in length, and these waves are present in power transmission, broadcast (shortwave, TV, FM, AM), radar (the longest), infrared, light, ultraviolet, x-, gamma, and cosmic (the shortest) rays. Light, however, is the only portion of the electromagnetic spectrum that is visible, and it travels at a speed of 186,282 miles per second (299,792.4 kilometers per second) in all directions as a transverse wave (Figs. 1–1 and 1–2).

In spite of their speed, lightwaves can be measured. Physicists deal with the length of the waves as angstrom units (Å) [named after Anders Jons Ångström (1814–1874, Sweden), noted for his spectrum analysis], but scientists use the metric *nanometer* (nm) as a unit of measurement. One nanometer is equivalent to ten angstroms. Often the term *millimicron* (μm) (one-millionth of a millimeter) is used interchangeably with nanometer — they are synonymous measurements.

When the energy in a light beam is measured, it is separated on an instrument called a *spectroradiometer*. Wavelengths, in and of themselves, have no color. However, when viewed through the spectroradiometer, a combination of the cones of the eye and the receptors of the brain enables

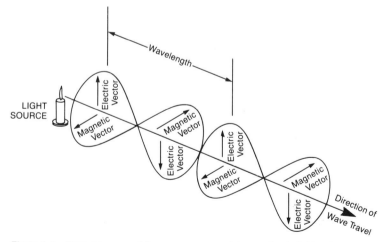

Figure 1–1 Transverse wave. A transverse wave contains an electric field and a magnetic field. Both fields radiate at right angles (called *vectors*) to the direction of light travel. This illustration shows only two of the field vectors out of the millions that are normally present in a single light beam.

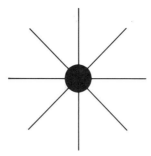

Figure 1–2 End view of light beam. A schematic end view of the line of travel of a light beam. The added vectors indicate the random electric and magnetic fields. If the millions of vectors in the light beam had been sketched in, the end view would appear as a solid black dot.

an individual with normal vision to perceive each wavelength as a specific "color."

NOTE: The cones and receptors of a totally *color blind* person will fail to register wavelength "colors" as anything other than gradations of gray. A *color-deficient* person will register some wavelengths as gray, but will see other colors. A few individuals have *monochromatic vision:* they perceive only one color.

Figure 1–3 illustrates how the various wavelengths of the visible spectrum appear as separate hues in the spectroradiometer. When not viewed through the spectroradiometer, all wavelengths are combined and light becomes desaturated; the color of each wavelength cancels out the color of all other wavelengths and light is perceived as color*less,* or white.

Since the frequencies of the wavelengths vary and can be viewed as colors on the spectroradiometer, the short wavelengths (violet, indigo, blue) are referred to as the *blue end of the spectrum;* the medium wavelengths (green and yellow) are called the *yellow-greens;* and the long wavelengths (orange, red) are know as the *red end of the spectrum.* These terms are commonly shortened to *blues, middles,* and *reds* to indicate the predominant color-rendering aspect of a light source.

Wavelengths shorter than violet are *ultra*violet *(ultra:* "above"); wavelengths longer than red are *infra*red *(infra:* "beyond"). Both are invisible to the eye, but lighting persons need to remember that the ultraviolet and infrared are not invisible to the film or target, and will often have an effect on the color rendition of film emulsion and/or the video target area (see Fixture Filters, Ch. 14).

1.3 CONTINUOUS SPECTRUM

When all the wavelengths of the visible spectrum are present in a light source, it is considered to be a light source with a *continuous spectrum,* and this is represented on a graph as an unbroken line. Graphs such as those in Figure 1–4 are called *spectral energy distribution* (SED) graphs. These are nothing more than diagrams that illustrate how the total energy in a particular light source — be it filament, arc, sunlight, or daylight — is divided among the wavelengths.

A lighting person will need to refer to an SED graph to determine if the light source it represents fits his or her requirements. When it does not, there are a number of options:

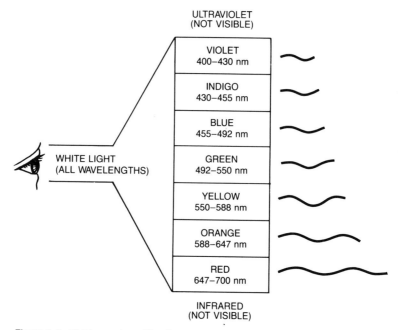

Figure 1–3 Visible spectrum. The shorter a wavelength is, the higher its frequency. The longer a wavelength is, the lower its frequency. Thus, the violet wavelength (400 to 430 nm), is the shortest and has the highest frequency. The indigo (430 to 455 nm) is longer and therefore lower in frequency. The blue (455 to 492 nm) is longer yet, so even lower in frequency. Green (492 to 550 nm), yellow (550 to 588 nm), and orange (588 to 647 nm) waves increase in length and decrease in frequency until finally reaching red (647 to 700 nm) which is the greatest in length and lowest in frequency in the visible spectrum.

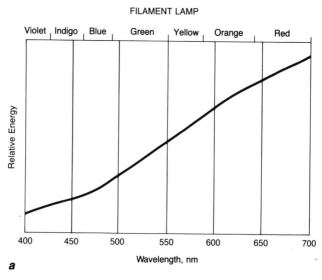

Figure 1–4 (*a*) SED graph of a continuous-spectrum filament lamp. Tungsten filament lamps are low in "blue" and relatively high in "red." (*b*) (facing page) SED graph of a continu-

DICHROIC LAMP

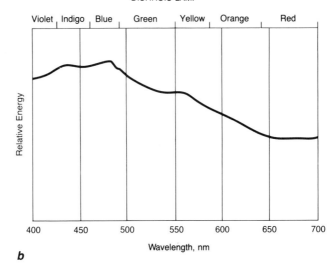

b

SKYLIGHT

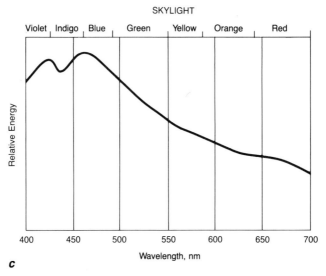

c

Figure 1–4 (*continued*)
ous-spectrum dichroic lamp. A dichroic-blue filtered light source is low in "red" and relatively high in "blue," as is skylight; it is used to supplement daylight lighting. Note its similarity to Fig. 1–4(*c*), natural skylight. (*c*) SED graph of continuous-spectrum skylight. Natural skylight is relatively high in "blue" and very low in "red." Note the similarity of a dichroic-blue filter to it. In all SED graphs the horizontal base represents the wavelengths in nanometers. The left vertical side of the graph represents the relative energy of the wavelengths. Unless otherwise noted (e.g., that the measurement is to a definite scale), the height of each wavelength indicates its strength in relation to the other wavelengths in the spectrum.

1. Select a different light source, such as one that has a continuous spectrum.
2. When using film, select an emulsion compatible to the particular light source represented by the graph.
3. Filter the present light sources so as to bring the color temperature and continuous spectrum into balance.
4. Place a filter on the camera lens (which will achieve the same result as filtering the light source).

An SED graph with a continuous spectrum will indicate the relative strength of short wavelengths (blues) to the relative strength of long wavelengths (reds) for the light source it represents. It can be seen from Figure 1-4a that a filament lamp of a 3200K to 3400K (Kelvin) light source is high in the red end of the spectrum and low in the blue end of the spectrum. The lamp could be used on an interior lighting project but could not be used as a supplementary exterior light because it is not matched for daylight.

Conversely, Figure 1-4b shows that a lamp with a coating that cancels out most of the red wavelengths and permits a great deal of blue to be transmitted (see Fixture Filters: 3200K to Daylight, Ch. 14) emits a light that resembles daylight. (Compare this with Fig. 1-4c, which is also high in blues and low in reds.) Thus, the graph reveals that the dichroic lamp (Fig. 1-4b) could be used to supplement exterior light but could not be used for interior work.

SED graphs are compiled by the lighting industry for each type of light source fabricated. This includes those that do not have a continuous spectrum (Fig. 1-5; see also Industrial HID Lamps, Ch. 10), as well as those that have a predominance of one or two wavelengths over and above the others (Fig. 1-6; see also The Fluorescent Lamp, Ch. 9). Manufacturers make these graphs available so that a potential user of the lamp can "see" the spectral characteristics of a given light source.

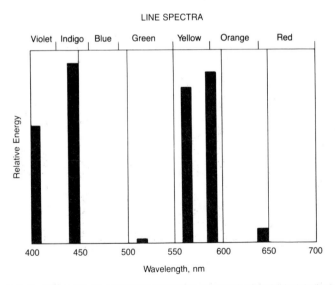

LINE SPECTRA

Figure 1-5 SED graph: Line spectrum (HID lamp). The width of each block indicates the size of the spectroradiometer slit used in the measuring of that particular wavelength. The space between spikes indicates the absence of light rays.

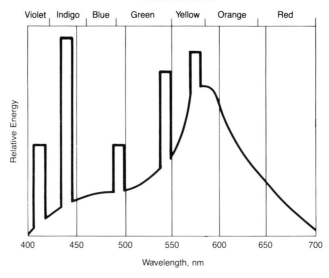

HYBRID SPECTRA

| Violet | Indigo | Blue | Green | Yellow | Orange | Red |

Relative Energy

400   450   500   550   600   650   700

Wavelength, nm

Figure 1-6 SED graph: Hybrid spectrum (standard fluorescent lamp). The continuous spectrum renders colors normal, but an overall hue of the spikes will predominate.

1.4 COLOR TEMPERATURE AND COLOR BALANCE

The human eye is color adaptive and will often accept some illumination as "white light," even though the light source that emits it does not have a continuous spectrum or is dominated by a few wavelengths. Unlike the eye, film emulsions and video targets are *not* color adaptive, and they will register color as they "see" it, in other words, as it really is, as either deficient or predominant in given wavelength "colors." For this reason, two additional factors must be taken into account: (1) the color temperature of the light source, and (2) the color balance of the emulsion or target face.

1.4a Color Temperature

The British scientist Lord William Thompson Kelvin (1824–1907, Ireland) was well-known for his work in electricity and thermal energy, and he devised a scale whereby the "color temperature" of a light source with a continuous spectrum could be measured. His scale (called the *Kelvin scale)* compares the *visual appearance* of a light source (candle, photoflood, arc, sky, etc.) with the emitted light of a "perfect black body" that has been heated.

NOTE: A *perfect black body* has an emissive power equal to its absorptivity. In other words, if it emits zero light and absorbs 100 percent light, it is a so-called perfect black body.

Of course, in the actual manufacture of light sources, no one heats up theoretical black bodies to determine that light source's color temperature. But to illustrate, consider the following:

At room temperature, the theoretical radiator, which is black, will emit no light. If a measure of heat is applied to it, the black body will turn a dull red; if more heat is added, it will shine orange; additional heat will cause it to glow white hot, then pale blue, and finally brilliant blue, as its highest temperature is reached. At the moment the color of the luminous radiator *visually matches* the hue of the light source with which it is being compared, the temperature of the glowing "black body" is measured, and that reading is noted in degrees Celsius (°C). The reading in Celsius is then converted to the Kelvin scale.

On Kelvin's thermometric scale, absolute *zero* is equivalent to −273°C, so in order to convert the Celsius reading to Kelvin, +273°C must be added.* The sum is then declared to be the *color temperature* of the light source, in degrees Kelvin (K). For instance, a black-body radiator heated to 2927°C is considered to have a color temperature of 3200K (2927°C + 273°C = 3200K). The term *degrees* is not used when referring to color temperature of a light source. It is simply called Kelvin or abbreviated to K.

Light sources are constructed in such a manner as to assure users−in combination with the use of instruments of measure−that the light sources are within ±50K in relation to tungsten filament lamps and ±500K in relation to "daylight-type" tungsten filament lamps with blue dichoic coatings. Again, it is important to remember that color temperature applies only to light sources that have a continuous spectrum. (The human eye has always been considered to have the ability to discern accurately a variance of ±200K, and so a 50K shift would not be perceived.) Figure 1-7 indicates color temperature ratings of familiar artificial and natural light sources.

1.4b Color-Temperature Meters and Possible Pitfalls

Some color-temperature meters are manufactured to measure the relative proportion of the radiation from two colors of the spectrum (blue and red), while others are capable of measuring the proportions radiating from three colors (blue, green, and red). While the latter type of meter is more accurate, neither instrument is perfect when measuring predominant-wave or discontinuous light sources (see The Fluorescent Lamp and/or Industrial HID Lamps, Chs. 9 and 10, respectively), which are rated with a correlated color temperature (CCT). Most CCT light sources are classified as "warm" or "daylight," which are their *apparent* color temperatures and refer only to the *visual appearance* of their light, not to the *actual* color temperature.

In rare instances, a color-temperature meter aimed at a fluorescent warm or "daylight light" source, such as high-pressure sodium, metalhalide, or a white mercury, will indicate a Kelvin rating compatible with the emulsion or target (see Color Balance, following). However, because that light source lacks a continuous spectrum, it will create havoc with the emulsion, which is not adaptable. Heavy filtering is necessary. This often isn't discovered until after the film has been shot and is being viewed in the screening room. When working with video, the off-color results could be mistakenly seen as an electronic malfunction. Watch out for this.

1.4c Color Balance

Film Once again, emulsion does not adapt to light source changes as the human eye does. For that reason, color film manufacturers balance their emulsions on film stocks for either interior or exterior use and mark them: "balanced for light of 3200K," or "balanced for light of 3400K," or "balanced for light of daylight quality (5500+K)."

The phrase *balanced for light of* _____ refers to the optimum color rendition of that particular emulsion when it is subjected to a specific color

---

*Absolute zero is a specific measurement used in physics to denote the temperature at which all molecular movement ceases (−273°C). Color temperatures were originally expressed and are still expressed in terms of degrees on this Absolute (or Kelvin) scale.

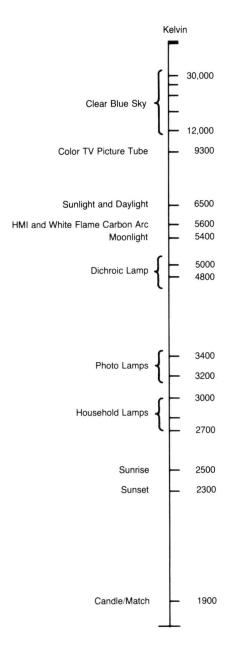

Figure 1–7 Samples of color temperatures.

temperature (3200K, 3400K, or daylight 5500+K) that has a continuous spectrum.

To achieve the best results when shooting interiors in color, an emulsion should be used that has been balanced for either 3200K or 3400K light sources. However, it is not necessary to use only 3200K light sources with 3200K balanced film, or only 3400K light sources with 3400K balanced film. These two different Kelvin temperatures can be safely mixed because film and the eye can tolerate a great deal of Kelvin difference. It is unnecessary to replace a 3400K light source, for example, simply because the emulsion in use is balanced for 3200K, or vice versa.

EXAMPLE: Consider the following illustration. Voltage on most studio stages is constant, with only a variable of ±5 percent, but on many locations where electricity is tapped from the main lines, there might be surges of power that increase or decrease input by as much as 20 percent. For every 1 volt in *excess* of the voltage rating of the lamp, there is an increase of 10 Kelvin; for every 1 volt *below* the voltage rating of the lamp, there is a corresponding decrease of 10 Kelvin. Therefore, if the voltage to a 3200K lamp rated at 120 volts rises to 140 volts, the lamp will have a color temperature of 3400K, but if the voltage drops to 100 volts, the lamp's color temperature will be 3000K. (The only exception to this is the HMI arc; see The HMI Lamp, Ch. 8.) If film stock had no "tolerance range," it would be impossible to shoot pictures, but in this case the variance is acceptable.

This does not mean that color temperature should be ignored; it does mean that a few hundred Kelvin plus or minus is no excuse for relamping an entire set because "We can't shoot unless it's 3200K exactly."

Color temperature differences *are* extremely important when an emulsion balanced for interiors (3200K to 3400K) is to be used in filming exteriors. Outdoor color temperatures range from 5000+ to 30,000+K. In this case the camera lens must be filtered to withhold the predominantly blue end of the spectrum. A no. 85 filter converts the 5500+K to 3400K; an 85B filter converts the 5500+K to 3200K.

Neutral density (ND) filters may be required on a lens in addition to the conversion filter to compensate for strong exterior light. Unlike conversion filters, they do not affect color temperature (see Fixture Filters, Ch. 14).

When an emulsion balanced for daylight (exteriors; approx. 5500+K) is used for filming interiors, either the lamps used must be converted to daylight color temperatures (5500+K) or the *lens* itself must be filtered to bring the *film* into balance with interior light sources.

NOTE: To use daylight film stock with 3200K lights requires the placement of an 80A filter on the lens in order to convert the color balance of the light to 5500K; to use the same film stock with light sources of 3400K requires the placement of an 80B filter on the lens so as to convert the color balance of the light to 5500K. Since the 80A filter also requires a 2-stop exposure compensation and the 80B a 12/3-stops exposure compensation, it can be seen that twice as much light must be employed to obtain the same aperture setting as would be required if using film balanced for 3200K to 3400K. Therefore, either a number of lighting units must be added to those already in use in order to bring up the light level or the filming must be done at wide-aperture settings with consequent loss of depth in the scene—or by adding a few fixtures and opening up the lens, which is a compromise between the two extremes.

Video The video target, like emulsion, also has limitations. Quite often, corrections within ±500K can be compensated for electronically, either in the camera itself, or in the control room. Color-balance problems should *not* be left to the engineer for a "save"; discrepancies are readily discernible on a monitor and need to be checked out immediately.

Video pickup tubes are balanced for optimum interior color rendition based on the fact that most studio light sources are rated at 3200K. Electronic cameras, as well as film cameras, utilize no. 85 filters and neutral density filters when used to telecast daylight exteriors where color temperatures are 5500+K. Some filters are "built-in" to the camera and can be dialed into position; when filters are not built-in, the filter must be placed on the lens.

Theater stage   The only theaters that utilize light sources of 3200K are those whose performances are frequently telecast or filmed. Most theater stages use lights with color temperatures ranging from 2000K to 3000K because they have a longer life. The lower-rated lamps do not require as frequent replacement as the higher-rated Kelvin units, and as a result they better meet low-budget needs. Moreover, gelatine filters of various hues, when placed over the front of a theater light lens, alter its color condition more, rendering the Kelvin even lower.

When working with electronic or film cameras on a theater stage where telecasting or filming is uncommon, the addition of auxiliary 3200K lighting units would raise the color temperature, which would render good skin tones for actors. As for the rest of the stage, the light "spill" from the auxiliary fixtures when mixed with that of the lower-rated theatrical units already on the stage will render a "tolerance range" acceptable to the target area and/or emulsion.

Of course, it is possible to use the existing units without adding higher-rated Kelvin units: An 82B filter could be placed on the lens, which would then raise all 2900K color temperatures to 3200K. The filter, however, requires a 2/3-stop exposure compensation. When using tape or the new fast negative, this is hardly a problem. Reversal, or slow negative, film stock may not be so easy to expose.

In some instances, lighting people have been known to ignore both the higher-rated Kelvin units *and* the compensating filter and let the laboratory correct for skin tones when printing.

chapter 2

The Fixture

In the early days of theater, indoor stages were lit by candlelight. In order to achieve an overall illumination, candleholders were placed in niches at different levels around the sides and tops of the proscenium, as well as at the footlights. Still later, candleholders were tied to ropes and hoisted into position. Between acts, the holders had to be recandled or the wicks trimmed, a time-consuming job.

Rising smoke from the flames was always a problem for the viewers; when the theater was drafty, the candles were most likely to blow out or the light flickered continuously, much to the annoyance of the audience. Because the level of illumination was so low, the actors had to wear costumes made of materials that would catch and reflect the light. Most of the time, actors would step toward the footlights in order to be seen as they delivered their lines, a tradition which, although it took away from the naturalness of the scene, was continued long after lighting methods were improved.

When oil lamps came into use, the units were so designed that a number of lighted wicks were fed from one dish of oil. Again, each "oil basket" was placed at a different level, but this time on movable racks as well as ropes. These portable "trees" at the sides of the proscenium were the precursors of the motion picture and TV light stands as we know them today.

Then came gaslight, and while gas was an improvement over candle and oil flame, especially with regard to the hazard of fire, it was still inferior to the invention of limelight.

Limelight used a mixture of oxygen and natural gas, had a filament of limestone (calcium oxide), and produced an intense light. In connection with the lens (see Fixture Lenses, Ch. 3), and reflector (see Fixture Reflectors, Ch. 4), the long-dreamed-of idea of using a fixture to emphasize and enhance *selective* lighting became a reality. Once the lens and reflector could be utilized in a housing, it was only a short time until the tilt-and-swivel aspect of a fixture came into being.

The use of limelight in the theater was phased out with the advent of the arc (see Carbon Arc, Ch. 7). Because emulsions were so slow in the early days of film, "interior" sets had to be constructed outdoors; in many instances, the sets were placed on revolving platforms so they could be turned to "follow the sun." To diffuse or soften the harshness of the sunlight or daylight, gauze was often stretched across the top of the set.

Although arcs had been in existence for some time, they were not used for filming until emulsions capable of handling the high actinic (green to ultraviolet) rays of the arc light were manufactured. Newer emulsions, coupled with filters that absorbed the high end of the spectrum (see Carbon

15

Figure 2-1 (*a*) The 18K HMI fixture. Unless properly cooled internally while in operation, its lamp has been known to warp reflectors, crack lenses, and vaporize interiors of the fixture, as well as to melt electrode tips. Courtesy of DN Labs, Inc. (*b*) (facing page) An 18K HMI fixture is fitted with foamed aluminum heat sinks and cooling airjets (not visible). Its modified parabolic reflector is designed with a highly polished cone at its center point. The cone reflects

Arc, Ch. 7), then made it possible for the fledgling film industry to abandon exterior sets and move indoors.

The use of incandescent lights to illuminate a set had to wait for many years after Edison's invention (see Filament Lamps, Ch. 6) because of the incandescent's low output.

Also, in the early days of video, sets had to be "flooded" with a "base light" in order to achieve an image on the target; then more lighting was added to emphasize light directions, moods, etc. This was an electronic problem, however, not a fixture deficiency.

Over the years, of course, lighting fixtures have been developed, designed, and redesigned to meet new challenges. Almost every day new products are brought to market to help solve illumination problems. How these present-day instruments are constructed, and the purpose they serve, is outlined on the following pages.

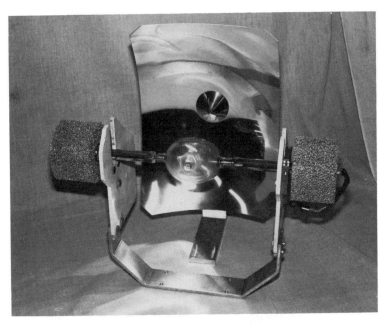

Figure 2–1 (*continued*)
any light emitting from the lamp to the outer surfaces of the reflector rather than back toward the lamp. Because of its configuration, light is re-directed from the reflector in parallel rays toward the fixture's lens; almost no light is radiated back through the lamp, which, in all fixtures, adds to additional heating and subsequent deterioration of the lamp. Courtesy of DN Labs, Inc.

2.1 HOUSING WITH ADJUSTMENT CONTROLS

A fixture housing is generally constructed of sheet steel and/or aluminum (sometimes of plastic), is light in weight, and is impervious to heat. It is fitted into a *yoke* — a Y- or U-shaped bracket of tubular or flat steel that has a spud or C-clamp at its center so that the fixture may be placed on a stand or hung from an overhead pipe. In addition, a lock knob on one arm of the yoke (either at the right or the left side) permits the unit to be tilted and secured at a desired angle.

2.1a Enclosed-Type Housing

While enclosed-type housings are often round (Fig. 2–1), some newer housing designs have taken on a "planes-of-angles" look (Fig. 2–2). An *enclosed-type housing* is designed as such because it is fitted with a condenser lens so that the unit's light source is surrounded by metal and glass (the lens). Three brackets are attached to the housing in front of the lens to hold scrims, filters, and other attachments (see Light Modifiers, Ch. 13 and Fixture Filters, Ch. 14). The rectangular section forming the base of the housing encloses a light-source socket and its reflector-holder, both of which are attached to an exterior adjustment control (see following) for focusing. Internal wiring and an exterior switch, cable, and plug (see The Powerline, Ch. 15) complete the unit.

A fixture of great intensity, such as one fitted with a carbon-arc light source (Fig 2–3; see also Carbon Arc, Ch. 7) is usually "double-walled";

Figure 2–2 12K HMI fixture. This unit contains a 12,000-watt lamp. Courtesy of Ianiro S.P.A.

Figure 2–3 Carbon arc fixture. The carbon arc is often designated by the amperage it draws, such as a 170 (obsolete) or a 225 Brute, or a 350 Titan. There are three different 225 Brute arcs that draw the same amperage, however they differ in weight and size: "Heavy Brute" (type 450), "Litewate Brute" (type 4951) shown, and "Baby Brute" (type 4611) almost obsolete. Courtesy of Mole-Richardson Co.

i.e., the exterior housing covers an interior metal liner with insulation between. This liner protects the outside wall from the great amount of heat generated by the arc flame; thus one can touch the unit and make adjustments without the danger of being burned. Both liner and housing are vented to permit the escape of heat through a "chimney" at the top. Viewing ports at the side and/or rear of the housing permit the monitoring of the burning carbons.

A standard incandescent fixture is not insulated; the liner and the outer housing are separated only by an air space, and both the liner and housing are vented. The exterior housing is either perforated or slotted for ventilation, and the opening is covered by metal channels. The channels serve a dual purpose: They absorb and disperse the heat given off from the light source and, since they cover the openings, they prevent unwanted light from spilling onto the set.

Access to the interior lamp socket and its reflector on most enclosed-type fixtures is through the front of the unit. The condenser lens and its three diffuser holders are an integral part of the hinged frame that make up the access door. There are units, however, with a door at the rear of the housing that tilts back for access to the lamp socket and its reflector. Access to a socket/reflector in a tiny fixture with a 250-, 100-, and/or 50-watt lamp is obtained either by swinging the top up and back or by removing the condenser lens.

2.1b Adjustment Controls

In enclosed-type fixtures (such as those shown in Figs. 2–1 through 2–9), the light socket and reflector are mounted together on rails that are mechanically connected to an exterior focus adjustment control knob. The focus knob at the front and/or rear base of the fixture is either a *paddle,* sometimes called a *rudder,* that rotates in a restricted arc, a *screw knob* that rotates clockwise and/or counterclockwise, or a handle that slides laterally.

Regardless of type, the purpose of the focus adjustment knob is to move the socket and its reflector in unison *toward* the condenser lens to achieve flood position or *away* from the condensor lens to achieve *spot* position.

2.2 DESIGNATIONS

Lighting units are generally considered to be "large" if they are equipped with either a carbon arc or an 18,000-, 12,000-, 6000-, 5000-, or 4000-watt lamp. They are designated "medium" if they are fitted with a 2500-, 2000-, 1500-, or 1000-watt lamp; "small" if they house a 750-, 650-, or 500-watt lamp. However, note that quite often a 1000-watt lamp and a 750-watt lamp will fit in the same housing; in that event, the size of the lamp inside the housing determines how the fixture is to be designated. When a unit accepts a lamp 200 watts or less, it is classified as a "tiny."

At the rear of the base of most large fixtures are recessed male pin-plug connectors that accept separate electrical power cables fitted with female pin-plug connectors. The male end of older cables has a full-stage plug (slowly being phased out), while newer cables have male pin-plug connectors at the feed end, where they connect to the powerline. Exceptions are the large HMIs and some 5K skypans; their cables are directly connected to the fixture.

Power cables of medium and small fixtures are directly connected to the on/off switch in the housing. At the feed end, many older cables are fitted with a half-paddle stage plug (fast becoming obsolete), while newer cables have a male pin plug. Many older *and* newer cables are also fitted with a twistlock plug, or an edison plug with ground, instead of a stage or pin plug

Figure 2-4 HMI arc. An HMI arc is referred to by its wattage and initials. For example, the 200 watt is called a "200 HMI," the 1200 watt is a "1200 HMI," and the 2500 watt is a "2500 HMI." However, the 4000 watt is called a "4K HMI" and the 6000 watt is called a "6K HMI," the 12000 watt is called a "12K." Courtesy of LTM Corporation of America.

(see The Powerline, Ch. 15). Tiny fixtures usually have an in-line switch in the cable instead of on the housing.

For ease of communication on a set, most incandescent fixtures are referred to by the wattage of the lamp contained within them. The symbol K, for kilowatt, is used to represent each 1000 watts of a lamp, e.g., 2K = 2000 watts, 5K = 5000 watts, etc. The K, for kilowatt, should not be confused with the K used to designate Kelvin, as explained in Chapter 1. In one instance the K stands for an electrical measurement, in the other, K stands for color temperature.

A fixture is also given a designation according to its amperage, size, shape, or effect. Figures 2–1 through 2–21 show some of the more popular lighting units used on film, TV, and theater stages and their common designations.

One manufacturer produces what is called a "baby line." Using a standard housing, the manufacturer has added a deepened base so as to accommodate larger lamps, sockets, and reflectors. By adding these modifications to the standard "studio-sized" line there is an increase in the wattage accommodation while retaining a smaller-sized housing. The "baby line" is often used on "location shoots," where compactness and weight are factors.

Obviously, the manufacturer's purpose is to accomplish the same intensity and coverage as "studio-size" fixtures without increasing the size of the housing. In practice, however, this is not the case. The "baby tener" and "baby junior" produce less intensity and coverage than do the comparable studio-sized fixture, whereas the "baby senior" produces slightly more than

Figure 2–5 A 10,000-watt incandescent fixture. A studio 10,000-watt fixture is either called a "10K" or a "tener." A 10K fitted with an extra-large condenser lens is referred to as a "big-eye." A baby-line unit is called a "baby 10K." Courtesy of Mole-Richardson Co.

its studio-sized counterpart. The "baby baby" produces about the same intensity, but has less coverage than a comparable studio-sized fixture.

2.3 ELLIPSOIDAL FIXTURES

The *ellipsoidal fixture* (in some areas called a "Focus Spot" or "Focal Spot"; see Fig. 2–10) is a unit that contains one or two plano-convex lenses (see Fixture Lenses, Ch. 3), and an ellipsoidal-type reflector (see Fixture Reflectors, Ch. 4). The combination of lens(es) and reflector provides a long throw and is more efficient for covering distances or projecting a pattern on a given area.

An ellipsoidal housing is also fitted with four framing shutters located between the light source and the lens(es). These framing shutters can be adjusted to interrupt the light beam, and they project hard, defined lines — to form a square, define a rectangle, or intersect just a small segment of the beam (Fig. 2–10, *insert*). The variations are almost endless. The front of an ellipsoidal snoot is also fitted with a holder for filter and/or pattern frames.

2.3a Ellipsoidal Adjustment Controls

Focus of the circular beam or projected pattern is achieved by sliding the front telescopic tube, which adjusts the lens(es) to the aperture. A screw-type knob locks the tube in place.

Intensity of the circle or projected beam can be further balanced (stronger or weaker) by adjustment of the lamp in relation to its reflector. If the reflector gets out of alignment, an egg-shaped or flattened arc will be

Figure 2–6 A 5000-watt incandescent fixture. A 5000-watt unit is either called a "5K" or a "Senior." Courtesy of Arriflex Corporation.

projected. A perfect circle can be formed again by adjusting the knobs located at the rear of the unit to reposition the reflector. On some ellipsoidals these are finger-adjustable; most require the use of a screwdriver.

2.4 FOLLOW SPOT

A *Follow Spot* (Fig. 2–11) is usually mounted on a stand, either portable or permanent. Unlike the ellipsoidal fixture, the follow spot is provided with horizontal framing shutters only (no vertical). The framing shutters can be used to intercept the light pattern from the top and/or bottom, or both, and they can also be tilted singly or together to give a 45-degree cutoff pattern.

The fixture has an on-off switch, a quick-focus handle, an iris, and a front housing, called a *boomerang,* which contains a set of filter holders. The filter(s) can be quickly inserted to intercept the light beam, which, of course, affects color, pattern, and/or fade effects. There is also a *douser* for complete blackout of the beam; on a large follow spot, the boomerang is mounted on the front of the unit.

Whenever it is necessary to use a follow spot on a location/remote shoot, the lighting person should check the unit to ascertain its type of light source and its color temperature, which can either be an arc (5500 + K) or an incandescent (2800K, 3200K, or 3400K). *It must be checked personally!* Never rely on "second-hand" information. Many follow spot operators (who use the unit daily) do *not* know. Since follow spots with arc light

Figure 2-7 A 2000-watt incandescent fixture. A 2000-watt fixture is called either a "2K" or a "junior," or it is simply called a "deuce." When a 1500-watt lamp is placed inside a 2K housing, it is called a "one-and-a-half;" sometimes a "light deuce." When a 1000-watt lamp is placed inside a 2K housing, it is called a "one-kay;" some people curse it as a "gutless deuce." A baby-line unit is called a "baby junior." Courtesy of Colortran, Inc.

sources often have to be used in conjunction with fixtures in the 3200K color temperature range, the arc's Kelvin rating must be lowered.

To accomplish the lowering of the color temperature on a follow spot from 5500 + K to 3200K, an 85B filter must be inserted into the unit's light beam. The 85B filter will convert the arc color temperature to one that will be compatible with other 3200K units. The resultant beam will appear to have a "color cast"; however, the emulsion in a film camera, as well as the target area in a video camera, will accept the rays as "white light" instead of unfiltered blue.

Some follow spots contain built-in filters in the boomerang; if this is so, it is a simple matter to pivot the filter, intercept the light beam, and convert the light to 3200K.

On a follow spot with no built-in filter, a large camera filter (85 or 85B) can be placed in the front holder to convert the arc's color temperature from a high to a low Kelvin rating. When an 85 filter of the proper size is not available, as an emergency measure, a filter that compares in color to an 85 filter will work. The comparison should be made by holding the two

Figure 2–8 A 1000-watt incandescent fixture. A 1000-watt fixture is either called a "1K" or a "baby." When a 750-watt lamp is placed inside a "baby" housing, it is called a "seven-fifty" or a "light baby." When a 500-watt lamp is placed inside a "baby" housing, it is either called a "five-hundred" or a "weak baby." Courtesy of Arriflex Corporation.

filters side by side and viewing them through the direct beam of the follow spot, *not* through any other artificial light source and *never* in daylight.

Should none of the foregoing be available, the combination of a light amber and a light pink gelatin may bring the color temperature down sufficiently. Although it is not the same as "white light," it is better than a washed-out blue, which would result if the arc were unfiltered. With these measures, the film laboratory or the TV technician in the control room will have a better chance of correcting for color imbalance.

2.4a Follow Spot Adjustment Controls

A follow spot concentrates a light beam into a very distinct circle and is capable of a long throw, the distance depending on the size of its light source. The projected circle is called a *spot*. Control of the spot is accomplished by sliding the lever located below the optical housing away from the operator for a small circle and toward the operator for a large circle. The projected spot can be further fine-focused to a hard, distinct circle by adjusting the knurled knob forward of the sliding lever. The size of the circle is brought down to a pinpoint by adjustment of the iris control.

2.5 MODULES

A *module* (Fig. 2–12) is constructed to accept a single PAR lamp, so-named for its parabolic-shaped reflector (see Filament Lamps, Ch. 6). The PAR

Figure 2–9   A 200-watt incandescent fixture. A 200-watt fixture with fresnel lens is called a "mini" or a "midget." However, a 200-watt open-face unit is referred to as an "inky-dink." An enclosed-type fixture with a 100-watt lamp is also referred to as an "inky-dink." An enclosed-type fixture with a 100-watt lamp is called a "dinky;" an open-face 100 watt is often called an "inkie." In either type unit, a 50-watt light source automatically classifies it as a "peewee." Courtesy of Mole-Richardson Co.

lamp has its own on/off toggle switch, its own built-in reflector, is nonfocusable, and is either size 36 or size 64.

Modules are often clustered in tiers of two or three lamps. The cluster is then placed within a bracket in order to achieve a greater illumination output. Clusters can be made up of 2-, 4-, 5-, 6-, 9-, or 12-lamp modules. Small units (1 to 4 lamps) have cables attached to the housing with male pin plugs attached to the feed end (older units will have a half-paddle stage plug). Large units (5 to 12 lamps) have pin-plug sockets on the housing that accept detachable cables. Cables on these larger units are fitted with female pin-plug connectors that insert into the housing and male pin plugs on the feed end (older units have full-stage plugs).

2.5a Module Adjustment Controls
Each tier of lamps can be swiveled independently of the holding bracket, which permits greater beam control of the unit. In many units the lamp can also be rotated for fine-beam control.

Various Shapes Obtainable by Sliding
Adjustable Built-In Framing Shutters.

Figure 2–10 Ellipsoidal fixture. Ellipsoidals are usually mounted on overhead grids, ante-proscenium beams, or balcony rails and are connected to outlets worked from dimmer boards. Very few ellipsoidals are fitted with on/off switches. If, however, a switch *is* used, it would be an in-line switch and never be in the housing. Courtesy of Oleson.

Many tiered units (6, 9, and 12 lamps) will have individual lamp toggle switches as well as master switches that control the illumination of the lamps in *each* tier. Other units have a master on/off switch that controls *all* the lamps in the unit.

2.6 OPEN-FACE FIXTURES

An *open-face fixture* (Fig. 2–13) is so designated because it is lensless. Its light source is visible and easily accessible. Light rays are directed by the shape of the unit's reflector (see Fixture Reflectors, Ch. 4). As a rule, an open-face fixture is more efficient as far as output per watt is concerned than an enclosed-type unit.

An open-face fixture is placed in one of five general categories depending on its purpose:

Figure 2–11 Follow spot. A follow spot concentrates a light beam into a very hard circle and is manufactured with a light source of either carbon arc, xenon arc, or incandescent (tungsten or tungsten halogen). Courtesy of Strong Electric Corp.

- Prime
- Fill (scoop and broad)
- Backing (pan and cyc strip)
- Indirect (softlite)
- Compact

2.6a Prime Fixtures

The housing of a *prime* open-face fixture is round, has no base, and is either fluted or perforated at the top to permit escape of the intense heat from the lamp socket. Additionally, much of the heat generated by the light source is dissipated at the open face.

Since a prime housing has no condenser lens, the light source is easily accessible from the open front; its reflector is stationary.

Some units have an on/off switch in the housing; most have the power cable attached to the housing with an in-line switch of the rocker or toggle type (see The Powerline, Ch. 15). At the feed end is either a twistlock plug or an edison plug with ground. Occasionally, a half-paddle stage plug is encountered, but that connector is fast being replaced by the safer pin plug.

For ease of communication on a set, a prime open-face fixture, like the enclosed-type, is referred to by the rating in wattage of its lamp, as well as the name given to it by its manufacturer. For example:

Figure 2-12 Modules. Modules are referred to by the number of lamps in the cluster. For example, a four-lamp cluster is called a "four-light;" a nine-lamp cluster a "nine-light;" etc. Courtesy of Mole-Richardson Co.

- A 2000-watt fixture (Fig. 2–13) is called a "2K," sometimes a "mighty" or a "multi-twenty," and is often equipped with a male pin plug at the cable's feed end. Older units can still be found with half-paddle stage plugs.
- A 1500-watt fixture is called a "fifteen-hundred" or a "1½K." It, like the others that follow, is usually fitted with male pin plugs or twistlock or edison connectors at its cable's feed end.
- A 1000-watt unit is called a "1K," or sometimes a "mickey" or a "multi-ten."
- A 750-watt unit is called a "seven-fifty."
- A 650-watt unit (Fig. 2–14) is called a "six-fifty," sometimes a "teenie" or a "multi-six."
- A 600-watt fixture is called a "six-hundred," sometimes a "teenie-weenie."
- A 500-watt fixture is called a "five-hundred."

Prime adjustment controls A focus control at the rear of an open-face fixture is either a *screw-knob* or lateral-moving *slider* handle. Occasionally, a focus control is found at the side of a unit. Focus controls move the lamp only; *toward* the stationary reflector to achieve *flood* position and *away* from the reflector to achieve *spot* position.

2.6b Fill (Scoop and Broad) Fixtures
Scoops and *broads* (Figs. 2–15 and 2–16) are utilized for soft fill light.

Fill adjustment controls Some scoops are focusable. A screw-knob moves the light source toward or away from the stationary housing that acts as the light source's reflector (see Fixture Reflectors, Ch. 4).

A single broad is nonfocusable. A multibroad (containing more than one light source) is focusable. As with a scoop, turning a screw-knob moves the light sources in unison toward or away from the interior housing.

Both the scoop and broad fixtures have attached cables, switches in the line, and either pin, twistlock, or edison (with ground) plugs at the feed end.

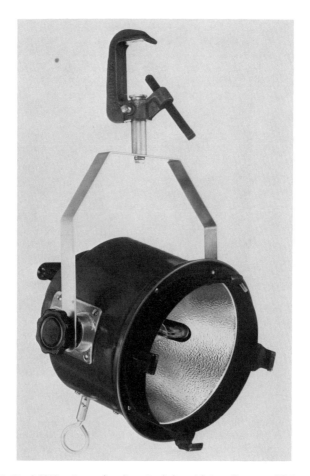

Figure 2-13 A 2000-watt open-face (tungsten-halogen) fixture. Courtesy of Colortran, Inc.

2.6c Backing (Pan and Cyc Strip) Fixtures

A *pan* (not shown) is used for lighting up scenery outside a window or door on a set. A pan is a circular unit with a slight lip around its perimeter. Laid flat, it appears similar to a frying pan without a handle. A detachable socket clamps to the lip and positions the lamp filament in the center of the pan.

Most pans have an on/off switch in the detachable socket. Some sockets have the cable attached, while others have detachable cables. A male pin plug is at the feed end. On older (and unsafe) models, a full-paddle stage plug will be found at the feed end.

A *cyc strip* (Fig. 2-17) is used to light cycloramas. A cyc strip ranges from a single unit to multiples of 12, with only one connector for all the lamps. There are no switches (the unit usually works off a dimmer), and there is a grounded plug at the feed end. Multiple units may have more than one circuit, so the entire unit will be operational if one lamp blows out.

Backing adjustment controls A pan is nonfocusable, as is a cyc strip.

Figure 2–14 A 650-watt open-face (tungsten-halogen) fixture. Courtesy of Colortran, Inc.

2.6d Indirect (Softlite) Fixtures

In a *softlite* fixture (Fig. 2–18), the light source is shielded; its beam is directed into the housing, as opposed to all other units, which utilizes the lamp itself for directing illumination toward the subject. The interior of a softlite housing is either of aluminum or baked white enamel and reflects a shadowless light (see Fixture Reflectors, Ch. 4).

While most indirect-type units have attached cables, others are 4- and 8-quartz-light units with male pin-plug sockets that accept detachable power cables. These larger unit cables are fitted with female pin-plug connectors and have pin plugs at the feed end. Older units may be around that have the obsolete full-paddle stage plug.

Indirect adjustment controls Indirect-type fixtures are nonfocusable; their intensity is controlled either by moving the unit toward or away from the subject and/or switching one lamp at a time on or off, or by lessening the intensity by adding scrims and diffusers (see Light Modifiers, Ch. 13).

2.7 COMPACT FIXTURES

The term *compact* encompasses a variety of fixtures originally intended for use on small location jobs. However, they are being used more and more on soundstages because they can be handheld for "quickie" shots, as well as taped and/or tucked into places ordinarily inaccessible to other types of units.

A compact fixture is so-called because of its small size, light weight, and

Figure 2-15 Scoop. A scoop is either bowl- or bell-shaped and utilizes the lamp as well as the housing for illumination. The housing also serves as the unit's reflector. Courtesy of Strand Lighting, Inc.

ease of handling. Its small configuration makes it easy to ship (usually in a "suitcase") and/or stow in the trunk of an automobile.

Figure 2-19 shows but one of many open-face compact fixtures. The Omni™ is focusable, has interchangeable reflectors (specular, diffuse, gold), interchangeable lamps of varying wattages (from 250 to 650 watts), and can be powered at 30 volts, 120 volts, or 240 volts AC/DC. Among other open-face units in the manufacturer's line (not shown) are the focusing Pro-Light, which can utilize interchangeable 250-watt 120-volt, 200-watt 30-volt, or 100-watt 12-volt AC/DC lamps, and the focusing i-Light, which can utilize interchangeable 100-watt 120-volt, or 100-watt 12-volt AC/DC 3200K lamps. The latter compact also has a built-in dichroic filter and four-leaf barndoor.

Figure 2-20 shows yet another type of open-face fixture. The non-focusable Stik-Up compact weighs 9 ounces with its power cord, and utilizes an interchangeable 100-watt 120-volt AC/DC lamp, or 100-watt 12-volt AC/DC lamp, or 100-watt 230-volt, AC/DC 3000K lamp. Since the unit is not intended for mounting on a stand, the Stik-Up lacks a yoke or spud, and is mounted into position by either tape, wire, alligator clip, or clothespin.

Figure 2-21 is a focusable fresnel fixture. The Pepper 100 (shown) can utilize interchangeable 100-watt and 200-watt 120-volt, AC/DC, 3200K lamps. Other fixtures in the compact Pepper line (not shown) are the Pepper 200 (interchangeable 100-watt, 150-watt, 200-watt, and 250-watt 120-volt AC/DC lamps), the Pepper 420 (interchangeable lamps of varying wattages from 100 to 420 watts powered at either 12, 24, 30, or 120 volts

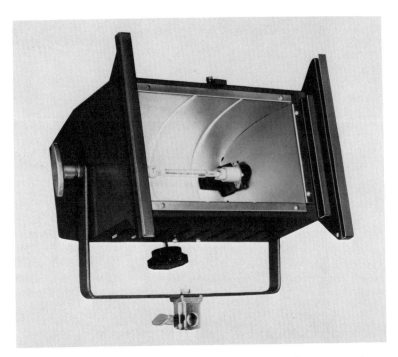

Figure 2-16 Broad. A broad is rectangular, has a reflector, and can utilize one or more lamps for illumination. It is fitted with front diffuser-holder brackets. Courtesy of Colortran, Inc.

Figure 2-17 Asymmetric 500-watt backdrop/cyclight fitted with gel holder. This particular unit is available in one; three; or four-light strip configurations. The yoke enables it to be either top- or bottom-mounted. Courtesy of Strand Lighting, Inc.

Figure 2–18 Softlite. Softlite units very early on acquired names that classify them quite well: A one-quartz softlite unit is called a "single soft"; a two-quartz unit is called a "half-gallon"; a four-quartz unit is called a "gallon"; and an eight-quartz unit is called a "two-gallon." Courtesy of Mole-Richardson Co.

AC/DC), the Pepper 650 (interchangeable lamps of varying voltages from 100 to 650 watts powered at either 12, 24, 30, 120, 220 volts AC/DC), and the Pepper 500/1K (interchangeable lamps of varying wattages from 100 to 1000 watts powered at either 120 or 220 volts AC/DC). Additional Pepper fixtures and accessories include a 400-watt 120-volt AC/DC soft light, a focal spot attachment with framing shutters and a pattern holder for projecting light and shadow patterns much like an ellipsoidal (but only for the 100, 200, and 420 fixtures), and miniature one-channel and three-channel 1000-watt-capacity 120-volt AC dimmers. Figure 2–22*a* is a focusable fixture with an external plano-convex lens and an internal meniscus lens. The Dedolight utilizes 12-volt AC/DC lamps in the following wattages: 100-watt, 50-watt, and 20-watt. Lamps are either powered through a standard 12-volt battery (camera, belt or automobile — via a cigarette lighter adapter) or through a fused (10-amp) power supply unit (Fig. 2–22*b*) that services four Dedolights. A selector switch at the side of the unit allows for utilization of AC power mains of either 110, 120, 220, 230, or 240 volts. Additionally each fixture can be separately switched to four positions: Off; Low (3000K); Medium (3200K); or High (3400K). (Because of the fixture's optical system, a 12-volt 100-watt lamp at High [3400K] is approximately equal to the luminous flux of a 300-watt fresnel). Cables intended for use with the power supply are fitted with three-pin cannon plugs, whereas cables intended for use with batteries are fitted with either four-pin or five-pin can-

Figure 2–19 The Compact Omni fixture. Courtesy of Lowel-Light Manufacturing, Inc.

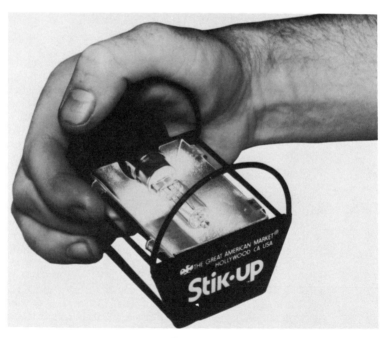

Figure 2–20 The Ultra-compact Stik-up™ Fixture. Courtesy of The Great American Market.

Figure 2–21 The compact Pepper 100 fixture. Courtesy of LTM Corporation of America.

non plugs (to match the battery outlet plug — *important to know*!) and in-line switches. A special power supply unit (not shown) has an additional 12-volt outlet that can be utilized to power a film or video camera or a fifth Dedolight. If powering a fifth fixture, unless the wire of its three-pin connector is fitted with an in-line switch, the Dedolight's plug must be inserted or pulled from the unit's receptacle when turning it on or off.

Additional Dedolight accessories includes a focusable projection attachment with framing shutters much like an ellipsoidal, an iris attachment, and a pattern holder for projecting light and shadow patterns, a flat holder with articulated arm for mounting the unit on a pipe or taping it to a wall or wedging it into a bookcase, as well as a swivel-jointed vacuum holder that allows a Dedolight to be attached to a wall, window, car hood, or any other flat surface.

Barndoors, scrims, gel frames, snoots, adaptors, holders, stands, etc., etc., are made for most of the fixtures mentioned. Detailed lists of accessories are available from the manufacturers.

2.8 PEANUT FIXTURES

A *peanut fixture* (not shown) is a tiny 25- to 100-watt lamp of short life and high intensity that can be taped to a slender or small object to give the illusion that the illumination emanates from the object. It is used mostly for effect lighting (see Using the Fixture, Ch. 17).

Figure 2–22a The compact Dedolight fixture. Courtesy of Dedo Weigert Film GmBh.

2.9 SPECIAL LIGHTING UNITS

2.9a Stroboscopic Units

Stroboscopic lights are used in conjunction with high-speed photography when a motion analysis is needed. For example, when a technique is used by a speed runner and one wants to "slow" the action for study, strobe lights will freeze each frame for that purpose. These lights will also eliminate blur, thus enhancing the aesthetic value of the images. Stroboscopic lights are frequently used in commercials to point up and/or magnify the action of drops of liquid.

The Unilux stroboscopic light (Fig. 2–23) requires a minimum power source of 208 volts AC, 50 or 60 Hz. The lamp pulsates anywhere from 48 pulses per second (pps) up to 2000 pps. In video applications, the camera records at either 60 frames per second (fps) or 120 fps only. Unilux's modular video strobe unit uses integrated circuitry: a power supply panel monitor, camera, and video disc. In film applications, a camera can run at speeds anywhere from 24 fps to 400 fps. A number of units plugged into a power panel can be synchronized with the camera once a sync cable (between the strobe power supply panel) and a sync control panel (that at-

Figure 2-22b The compact Dedolight Power Supply Unit. Courtesy of Dedo Weigert Film GmBh.

taches to the camera drive mechanism) are connected. The CCT of a Unilux strobe light is 6500K. A trained technician usually accompanies the unit.

The Clairmont stroboscopic light (Fig. 2-24) requires a minimum power source of 110 volts AC, 50 or 60 Hz. It was intentionally designed for table-top filming and to only work with certain cameras (35mm Arriflex 3, BL [models 1, 2, 3, and 4] Mitchell Mk 11, Fries high-speed, and the 16mm Arriflex SR) that have been special-wired by Clairmont to accept a pulse signal from the power pack to the shutter. Integrated with any one of those cameras, the lamp is capable of firing in sync at speeds ranging from 1 fps up to 120 fps (35mm) or 1 fps to 150 fps (16 mm). The CCT of a Clairmont strobe light is 7000K. A "power pack," which can be plugged into any ordinary household wall plug, is required for each fixture. A user's manual usually accompanies the unit.

Regardless of manufacturer, when using a strobe light it is necessary to use a special "strobe meter" in order to determine exposure. At 60 pps, or more, the strobe appears as a steady light and a reading can be obtained; at fewer pps the flashes are visible.

Care must always be taken that a stroboscopic unit, whether used with film or video, is not pulsed at less than 30 pps. A warning is appropriate on

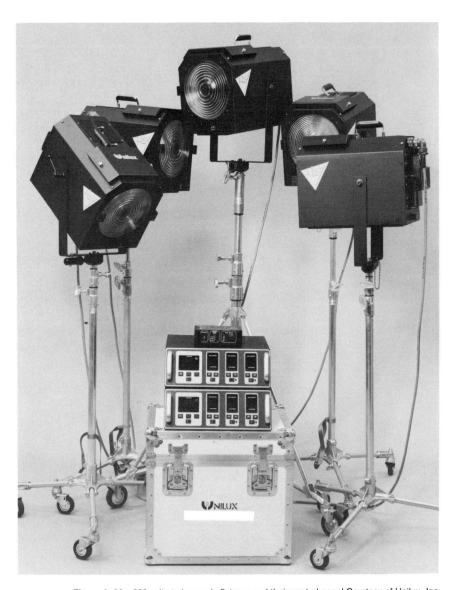

Figure 2–23 208-volt stroboscopic fixtures and their control panel.Courtesy of Unilux, Inc.

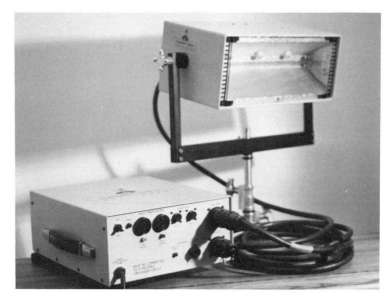

Figure 2-24 110-volt stroboscopic fixture and its "power-pak." Courtesy of Clairmont Camera, Inc.

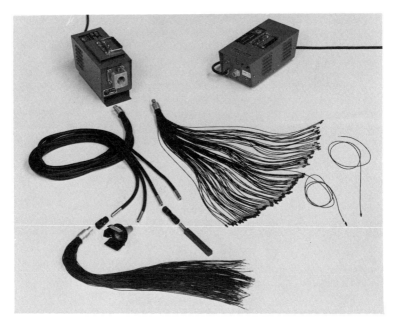

Figure 2-25 Fiber Optic Lighting Unit. Courtesy of LTM Corporation of America.

all soundstages: *At less than 30 pps, a person susceptible to epilepsy can be affected by a resultant sympathetic brain-wave response and go into convulsions.*

2.9b Fiber Optic Units

The fiber optic lighting unit (Fig. 2–25) is used extensively in commercials, special effects, and automobile "night shots." The unit consists of a power supply (ballast), light box, connectors and cables, and micro-lights consisting of a 2½-inch-diameter fresnel lens, a 6-light bar, and extension lenses.

The ballast operates at either 120 volts AC, 220 volts AC, or 12 volts DC (with an inverter). The light box contains a 250-watt gas-discharge lamp (related to the HMI family) with a color temperature of 5600K.

The cables carry the light through glass fibers, and because there is no electrical wiring and, consequently, no heat, the fibers and micro-lights can be submerged in liquid or used in proximity to delicate specimens and/or electronics.

Extension cables are either 8 feet in length (single strand) or 2½ feet in length (bundles of 100 tiny strands). Because of the composition of the fiber optics, extensions longer than 8 feet take on a green cast, which can be corrected by insertion of a 30 magenta or Tough Minus Green™* filter (see The Fluorescent Lamp; Filters, Ch. 9) into the light box or at the end of each cable.

---

*Manufactured by ROSCO, Port Chester, N.Y.

chapter 3

Fixture Lenses

In the early days of theater, lighting designers placed bottles of distilled water in front of candles in order to "spread" the light over a greater area, thus creating the effect of a lens. Fixture lenses as we know them today did not actually come into use until the invention of limelight, which had a light powerful enough to penetrate the thick glass and be concentrated into a beam.

Of course, the principles behind the construction of thin lenses had been known for years, eyeglasses having been invented around 1285 in Holland. At one time, the Dutch were the lensmakers for the world. In 1609, Galileo used Dutch lenses when he constructed his telescope for exploring the heavens. Antony van Leeuwenhoek (1623–1723, Holland) looked the other way — he invented the microscope, based on knowledge provided by fellow countryman Willabrod Snell, who had experimented with the refraction of light through air, water, and glass, findings that hold true to this day.

Which brings us to the lenses in use with today's filming and/or taping. The function of an enclosed-type fixture lens is to refract (bend) and project (direct) the rays emanating from the light source and its reflector (see Fixture Reflectors, Ch. 4) toward the subject. How this is accomplished in a fixture and how the characteristics of the rays are determined depends on the unit's focal point and focal length.

3.1 FOCAL POINT AND FOCAL LENGTH

A fixture lens, like a camera lens, has a *focal point* and a *focal length*.

3.1a Focal Point

With a simple plano-convex camera lens set at infinity, all parallel incident light rays that enter the lens are bent in such a manner that the light rays converge. The specific place where all the rays meet, where the image is in sharpest focus, is called its *focal point* (Fig. 3-1*a*).

With an enclosed-type fixture lens, this principle is reversed; i.e., a light source is placed at the point of sharpest focus, the focal point, so that when the radiant energy emanating from the light source via the reflector strikes the lens, the light rays are bent and projected as parallel rays (Fig. 3-1*b*).

3.1b Focal Length

Every lens has a *node of emission* (determined by optical engineers), which is an imaginary point where the light rays from the focal point leave the lens and pass through it as rays. The node of emission is in the lens itself never at the front or rear of the element, its placement dependent on the configu-

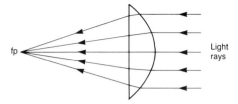

a Camera lens

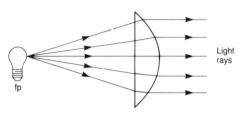

b Fixture lens

Figure 3–1 Utilization of the focal point of a lens in a fixture. (*a*) Path of light rays in a simple planoconvex lens set at infinity. (*b*) Path of light rays in an enclosed-type fixture lens. (Notice reverse direction of rays.)

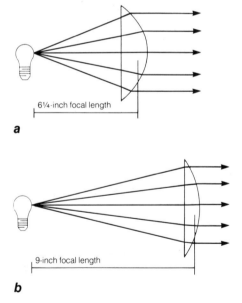

6¼-inch focal length

a

9-inch focal length

b

Figure 3–2 The distance from the *node of emission* to the *focal point* is called the *focal length*. Here are two examples of focal lengths.

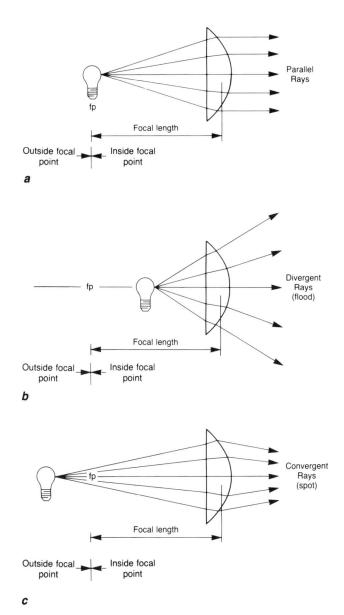

Parallel Rays

fp

Focal length

Outside focal point — Inside focal point

a

Divergent Rays (flood)

fp

Focal length

Outside focal point — Inside focal point

b

Convergent Rays (spot)

fp

Focal length

Outside focal point — Inside focal point

c

Figure 3-3 Types of rays formed by varying the light source in relation to the focal point. Parallel light rays (a) can be altered by moving the light source off its focal point. Divergent, or flood, rays (b) are formed by focusing within the focal length. Convergent, or spot, rays (c) are formed by focusing outside the focal length.

ration of the lens (whether it is plano-convex, concave, convex, symmetrical, asymmetrical, etc.) and on the characteristics of the glass (its thickness, radius of curvature, refractive index, etc.). The distance from the node of emission to the focal point is called the *focal length* (Fig. 3-2).

3.2 USING FOCAL POINT AND FOCAL LENGTH

In a focusable fixture, parallel light rays (Fig 3–3a) can be altered by moving the light source off its focal point. When focused *within* its focal length, the lens will produce divergent, or "flood," rays (Fig. 3–3b), and when focused outside its focal length, the lens will produce convergent or "spot" rays (Fig. 3–3c).

3.3 TYPES OF FIXTURE LENSES

An enclosed-type fixture usually has one of three types of lenses. The three most common fixture lenses in use today are the plano-convex, the fresnel, and the step lenses.

3.3a Plano-convex Lenses (Fig. 3–4a)

The plano-convex lens is glass, with one flat surface (plano) and one spherical surface (convex), and it is measured by its diameter and focal length.

Diameter is determined by the size of the fixture's opening, and focal length is determined by the size of the projected beam. For example, it is possible to encounter a 4½ × 6¼ inch lens, as well as one 4½ × 9 inches. Both will fit the same fixture, but the one with the short focal length (6¼ inches) will be thick and produce a wide beam, while the one with the longer length (9 inches) will be thinner and produce a narrower beam.

Because of its thickness, a plano-convex lens retains the heat generated by the fixture's light source. Such lenses have been known to crack if subjected to high-intensity light sources for long periods of times.

3.3b Fresnel Lenses (Fig 3–4b)

The fresnel (pronounced "fray-nell") lens was invented for lighthouses by a French physicist, Augustine Jean Fresnel (1788–1827, France). He took a plano-convex lens and cut away the bulk of the convex surface, and then he "duplicated" the convex contour on the remaining portion by recessing it with a series of sloped concentric rings.

The basic design has not changed since the early 1800s. Each sloped ring in the surface of the lens acts as a small prism, gathering the scattered radiant energy from the lamp and reflector and directing the light into parallel rays. In addition, the plano surface opposite the concentric rings is "stippled" so as to diffuse the lamp's radiant energy slightly and provide a

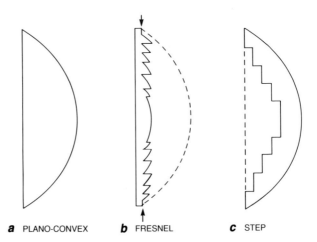

a PLANO-CONVEX   *b* FRESNEL   *c* STEP

Figure 3–4 Types of condenser lenses.

more "even" light. Because a fresnel lens is relatively thin and light in weight, it readily dissipates heat. It is therefore less likely to crack, even when subjected to an intense light source for long periods of time.

3.3c Step Lenses (Fig 3–4c)
A lens of the step type is halfway between the "evenness" of the fresnel lens and the "hardness" of the plano-convex lens. A step lens retains its convex surface; however, it is the bulk of the plano surface that is cut into concentric rings. The risers on each ring are sometimes opaque (either painted or sandblasted), which inhibits random dispersal of the lamp's energy and directs it into forward rays.

As with the plano-convex lens, the step lens is referred to by diameter and focal length. Diameter size is determined by the fixture's opening; the focal length is determined by the beam coverage desired [a thick lens will disperse (flood) the ray; a thin lens will produce narrow (spot) rays].

chapter 4

Fixture Reflectors

The lighting used on eighteenth-century theater stages left much to be desired, although experimentation was going on all the time and improvement was achieved. For example, flat mirrors were placed behind the footlight and proscenium candles, thus causing the light that formerly would have spilled onto the audience or theater walls to be redirected toward the stage. However, the rays were still uncontrollable, so light was thrown in a haphazard manner into areas unrelated to the action.

Then Antoine Lavoisier (1743–1794, France), a scientist and avid theater-goer, got into the act. Lavoisier is known today as the founder of modern chemistry. Few know that in 1781 he presented a paper before the Academie des Sciences, not on chemistry, but on the need for better lighting methods for theater stages, which greatly surprised and amused his peers, who urged him to go back to his laboratory and do something "worthwhile." He did.

Lavoisier constructed a fixture for the theater. He placed a large candle inside a box from which the front panel was removed. All interior panels (the two sides, the rear, top, and bottom) were mirrored. Thus the mirrors reflected and intensified the candle flame from side to side and top to bottom. The rear mirror reflected and directed the light forward. Then, by attaching a tube to the front opening the light was projected in the shape of an orb, and by adding a yoke, which allowed the fixture to swivel and tilt, Lavoisier had created an instrument with which the orb of light could be directed toward a specific area. In addition, his success encouraged other scientists to intensify their research in this field.

Today's fixture reflector is a curved metal plate with a polished surface. The manufacturer has placed the reflector behind the light source (or around it) in order to (1) redirect those light rays which radiate toward the back of the unit *forward,* and (2) intensify the unit's illumination. The reflector may be either fixed or moveable.

Reflectors are fabricated for the various types of fixtures they will fit; some reflectors are for use in enclosed-type fixtures, others are only for use in open-face (lensless) fixtures, while still others can be used in either type of fixture.

For reflectors to have maximum effectiveness, each must have its own polished surface, reflection factor, focal point, and shape.

4.1 POLISHED SURFACE

A reflector surface used in a fixture has been polished to meet one of the following specifications.

4.1a Specular

A highly polished mirrored surface that reflects hard rays which imitate a point source like the sun (Fig. 4–1*a*) is called a *specular reflector*. Specular reflectors are used in enclosed-type housings.

4.1b Specular Rays

Light intensified by a specular reflector emanates as "hard" rays. Since the source is a single one, the light can be easily controlled and its rays sharply cut with a barndoor or flag (see Lighting Controllers, Ch. 12) when in the flood position. This happens because the rays are divergent, making a sharp shadow possible. In the spot position, then, it is almost impossible to create a sharp shadow because the rays are convergent, or highly concentrated.

4.1c Diffuse

A smooth, dull-finish surface (often called *matte* or *etched*) that softens and reflects light rays uniformly (Fig. 4–1*b*) is called a *diffuse reflector*. The reflector in a broad is a good example.

4.1d Mixed

A surface that has both the characteristics of the specular and diffuse reflectors is called a *mixed reflector*. It reflects a mixture of hard-rays and diffuse rays (Fig. 4–1*c*). The enameled surface of a softlite is an example.

4.1e Scattered

A surface that is crinkled, stippled, or creased by the manufacturer in such a manner that incident light rays are broken up and reflected as though from a number of tiny mirrors (Fig. 4–1*d*) is called a *scattered* reflector. Most reflectors found in open-face housings are typical examples.

4.1f Diffuse, Mixed or Scattered Rays

Light intensified by either a diffuse, mixed, or scattered reflector surface emanates as a "soft" ray and is less controllable. A barndoor or flag tipped in to cut the rays leaves a soft, undefined shadow.

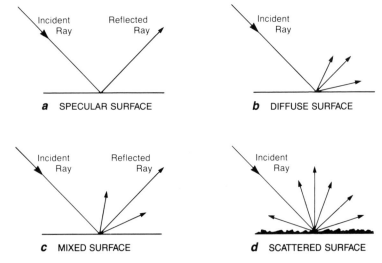

a SPECULAR SURFACE   *b* DIFFUSE SURFACE

c MIXED SURFACE   *d* SCATTERED SURFACE

Figure 4–1 Reflector surfaces.

4.2 REFLECTION FACTOR

A reflector will absorb a given degree of light regardless of its type of surface. The amount of light it absorbs depends on the material from which it is manufactured. Some materials are more porous than others and therefore will *absorb* more light and *reflect less,* giving a low reflectance factor to that surface. Less porous materials will absorb *less* light, giving a *higher* reflectance factor to that surface. Table 4–1 shows representative reflection factors of various materials used in the manufacture of reflectors for motion picture, video, and theater fixtures.

4.3 FOCAL POINT

The rays emanating from a lamp are more intense at the filament or arc than at the lamp's top, bottom, or sides. Therefore, in order to diminish the high-intensity rays at the center and augment the low-intensity rays at the edges, the center of the reflector has been curved *away* from the filament or arc and its edges bent *toward* the filament. With the curving (at point of manufacture), the redirected rays at the center of the reflector will be less intense because of their distance from the filament, and the edges of the reflector, having an inward curve toward the top, base, and sides of the lamp, will reflect more intense rays because of their proximity to the filament. Thus the closeness of the reflector's edges to the lamp and the intensity reflected are equal to the intensity reflected from the center.

The point at which a lamp is situated in relation to its reflector (so that the emitted rays from the center and edges of the reflector will be of equal intensity) is called the *focal point* of the reflector.

Rays from an off-center reflector are difficult to control. If an enclosed-type fixture has been damaged or not properly set at the point of manufacture, the light source might not be squared to the reflector, in which case the illumination will be uneven—the top, bottom, or one side of the beam could be more intense ("hotter") than another. It is sometimes possible, on the job, to pivot the reflector in its holder or bend the holder up or down to "even out" or at least reduce considerably the intensity of the offset rays.

When all the light rays are even, the lamp is in focus with the reflector. However, this does create a problem: With the reflector in focus on the filament, additional heat is created, causing the bulb to blister and the filament to deteriorate more quickly. Therefore, manufacturers shorten the dis-

Table 4–1 Representative Reflection Factors of Materials Used in Fixtures

Material	Percent Reflection
Alzak* aluminum—specular	80–85
Alzak* aluminum—diffuse	75–80
Baked white enamel	75–80
Porcelain enamel—gloss	62–79
Porcelain enamel—dull	60–77
Chrome—specular	60–67
Nickel	60–63
Stainless steel—specular	56–65
Stainless steel—diffuse	41–48

NOTE: Dust, dirt, and metal fatigue will alter the reflection factors considerably unless the surfaces are properly maintained.
*Alzak is a trade mark of the Aluminum Company of America.

tance between lamp and reflector slightly (a minute alteration of the focal point) so that the focus of the reflector is somewhere in the air space between the lamp and the lens.

An *enclosed-type* fixture usually contains a spherical reflector. Since a lens-fitted fixture is almost always focusable, the reflector and light source are mounted on a block by the manufacturer, with the reflector being at a fixed distance from the lamp. The block is coupled to the fixture's focus knob so that the combination lamp/reflector can be moved toward or away from the lens. Because they have been mounted on the block, the light source and reflector maintain proper focal length and realize maximum, or near-maximum, illumination no matter where the block is moved.

Maximum illumination is possible with an open-face fixture because the reflection factor of the polished surface of the reflector itself is utilized in conjunction with the intensity of the lamp. Should the unit be a focusable-type, the light source can be placed in one of several positions in relation to the focal point of the reflector: at, near, or away from the focal point. The various positions of the lamp control the amount of intensified illumination striking the surface of the reflector (spot or flood).

Since there are two sources of illumination emitted from the unit — the lamp itself and the redirected rays from the reflector — and, because most open-face fixture reflectors have a scattered-finish surface, the light emitted is a soft ray and less controllable. A sharp shadow is not possible when attempting to barndoor or flag the projected rays. At best, a double-edged soft shadow will be the result.

4.4 SHAPE

Numerous methods of light control become possible through controlling the shape of a fixture's reflector. The most common shapes are spherical (Fig. 4–2a), ellipsoidal (Fig. 4–2b), parabolic (Fig. 4–2c), and combination spherical/parabolic (Fig. 4–2d).

4.4a Spherical Reflector

The spherical reflector (Fig. 4–2a) is used most often in *enclosed-type* fixtures that utilize a lens for directing the beam of light; it is also used in *lensless scoops* (see The Fixtures, Ch. 2, and Fig. 2–15), where the housing itself, with a matte finish, may be used as the reflector. In an enclosed-type fixture, the reflector and light source are mounted on a block (see above).

When using a spherical reflector in a lensless scoop, and the light source is fixed and positioned *outside* its focal point (*away* from the reflector; to the right of the dotted line in Fig. 4–2a), the majority of the light rays will mainly scatter, reflecting almost no beam. When the fixed light source is *inside* the focal point (close to the reflector; to the left of the dotted line in the illustration), the light will be reflected as a narrow beam.

With a lensless fixed and/or *focusable* scoop, however, when the lamp is positioned *at* the focal point, the unit will emit "flood" rays. With a focusable scoop when the lamp is positioned *inside* the focal point, the unit will emit "spot" rays.

4.4b Ellipsoidal Reflector

The ellipsoidal reflector (Fig. 4–2b) is found in both *open-face* and *enclosed*-type fixtures. The focal point for this reflector is the same as for other reflectors except that, because of its shape, it has both a primary and a secondary focal point. A light source placed at the primary focal point will reflect a maximum amount of rays that converge and "meet" at a very narrow "pinpoint," which becomes its secondary focal point.

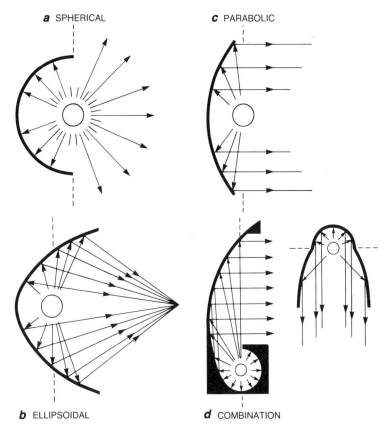

a SPHERICAL

c PARABOLIC

b ELLIPSOIDAL

d COMBINATION

Figure 4–2 Reflector shapes.

The distance at which the secondary focal point occurs depends on the size of the reflector. Once the rays meet at the pinpoint they widen again, or diverge. However, when working with a *variable-focus open-face* type of fixture, the construction is such that the light source can *never* be brought to the primary focal point and the resultant pinpoint. Instead, the *socket* containing the light source travels from a point slightly *short* of the primary focal point to slightly *beyond* the focal point.

By changing the position of the socket/lamp in relation to the reflector, the rays from the light source change and are then projected either as parallel rays, which is the flood position, or as an intense narrow beam, which is the spot position.

With an ellipsoidal reflector when the light source is *outside* the primary focal point in an *open-face* fixture (to the right of the dotted line in the illustration), the light rays will scatter widely and reflect almost no beam at all. When the light source is just *inside* its focal point (to the left of the dotted line in the illustration), the light rays will be parallel. When this type of reflector is placed inside an *enclosed*-type housing, the unit has an easily identifiable configuration, works in conjunction with plano-convex lenses, and is called appropriately an *"ellipsoidal"* fixture (see The Fixture, Ch. 2, and Fig. 2–10).

In an *enclosed*-type ellipsoidal fixture when the light source is *outside* its primary focal point (to the right of the dotted line in the illustration) the majority of the light rays will scatter and illuminate only the interior of the housing. As with the *open-face* fixture, when the primary light source is just *inside* its focal point (to the left of the dotted line in the illustration), the light rays will be parallel. In an *enclosed*-type ellipsoidal fixture the reflector's light source is fixed, i.e., nonfocusable, and the reflector is so constructed that the pinpoint is slightly beyond the four framing shutters. In this type of unit it is the lens(es) in the tube that is(are) brought back toward the pinpoint to achieve a focused beam of light.

4.4c Parabolic Reflector

The parabolic-shaped reflector (Fig. 4–2c) is found in light sources such as the PAR lamp used in modules (see The Fixture, Ch. 2, and Fig. 2–12) and units that are fixtures in themselves, such as the R-type lamps (see Filament Lamps, Ch. 6).

When the light source is placed at the focal point of a parabolic reflector the light rays will be parallel. When the light source is *ahead* of its focal point (to the right of the dotted line in Fig. 4–2c), the rays will converge. Depending on the size of the light source and housing, the rays will meet at some distant pinpoint (much like the ellipsoidal) and then diverge. When the light source is *behind* its focal point (to the left of the dotted line), the rays will diverge and project a wide beam.

4.4d Combination Spherical/Parabolic Reflector

This combination shape (Fig. 4–2d) is found in the bell-shaped scoop (Fig. 2–15) and the softlite (Fig. 2–18). The combination utilizes the spherical section in a nonfocusable softlite to reflect and increase the power of the light source, while at the same time the parabola reflects the rays as a parallel beam.

The light source in the spherical area of a focusable scoop is subject to the focal-point limitations of the spherical reflector, as described above, the parabolic area of it serving only to direct its rays.

4.5 OTHER REFLECTOR FUNCTIONS

A reflector can do more than redirect light. One particular open-face type is especially constructed to absorb either infrared or ultraviolet radiation while utilizing a 3200K incandescent light source. The infrared-absorbing reflector is color-temperature-corrected to 3200K. The ultraviolet-absorbing filter is color-temperature-corrected to 5600K.

Heat is absorbed through the rear of the infrared reflector. A person can place a hand within inches of the front element and feel very little radiation. Sinks—metal pieces that disperse the heat—and vents at the rear of the fixture become extremely hot, however, often hotter than a standard lighting unit would.

Such a reflector keeps the working area cooler, thus providing comfort for actors working on a closed stage. Additionally, it has value when used in the filming/telecasting of laboratory specimens, medical operations, or highly perishable foods, particularly where heat could "cook" the subject. The 5600K ultraviolet reflector is also used as an outdoor supplementary light.

chapter 5

The Lamp Socket

The socket in a fixture does more than just hold a lamp in place. It provides an electrical circuit either to a filament in an incandescent lamp, or to the cathode/anode in a gas-activated lamp, or to electrodes in a carbon-arc fixture. The flow of electricity through the socket can be interrupted by either turning off its switch, removing the lamp (or electrodes) from the socket, breaking the filament, burning the cathode/anode beyond its ionization point, or creating a wide gap between electrodes. Typical sockets for incandescent and gas-filled lamps are shown in Figure 5–1.

A socket for industrial use is ruggedly constructed and capable of abuse far beyond the life of the light source it will hold. Sockets are constructed of various materials (metal, ceramic, plastic, etc.) to accommodate high temperatures, and are of various configurations (Fig. 5–1) to accommodate lamp bases: screw, bayonet, bi-post, clamp, single-ended, etc. (see Filament Lamps, Bases, Ch. 6). The socket is perhaps the least appreciated part of a fixture, even though it is so vital to the efficiency and longevity of the lamp it holds.

In an enclosed-type fixture that is focusable, the socket and reflector have been mounted on a block by the manufacturer. The block allows the two to slide together on a pair of rods as one piece; one of the rods is attached to the external adjustment control knob on the fixture. A socket in an open-face fixture will accept either a single- or a double-ended lamp.

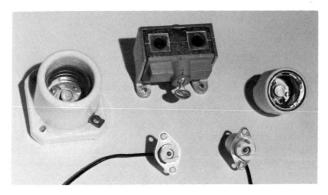

Figure 5–1   Types of lamp sockets. Courtesy of Mole-Richardson Co.

The socket and its bulb are moveable to a flood or spot position or can remain fixed (non-focusable). The reflector remains stationary. A single-ended lamp must have a base that conforms to the configuration of the socket. When a socket accepts a double-ended lamp, the bulb is held in place by either a spring action or by screws. In its position in a fixture, a socket is subject to intense heat and voltage variation, so periodically it must be carefully checked for the three most damaging factors to the fixture's lamp: Discoloration, pitting, and oxidization.

5.1 DISCOLORATION

A socket discolors as a result of a physical change in the metal caused by excessive heat. Undue heat generated in the socket indicates the holder either lacks adequate ventilation, is constructed of a gauge of metal incapable of withstanding the heat created by an electric current passing through it, or both. Too much thermal stress on a socket can melt soldered leads, crystallize the cement in a lamp base, weaken the holder springs, or cause the socket to crack, all of which will increase resistance to the voltage applied. Any or all of these conditions will impart an even greater temperature to the lamp and shorten its life considerably. A discolored socket should be replaced and the fixture provided with additional ventilation or a heat sink. A *heat sink* is a small piece of metal attached to the socket that "draws off" the heat, dissipates it into the air, and leaves the unit cooler.

5.2 PITTING

Small pits in the socket constitute a sign that excessive voltage has caused crystallization of the metal, which flakes off as "chips" and leaves tiny holes. Pits in a socket allow room for ionization, and the minute positive or negative charges will create an arc even in microscopic spaces. These charges keep "chipping" away at each pit, enlarging it until it is visible to the naked eye.

When a socket is already pitted and a new lamp is inserted, the force of the arc from the base socket will gouge tiny holes into the new lamp base. Therefore, when a socket becomes pitted, it should be replaced immediately; readings should be taken at the new socket to verify that the proper voltage is reaching the lamp. Connections should also be checked: A poor connection can cause voltage surge, starting the cycle all over again. By the same token, the placement of a lamp that has a pitted base into a *new* socket will permit ionization, and this will pit the new socket. Unless corrected, this action brings about premature lamp burnout. It is important that a lamp with a pitted base and/or a pitted socket in a fixture, be removed.

5.3 OXIDIZATION

When two different metals (e.g., aluminum and brass) come in contact and are subjected to excessive heat, as in a fixture, an electrochemical reaction between the metals called *oxidization* takes place. The metals are "welded" together, rendering both lamp and socket unusable.

The use of compatible metals is not always controllable. Manufacturers of lighting fixtures may use a given metal to fabricate sockets, while manufacturers of lamps may use a different type of metal, or alloy, for the lamp base. It is wise maintenance procedure to conduct periodic and frequent inspections to prolong the life of a lamp. Apply sperm oil to the base of a lamp and its socket to prevent oxidization. In an emergency, a rust preventative may be used. Although sperm oil is reputed to be odorless when heated (a rust preventative is not — it will smoke and smell), the fixture lamp should be burned a few minutes after application of the oil to burn off odor and smoke.

PART II

Light Sources

Artificial light sources used in film, video, and the theater are of two major types:

1. Incandescent Filament
   a. Tungsten Standard
   b. Tungsten Halogen
2. Arc
   a. Carbon
   b. Multiline Discharge

Artificial light sources not normally used but often encountered while location filming or remote videocasting are:

3. Predominate and/or Broken Spectra
   a. Fluorescent
   b. HMI:
      (1) Mercury
      (2) Medium Arc
      (3) Iodides
   c. High Intensity Discharge (HID):
      (1) Mercury
      (2) Metal Halide
      (3) Sodium

Tungsten standard, tungsten halogen, HMI, fluorescent, and HID light sources are encased in glass envelopes (bulbs) and are rated in watts. The carbon arc is not encased in a bulb; its light source is dependent on flame produced by an electric charge between two carbon electrodes. The carbon arc is rated by the amount of current, or amperage, it draws.

In order to light a lamp, make its filament glow, or excite its gas-filled interior, electromotive force, which is commonly called *voltage,* must be applied to it. Voltage will force electrons to flow. The flow, or *current,* is measured in *amperes.* The term *amperage* refers to the load-carrying capacity of generators, carbon, arcs, wires, etc.

The *rate* at which the electrons are moved through a wire is called *power,* and power is measured in terms of *watts.* The wattage rating of a filament, or gas-discharge, lamp indicates the intensity at which the filament, or gas, converts electrical energy into light (its output). For example, a high-rated lamp of 10,000 watts will produce more light than a 2000-watt lamp because it converts more electrical energy into light.

When a filament glows, what we see and call light is energy being transferred from the filament in the form of visible radiation. In lighting terms, this transfer of energy in the visible wavelength range is called *luminous flux* ("seeable" flow of light). Luminous flux is measured in *lumens*.

The term *lumens per watt* is used when referring to the *efficiency* of a light source. Lumens per watt indicates how much light will be emitted based on the amount of power expended in order to get the lamp to light; e.g., if a 500-watt lamp emits 5000 lumens, it is more efficient than a 500-watt lamp that emits only 2000 lumens. The ratio of the first lamp is 10 to 1 (10 lumens emitted for every 1 watt of power moving through the wire); the second lamp only has a ratio of 4 to 1 (4 lumens emitted for every 1 watt of power moving through the wire).

Efficiency refers to the light source itself and has nothing to do with comparative values or unit size. For example, a 750-watt lamp that emits 7500 lumens (10 to 1 ratio) is more efficient than a 2000-watt lamp that emits 10,000 lumens (5 to 1 ratio), although the latter will have more intensity and "throw" its beam farther.

Most gas-filled lamps — such as the HMI, fluorescent, metal-halide, and mercury vapor — are more efficient, size for size and watt for watt, than filament lamps, such as the tungsten standard and tungsten halogen. The gas-filled unit will generate less heat, resist the flow of current less, and therefore be more economical to operate.

chapter 6

Filament Lamps

Joseph Swan (1824–1914, England) built the first practical carbon filament lamp in 1878. Whether Thomas A. Edison (1847–1931, United States) was familiar with Swan's work is not known, but using a similar method and forming his carbon filament in the shape of a loop (Swan's filament was linear), Edison created a lamp that emitted double the light of Swan's and was longer lasting. Edison patented his lamp in 1879; later, the two men became partners in the Edison & Swan United Lamp Company and enjoyed a monopoly in England for years. The filament of Edison's design, however, was not strong enough for use in the infant motion picture industry.

Although it was known that tungsten was far superior to carbon and other metals that were used as filaments, it was not until 1909 that William David Coolidge (1873–1975, United States) perfected a method for softening tungsten so that it could be formed into various shapes and patterns. It was heated close to its melting point of 3400°C (6120°F) without disintegrating, which permitted four times as much wire filament to occupy a space that previously accommodated only one loop and was still capable of producing *more* light. Still, Coolidge's newly designed filament lamp was ineffective on the slow emulsions used in the film industry.

The next development in lamps, the one that brought electric lighting to film stages as a supplementary illumination to the arc light (see Carbon Arc, Ch. 7) was the work of Irving Langmuir (1887–1951, United States). In 1913, he developed the gas-filled lamp: The gas inhibited the deterioration of the tungsten and allowed for an increase in filament temperature, which again doubled the light output of the tungsten lamp.

In 1934, the coiled-coil filament tripled the output of all previous lamps and eventually replaced carbon arcs with all-electric fixtures on the sound stages.

A group of scientists and engineers at General Electric in the 1950s was working to perfect an infrared linear lamp. In order for the lamp to generate the heat necessary to accomplish its intended purpose, a filament was placed inside a newly developed glass envelope of quartz glass instead of borosilicate. The bulb walls were thick and blackened rapidly, which in turn retarded the heat and intensity of the lamp. It seemed to be a losing proposition. Someone then recalled that in 1880 Thomas Edison had postulated a theory: Iodine, or one of the related regenerative elements, could be placed inside a glass bulb and the filament would burn at a temperature of at least 3000°C, the tungsten would combine with the element, be restored on the filament, and the bulb would not blacken. In Edison's day there was no glass in existence that could withstand the internal temperature that was generated. Fortunately, nearly three-quarters of a century later, General Electric *did* have the quartz-glass envelope that Edison had only theorized about. So iodine was added to the lamp's interior just to see what would happen. (Had he been alive, the taciturn Edison might have said, "Knew it would work.")

It took several years of development and experimentation, but in 1959 the first of the halogen-filled lamps—the *quartz iodine* lamp—made its debut in film and video work. Because of its regenerative qualities and the advantage of reduced size, the tungsten-halogen lamp bulb has all but replaced the standard filament lamp. Almost, but not quite. It is essential to those involved in lighting to know the similarities and differences of both types of filament lamps.

6.1 THE LAMP

Visible radiant energy emitted by any heated material is called *incandescence.* A filament lamp "lights up" because as an electric current passes through it, its light-emitting wire becomes so hot it "glows." However, in order to incandesce, the wire must be in an airless container (bulb). Air reaching the filament causes the filament to oxidize and evaporate. In a vacuum, and/or in a gas-filled bulb, the more electricity applied to a filament, the higher is its light output and its color temperature. Of course, too much current will cause the filament to heat up beyond its tolerances and "blow out."

The term *incandescent* applies to both tungsten-standard and tungsten-halogen lamps. The term *tungsten standard* refers to a tungsten filament lamp that has a gas (nitrogen or argon) sealed within the bulb. The term *tungsten halogen,* however, refers to a tungsten filament lamp that contains not only argon and nitrogen, but also one of the regenerative elements (bromine, iodine, chlorine, fluorine, or astatine) sealed within the bulb. An SED graph of a typical tungsten halogen lamp is shown in Figure 6–1. The graph is similar to that of a tungsten-standard lamp.

Motion picture, video, and theater filament lamps are comprised of three basic parts: (1) the bulb, (2) the filament, and (3) the base.

6.1a Bulb

The bulb of a tungsten-standard lamp is made of either borosilicate or silica glass. The tungsten-halogen bulb is made of fused quartz, a high form of silica glass that can withstand a high degree of heat.

With either type, most bulb shapes are formed by heating a tube of glass to near melting point. The glass is then inserted into a mold and warm air is pumped into the tube, forcing the glass to expand and adhere to the contours of the mold. Some bulbs, such as the PAR lamp, are pressed into molds.

Bulbs vary in shape and size (Fig. 6–2) and are easily recognized by their configuration as either the tungsten-standard type or tungsten-halogen type; the PAR of either type has the same configuration. Whether the PAR contains just gas or the added regenerative halogens is learned by consulting Table 6–1.

Most tungsten-standard and tungsten-halogen bulbs are of clear glass (manufacturer's symbol CL); the filament and its support are visible and can thus be readily inspected. The filaments of other units are obscured by an inner coating or the thickness of their glass.

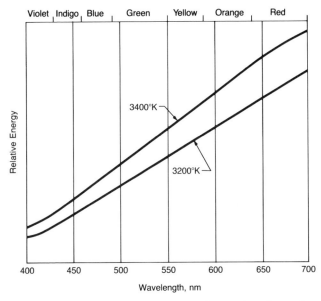

| Violet | Indigo | Blue | Green | Yellow | Orange | Red |

Relative Energy

3400°K

3200°K

400   450   500   550   600   650   700

Wavelength, nm

Figure 6–1 Typical filament lamp (tungsten-halogen) SED graph. A filament lamp has a continuous spectrum high in the "red" area.

Coated bulbs: Tungsten standard A tungsten standard *inside frost* photoflood bulb (symbol "IF") such as an "A," or "PS" type has a white silica coating applied to its interior surface, giving it a milky appearance: It produces a light of 3400K.

When a tungsten standard photoflood is needed to supplement daylight, then a blue-glass photoflood lamp (symbol "B") is used.* A "B" lamp produces a light of 4800K.

Since the blue coating on a photoflood causes the lamp to lose a great percentage of its efficiency, it should be treated as a dichroic filter (see Fixture Filters, Ch. 14, Table 14–6). In other words, in order to obtain the same amount of footcandles normally obtained from a nonblue photoflood, one should use the next higher wattage daylight (blue) photoflood. For example, a no. B4 (blue) photoflood provides approximately the same light output as a no. 2 (nonblue IF) photoflood.

Reflector floods The tungsten-standard R-type lamp has a silvered inside bowl; the coating acts as a reflector, and with its lens, this lamp is consid-

---

*The use of the letter B applied to a blue photoflood lamp should not be confused with the single letter B that is applied to a common household lamp, which also has a milky inside frost (IF). The B of a blue photoflood *always* precedes the manufacturer's bulb-type letter. For example, a blue no. 2 photoflood is designated a no. B2; a blue PS52 is designated a no. BPS52, while a household lamp is simply listed as an IFB (Inside Frost, B-size). Again the household lamp is not blue-colored, and its comparative low light output and low Kelvin renders it virtually useless for motion picture, video, or theater fixtures. However, some lighting people do utilize household lamps in "practical" fixtures on a set because of the "warmth" of the light (especially in night scenes). Other people like to use the low-wattage household lamp (ranging from 15 to 60 watts), hiding them behind furniture or other objects so as to impart a subtle separation of object and wall. The general set lighting of normal quality will overlook the disparity in Kelvin.

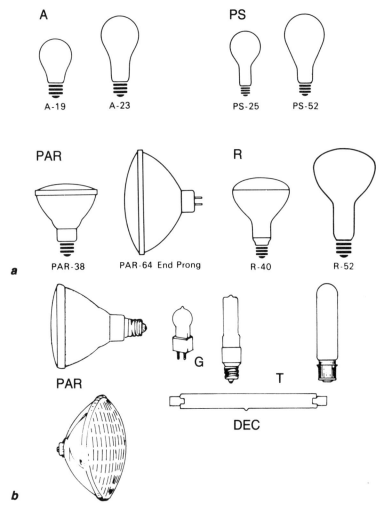

Figure 6-2 (a) Tungsten-standard filament lamps used in motion picture, video, and theatre fixtures. Manufacturers apply a code letter to bulb shapes; A = standard, PS = pear shaped, PAR = parabolic, R = reflector. Manufacturers also append a number which designates the maximum diameter of the bulb in eighths of an inch. Thus, an A-23 is a standard photoflood 23 eighths of an inch, or 2 7/8 inches in diameter; a PAR-38 is 38 eighths of an inch, or 4 3/4 inches in diameter; an R-40 is 40 eighths, or 5 inches in diameter. (b) Tungsten-halogen filament lamp bulb shapes most commonly used in motion picture, video, and theatre. Manufacturers apply the same code letters to tungsten-halogen lamps, although the shapes are different; G = globe, T = tubular, PAR = parabolic, DEC = double ended contact. Courtesy of Phillips Lighting Company.

ered to be a fixture in itself. When the inside face of the lens is lightly milk-coated, the lamp is classified as a flood (symbol RFL); when the face is clear, the lamp is classified as a spot (symbol RSP).

Tungsten halogen frosted A frosted finish (symbol F) is given to a tungsten-halogen bulb by scarring it with the application of a dilute acid to the interior surface.

Table 6-1 PAR-Size Lamps, Wattage, and Type (Standard/Regenerative)

PAR Size	Wattage	Tungsten Standard	Tungsten Halogen
36	75–300	X	
36	650		X
38	75–300	X	
46	75–300	X	
56	75–300	X	
56	500		X
64	120–500	X	
64	1000		X

Tungsten standard and tungsten halogen, PAR type A PAR lamp of either type has a silvered bowl inside. Its face is also its lens. Since the conformation of the bulb is a parabola (hence the symbol PAR), the inside coating also acts as a reflector (see Fixture Reflectors, Ch. 4). In combination with the shape of the lens, this type of lamp is a fixture in itself. The filament is placed in relation to the unit's focal point so that, in combination with its lens, its projected rays will either be convergent, parallel, or divergent (see Fixture Lenses, Ch. 3).

The inside of the lens is then either clear (symbol NSP), which directs the rays into a narrow spot, moulded with a medium-size pattern (symbol MFL), which directs the rays into a medium flood, or molded with a wide pattern (symbol WFL), which directs the rays into a wide flood. When a PAR lamp is coated blue, it is considered to be a dichroic filter (see Fixture Filters, Ch. 14).

Leakers At point of manufacture, oxygen is always withdrawn from a bulb just before it is sealed. Most tungsten standard filament lamps of 40 watts or more have a gas (such as argon and nitrogen) injected to replace the oxygen. The gas helps retard deterioration of the filament. However, the inside of a bulb of less than 40 watts is a gasless vacuum.

Tungsten-halogen lamps are also filled with argon and nitrogen, with either bromine, iodine, chlorine, fluorine, or astatine added. If the slightest amount of air enters a sealed burning lamp, tungsten oxide is formed, and the inner surface of the bulb will discolor—either a yellow-white, blue-black, blue-white, or black-gray. Air leaks can be caused by rough handling of the lamp, or splashed water which will produce minute cracks on a hot bulb, especially in open-face fixtures. The lamp may not fail while burning, but once it has cooled, air *will* enter and the lamp will either "blow out" when the current is next applied or become discolored.

Blisters The following conditions cause glass to soften and a blister to form on a bulb at extreme temperatures: Moisture on the bulb (grease, perspiration, fingerprints, etc); excess voltage; a misaligned reflector (focal point is out of whack) focusing on the filament.

Blackening After long use a bulb with a standard filament has a tendency to blacken on the inside. This is caused by "boil off" of tungsten particles from the filament (see Filaments, below), which rise from the heat and adhere to the inner bulb wall. Large standard filament bulbs, such as the globular-shaped 10K or the 5K, contain a small amount of tungsten powder sealed inside the bulb for cleaning purposes. By slowly inverting the bulb and swirling the powder in small circles the deposit can be easily removed. Extreme care should be taken after the bulb has been cleaned to return the bulb slowly to an upright position so that the tungsten particles slide along the interior wall of the bulb and *gently* settle to the bottom. Rapidly inverting the bulb to an upright position will cause the particles to "rain" on and adhere to the filaments, which will cause an arc when the lamp is lighted and blow it out.

Medium and small standard filament lamps, such as the 2K, 1K, 750-watt, 500-watt, etc., do not contain a cleansing agent; they therefore blacken as they age. Blackening inside a standard filament bulb causes a reduction in light output and color temperature. Important: Bulbs should be checked frequently and either cleaned as outlined above or replaced.

Collectors Some standard incandescent lamps will contain a *collector,* which is a screen or grid located just above the filament. The collector is intended to catch the "boil off" of tungsten as it rises, thereby retarding the blackening of the bulb interior. However, some blackening is inevitable, since most fixtures on a studio stage are tilted down at angles of various degrees. The particles rising straight up miss the collector and the bulb blackens.

Tungsten-halogen bulbs, although they do not have collectors, do not blacken at all. They contain a regenerative element that inhibits blackening, and this is explained in greater detail under Filaments, Material (following).

6.1b Filaments

Filaments in a tungsten-standard lamp intended for studio use fall into three basic categories: (1) compact, (2) linear, and (3) planar. The most common forms are shown in Figure 6–3.

Manufacturers also apply a catalog code and catalog number to filaments.

- S is straight: a straight wire, sometimes corrugated.
- C is coiled: a straight piece of wire that has been wound around a round bar.
- CC is a coiled-coil: a coiled wire that has been coiled a second time; the double coil produces a greater amount of heat and incandescence (it takes 27½ inches of straight wire to produce a CC filament 1½ inches long).

The numbers that follow the first letter indicate the manufacturer's configuration of the filament used. Letters that follow the number are arbitrary designations set up by the manufacturer for internal use. Nowhere on the lamp is there a description of the configuration of the filament. In a lamp with a clear bulb, the filament can be readily seen; to find the type filament in a frosted bulb, consult Figure 6–3.

Material Tungsten is the best material for filament because of its great tensile strength and high melting point (approximately 3400°C, 6120°F). When tungsten is heated to incandescence, particles of the tungsten "boil off." With an incandescent standard lamp, these particles adhere to the inside of the bulb and blacken it (see Blackening, earlier).

With a tungsten-halogen lamp, however, the boiled off particles of tungsten combine with the halogen element (bromine, iodine, etc.) sealed within the bulb. When combined with a halogen, the tungsten will not adhere to the inner glass wall; it circulates within the bulb until it touches the glowing filament; when it does, the halogen burns off and recirculates, leaving only the tungsten particle. This regenerative cycle extends the life of the lamp and its color temperature by redepositing the tungsten on the filament, thus preventing the blackening of the bulb. The redeposit of tungsten is not even, however. Eventually, as with any incandescent lamp, the filament will boil off enough of its tungsten that it breaks and blows out.

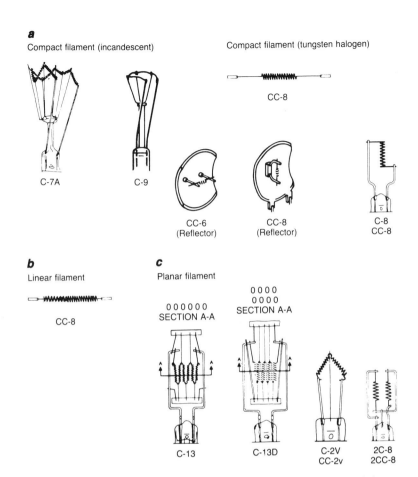

Figure 6-3 Filament forms most commonly used in motion picture, video, and theater lamps. (*a*) A *compact filament* in a tungsten standard lamp is arranged so that the filaments are staggered to distribute glow to all the inside surfaces of the bulb, or to its built-in reflector. Because of its shape, it is called a *crown filament,* a *carona filament,* or sometimes a *barrel filament.* A *compact filament* in a tungsten-halogen lamp (double- or single-ended) is a short-coiled coil, and is positioned in the center of the bulb. (*b*) A *linear filament* in a double-ended tungsten-halogen lamp is distinguished by the fact that it extends for most of the length of the bulb and has spacers at intervals that keep the filament from touching the inner bulb wall. The linear filament should not be confused with a tungsten halogen compact filament: the latter is short and does not have spacers. (*c*) A *planar filament* in either a tungsten-standard or tungsten-halogen lamp is arranged so that one or two rows of filaments are in one plane, i.e., lined up evenly. In parts *a* and *b,* each O represents a filament viewed from the top in relationship to the other filaments. Not all planar filament illustrations show this arrangement. A lamp with a planar filament requires the alignment of an external reflector behind the filament in order to increase and direct its beam forward (see Fixture Reflectors, Ch. 4). Courtesy of General Electric Co.

Color temperature   Filament lamps used in the film and video industries have an optimum color temperature of 3200K to 3400K. The color temperature of any lamp is predicated on specific filament design criteria: The material, the diameter of the wire, its length, and the degrees centigrade at which it glows.

Thus manufacturers using the same materials, configurations, and conformation to thermal tolerances can mass-produce lamps that are consistently in the 3200K to 3400K color temperature range that maintain a tolerance factor as well as lamp life (see below). A cooler-glowing filament lamp, one of low color temperature, is less efficient than a hotter-glowing lamp, which is one of high color temperature.

Bowing   Periodic inspection of filaments is important. If the filament bows away from or toward the fixture's reflector one of two things is indicated. First, the voltage is too high at the socket, producing extreme heat within the bulb, which in turn causes excessive heat to be "kicked back" by the reflector. The filaments are "pushed away" from the concentrated beam. Second, the reflector is misaligned, causing the filament to be focused on the bulb, which becomes overheated and "draws" the filament toward the inner wall of the bulb in the direction of the reflector. This will also cause bulb blister (see Bulb, earlier).

Some lamps can be reversed on the lamp socket so the filament can be "pulled" until it straightens out, but the unit must be inspected every day or it will begin to bow the other way. This will prevent the lamp from premature blowout, but it is not a permanent solution to the problem.

Vibration   Perhaps the greatest enemy of a filament lamp is shaking. Many fixtures are placed on rolling stands. A smooth floor poses little problem, but on rough surfaces the filament can be shocked to the breaking point, especially if it is still hot. It is good practice to *carry* a lighting unit over a rough surface.

Lamp life   A lamp is so designed that the higher its wattage rating, the heavier its filament. A 500-watt lamp may have a life of 2000 hours, while a 250-watt lamp may have 300 hours. The life of a lamp depends on a number of things: its handling, its manufacturing excellence, and proper usage.

A stipulated lamp life is just an approximation. Based on materials used in its manufacture and testing, a given number of life-hours is allotted for a lamp. Thus, a designated 10-hour lamp means approximately 9 to 11 hours.

The greatest factor affecting lamp life is voltage. The higher the voltage, the quicker the tungsten will "boil off," shortening the life of the lamp (see Table 6–2).

6.1c Base

The most common bases used in motion picture, video, and theater lamps are shown in Figure 6–4. A lamp should be removed from its socket from time to time to check for discoloration, pitting, and/or looseness. Any one of these signs indicates socket problems and must be corrected immediately (see The Lamp Socket, Ch. 5).

Base operating positions   Lamps used for lighting in studios will operate at optimum efficiency within certain limits. Bases are letter- and number-coded as follows:

Letters
- BD — base down
- BU — base up
- ANY — base may be in either position
  Numbers
- 30 and/or 45 indicates the maximum degree of angle from vertical the bulb can be burned for maximum results.

Table 6-2 Line Voltage vs. Life. Line voltages under 115 volts will increase lamp life but greatly reduce light output. Higher voltages more than 120 volts will drastically reduce lamp life.

If Line Voltage is Between:	A 100-Hour Lamp Will Burn:	A 50-Hour Lamp Will Burn:	A 25-Hour Lamp Will Burn:	A 15-Hour Lamp Will Burn:	A 10-Hour Lamp Will Burn:
115–120 volts	75–125 hrs.	38–65 hrs.	19–32 hrs.	12–18 hrs.	7–13 hrs.
121–125 volts	39–75 hrs.	23–39 hrs.	11–20 hrs.	7–12 hrs.	4–7 hrs.
126–130 volts	27–45 hrs.	14–23 hrs.	5–12 hrs.	3–7 hrs.	0–4 hrs.

Source: General Electric Co.

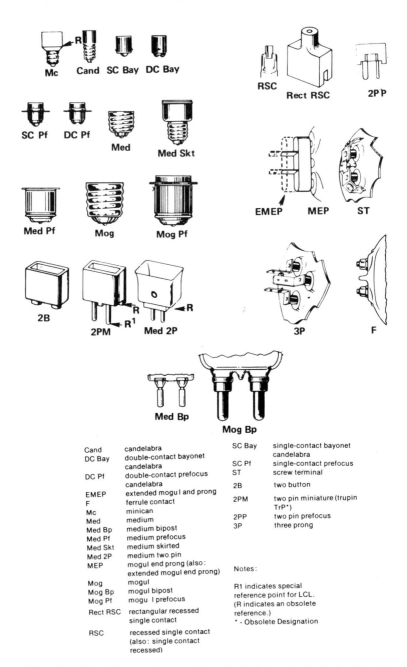

Cand	candelabra		SC Bay	single-contact bayonet
DC Bay	double-contact bayonet			candelabra
	candelabra		SC Pf	single-contact prefocus
DC Pf	double-contact prefocus		ST	screw terminal
	candelabra		2B	two button
EMEP	extended mogul and prong			
F	ferrule contact		2PM	two pin miniature (trupin
Mc	minican			TrP*)
Med	medium		2PP	two pin prefocus
Med Bp	medium bipost		3P	three prong
Med Pf	medium prefocus			
Med Skt	medium skirted			
Med 2P	medium two pin			
MEP	mogul end prong (also:		Notes:	
	extended mogul end prong)			
Mog	mogul		R1 indicates special	
Mog Bp	mogul bipost		reference point for LCL.	
Mog Pf	mogu l prefocus		(R indicates an obsolete	
Rect RSC	rectangular recessed		reference.)	
	single contact		* - Obsolete Designation	
RSC	recessed single contact			
	(also: single contact			
	recessed)			

Figure 6–4 Base shapes most commonly used on both tungsten-standard and tungsten-halogen filament lamps. The bases shown are used on both types of lamps, with the exception of the recessed single contact (RSC) and double-ended contact (DEC). The latter two are restricted to tungsten-halogen filament lamps only. A *bayonet base* has either one or two "bosses" on the rim of the base. The bayonet(s) insert into matching slots in the socket. A slight twist of the lamp locks it into place with the filament positioned accurately in relation to the reflector. A *recessed single-contact base* inserts into spring-loaded sockets. A *two-pin pre-*

For example: A lamp marked BD30 should be burned base down and at an angle not to exceed 30 degrees from vertical. A lamp marked BU45 should be burned base up and at an angle not to exceed 45 degrees from vertical. Most studio lamps are in the BD30 and BD45 categories. Lamps used in ellipsoidals, and some follow spots are in the BU30 and BU45 categories. Most photofloods, R, and PAR lamps will be in the ANY position category.

Occasionally, a lamp will have BDBU marked on it, but it would rarely be used in a studio. Slide and film projectors can take a lamp marked BDTH (base down, theater), but that is beyond the scope of this book.

Other measurements Manufacturers apply two other measurements to tungsten-standard and tungsten-halogen lamps:

- LCL—light center length
- MOL—maximum overall length

Light center length applies only to single-ended lamps. LCL is the distance from the filament center to a given reference point on the lamp base. The measurement varies with the type of lamp, as shown in Table 6–3.

Maximum overall length on a single-ended lamp is measured from top to bottom, including the pins, buttons, ferrules, screws, etc. MOL on a double-ended tungsten-halogen lamp is measured from tip to tip.

Both measurements are of importance when changing lamps or replacing them with a different type. For example, when replacing a single-ended tungsten-standard lamp with a single-ended tungsten-halogen lamp, the center of the filament must have the same measurement in order to be in

Table 6–3   LCL Measurement Points

Type of Lamp	From Center of Filament to:
Mogul bipost	Shoulder of post
Medium bipost	Bottom of bulb
Bayonet base	Top of base pins
Prefocus base	Top of pins
Screw base	Bottom of base
Two-pin prefocus	Bottom of base

Figure 6–4   *(continued)*

focus base has pins of uneven diameter so that the lamp fits into its matching socket in one position only. A *prefocus base* (mogul and medium) is fitted with uneven "bosses," i.e., fins, located just below the bulb so that the base is to be placed into its matching socket in one position only. It is locked in place by giving the bulb a short turn in the socket. The position of the filament is then automatically aligned with the reflector. A *screw base* (mogul and medium) is the most common in use. To prevent breaking it at the juncture of glass and metal, a screw base lamp should be fitted into a socket carefully so that it is just snug (not too tight). A *medium skirted base* (known in some areas as mogul-to-standard adapter), is attached to large size bulbs that would normally utilize a mogul screw base. By fitting the medium-skirted base to the lamp, the unit can then be used in a medium socket. *Extended mogul end prongs* insert into a flat-blade socket inside the housing. Lamps with the shortened *mogul end prongs* are rarely used in motion picture, video, or theater fixtures. *Screw terminals* require the wires of the incoming feed cable to be attached to each side of the lamp; they are then held in place by tightening the screws. *Ferrule contacts* on a lamp insert tightly into matching sockets. A *bipost base* (mogul and medium) has two contacts imbedded in glass and fused to the bulb. The posts in the base can be placed in a matching socket with no regard for the positioning of the filament with respect to the reflector since the alignment is automatic either way. Courtesy of GTE Products Corp., Sylvania Lighting Division.

alignment with the reflector, even though the tungsten-halogen globe is a smaller size than the standard globe. Double-ended lamps must be replaced with units of the same length.

6.2 ANSI FILAMENT LAMP DESIGNATIONS

Under the auspices of the American National Standard Institute (ANSI, 1430 Broadway, New York, NY 10018), manufacturers have agreed to a designation system that ensures easy identification and interchangeability of fixture lamps with those of like code from all manufacturers who use the code.

ANSI-coded interchangeable filament lamps have a three-letter code (BTA, DXH, FFS, etc.) that is for convenience only. Information regarding the lamp's characteristics must be obtained from the manufacturer.

It is good practice to pronounce each letter of the code separately rather than phonetically. For example, an FEY is a 2000-watt double-ended 3200K lamp, but an FAY is a 650-watt PAR 5000K lamp, and although the names "FEY" and "FAY" *sound* alike, one bulb cannot fit in the fixture of another.

chapter 7

Carbon Arc

The arc lamp was invented in 1801 by Sir Humphry Davy (1778–1829, England). For many years its main uses were to light construction projects, to illuminate night rescue efforts along the coastlines, and to provide the light to dazzle spectators at fairs and exhibits. The arc was introduced to theater stages about 1849. Later, in the early 1900s, filmmakers were able to move their sets indoors because of the arc; the intensity of the flame provided enough light to "bite" into the slow emulsions in use at that time.

In the beginning, arcs were used for general fill, but as always, through trial and error as well as experimentation, lighting people discovered how to tame and direct the rays of the arc by incorporating the iris, the barndoor, scrims, shutters, and so on (see Lighting Controllers and Light Modifiers, Chs. 12 and 13, respectively), thus enhancing the art of lighting for the screen.

In the early days of cinema, arcs had to be handcranked in order to produce light; the electrician who did the "trimming," as the cranking was called, had to be as skillful as the cinematographer handcranking the camera in order to maintain a flickerless light. Back then, on many a job the arc lamp was rented as a package that included the person to "trim" its carbons as well, and to distinguish the person as an "arc specialist," he was known as a *Lamp Operator,* a term still used today to denote a studio electrician, male or female. Arc electrodes are now fed by motor; the firing, adjusting, and other operating procedures of an arc are considered part of every journeyman electrician's duties.

A carbon arc fixture (Fig. 2–3) used in motion picture or video work is called a *studio arc* to distinguish it from a projector-type fixture, such as a theater follow spot or a searchlight.

NOTE: A *follow spot* has an ellipsoidal reflector (see Ch. 4) that concentrates the light from the carbons toward a small aperture; the rays in turn are transmitted through an optical system that filters the ultraviolet rays given off by the burning carbons. A *searchlight* contains a polished parabolic reflector (see Ch. 4) that concentrates and directs the light into parallel rays; the front of a searchlight is fitted with plane glass that filters the ultraviolet rays.

The high-intensity light emitted by a studio arc produces sharp shadows and is useful as a single-source keylight where sunlight or moonlight effect must be duplicated in either exterior or interior settings; it is also used as an exterior fill light where dark shadows produced by the sun must be diluted.

Although the arc scatters light in all directions within the enclosed housing, it is the fresnel lens (see Fixture Lenses, Ch. 3) at the face of the fixture that directs the light into a controllable beam. The carbon arc is focusable and can be "spotted down" whenever a long throw of light is required.

The unit's angle of tilt is limited, since it can only be burned at an angle of ±45 degrees from level. An angle greater than ±45 degrees will damage either the feed mechanism or the fresnel lens.

A studio arc depends on three components for its operation: (1) electrodes, (2) feed mechanism, and (3) grid (resistor).

7.1 ELECTRODES

Two carbon electrodes, a negative and a positive, are necessary to maintain the arc (Fig. 7-1). Electrodes vary in diameter and length depending on the amperage rating of the fixture (see Table 7-1). Carbon electrodes also fall into two light-emitting categories: White flame and yellow flame. The light emitted from both the white-flame and yellow-flame carbon arc has a continuous spectrum, but it is high in ultraviolet. Therefore, the light requires filtering in order to bring it into color balance (see Filtering the Arc, following).

7.1a Negative Electrode

When current from the grid (see The Grid, following) is applied to the negative electrode at its butt end, the copper jacket, being a greater conductor of electricity than the carbon encased within it, serves to carry most of the current along the outside of the electrode shaft. Its bullet-nose shape directs the current that flows along the copper jacket to the tip, where the electrons are concentrated into one steady steam aimed at the lower lip of the crater on the positive electrode carbon. The copper jacket of the negative oxidizes and drops away as the negative burns down.

7.1b Positive Electrode

The current flows across the ionized space between the two carbons to the positive electrode and is then diverted through electrical contacts, called brushes, located in the feed mechanism (see Feed Mechanism, following). The brushes are situated near the positive carbon's cratered end to minimize the heating of the positive, which could otherwise burn along its entire length.

7.1c Interaction of Negative and Positive Electrodes

The stream of electrons from the bullet-nose negative causes the solid material of the cratered positive to become a gas, and this action produces the arc flame. Close observation of a burning negative through a safety glass viewing port will reveal a small tongue of flame spurting from its tip. It is this flame, in addition to the rotating action of the positive carbon, that continues forming the crater in the positive electrode as it burns down.

7.1d Carbon Electrode Placement

The burning time of an electrode varies depending on its length, how quickly it is trimmed, and on the gap being properly maintained (Table 7-2).

Access to the interior of a studio arc is obtained, whenever electrodes are to be changed, by tilting the lamp mechanism out from the rear of the housing. On older models, an access door at the right of the housing lifts up to reveal the mechanism.

A word of warning, however. Although the voltage is low, the amperage in a studio arc is extremely high. One must bear in mind at all times: High amperage is a killer. Therefore, ALWAYS TURN OFF THE POWER SWITCH BEFORE CHANGING CARBONS.

Table 7-1 Electrode Sizes

Type of Arc	Amps	Flame	Positive		Negative	
			English (inches)	Metric (mm)	English (inches)	Metric (mm)
Titan	350	White	0.63 × 25	16 × 640	11/16 × 9	17.5 × 230
		Yellow	0.63 × 25	16 × 640	11/16 × 9	17.5 × 230
Brute*	225	White	0.63 × 22	16 × 560	17/32 × 9*	14 × 230
		Yellow	0.63 × 22	16 × 560	17/32 × 9*	14 × 230
Litewate Brute	225	White	0.63 × 22	16 × 560	17/32 × 63/4	14 × 170
		Yellow	0.63 × 22	16 × 560	17/32 × 63/4	14 × 170
Baby Brute	225	White	0.63 × 22	16 × 560	17/32 × 63/4	14 × 170
		Yellow	0.63 × 22	16 × 560	17/32 × 63/4	14 × 170
150	150	White	0.63 × 20	16 × 510	1/2 × 81/2	13 × 220

*Some Brutes have been fitted with negative electrodes 63/4 inches (170 mm) in length.

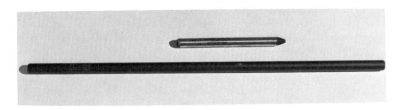

Figure 7–1 Carbon electrodes. The negative carbon is copper-jacketed. The arc end of the negative is bullet-nosed. The positive carbon, the longer and greater in diameter of the two, contains a core of material that volatizes and becomes incandescent when it is bombarded with electrons. The core consists of compounds of the cerium group of rare earth metals combined in a mixture with carbon. The arc end of the positive has a concave depression referred to as a *crater*. Courtesy of Mole-Richardson Co.

Table 7–2 Burning Time of Carbon Electrodes per Hour

Amperage	Positive	Negative
350	20 inches (510 mm)	10 inches (254 mm)
225	20 inches (510 mm)	10 inches (254 mm)
150	9 inches (228.6 mm)	4½ inches (114.3 mm)

Note: The positive burns faster than the negative; a rough rule of thumb is 2 positive carbons to 1 negative per hour.

The interior of an arc housing becomes very hot when the carbons burn. To prevent receiving severe burns to the hands when contacting hot metal, one needs to develop a routine practice of using pliers to depress levers and to remove and/or replace carbons, etc., when working on an arc *even when the housing is cold.*

7.1e Inserting the Negative Electrode

When the dimpled release lever is depressed (Fig. 7–2), the negative carriage drops down to its extreme retracted position. Near the dimpled release lever is a spring-levered negative carbon holder; when one side of the carbon holder is depressed, the roller is lifted; the butt end of the negative carbon is then inserted into a V-block against the stop. Upon releasing the holder, the roller will lower against the shaft of the negative carbon and clamp it in place.

7.1f Inserting the Positive Electrode

A *camming lever* is located inside the rear of the housing. (On older models, it may be a knob outside the rear housing.) When the lever is rotated clockwise, the brushes that clamp the positive carbon will then spread, permitting the positive to be slid into position from outside the arc housing. The outside *striker lever* (beneath the control box) on the rear plate must then be depressed. This action brings up the negative carbon so that its tip will point at the hole of the positive brush assembly.

While holding the striker lever depressed, one inserts the positive carbon through the tube in the control box at the rear of the housing, crater end first, and pushes through *gently* until the crater touches the negative carbon. With the positive carbon positioned in this manner, the negative carbon will make contact with the center of the positive carbon during the arc strike rather than on the underside of the carbon shell. The negative must

Figure 7–2 Carbon-arc mechanism. Courtesy of Mole-Richardson Co.

NEGATIVE CARBON HOLDER

ROLLER

NEGATIVE DRIVE GEAR

NEGATIVE BAFFLE PLATE

DIMPLED RELEASE LEVER

POSITIVE BAFFLE PLATE

POSITIVE BRUSHES

FEED GEAR

CAMMING LEVER

POWER LEADS

MOTOR

GEARBOX

WORK LIGHT

MANUAL NEGATIVE HANDCRANK CONNECTING SHAFT

STRIKER LEVER ARM

MANUAL POSITIVE HANDCRANK CONNECTING SHAFT

be centered so that the positive will not shatter the crater lip when the arc strikes.

After centering, the striker lever is released and the negative carbon is allowed to drop down into its burning position. Next, the camming lever has to be rotated counterclockwise, so that the feed gears of the mechanism (see Feed Mechanism, following) as well as the brushes will grip the positive carbon.

The arc is now "carboned." In preparation for striking the arc one needs to tilt and latch the lamp mechanism back into place. On older models, one only has to close and latch the access door.

7.1g Striking the Arc

With the unit's switch turned to "on," so that current will flow, the striker lever is *gently* depressed until the negative carbon touches the positive carbon. When contact is made the striker lever must be released immediately. If polarity is correct (see Polarity, following), the arc will fire; if incorrect, and a sputter and hiss results, the switch should be turned off, the cables from the grid reversed, and the arc restruck.

7.2 THE FEED MECHANISM AND "TRIMMING" THE ARC

Once the arc has been struck, the positive carbon is cranked approximately three half-turns clockwise to advance the carbon to its nearly correct burning position.

As the electrodes burn away, they must be fed by motor toward each other in order to maintain a constant distance so that the most efficient flame will be maintained.

An *external rheostat* controls the rate of speed of a small electric motor within the housing; the motor controls the feed and rotates the positive carbon.

If the speed of the motor is too slow, the electrodes will part, resulting in loss of light. If the speed is too fast, the gap will shorten, causing an increase in current that will overload the carbons and result in unsteady "flicker." By turning the rheostat to adjust the speed (fast or slow), the operator can easily cure the "flicker" problem and produce a steady flame.

In addition to the rheostat, *manual hand cranks* outside the housing are connected to overriding clutches so that either carbon can be trimmed and adjusted independently of the motor.

It takes a few finite manual adjustments to set the gap to its proper distance (see Striking the Arc, earlier) once proper speed is established.

The upper handcrank trims the positive; the lower handcrank adjusts the negative (see additional reference to the rheostat and handcrank in Feed Mechanism, following).

7.2a Flame Characteristics

In a properly trimmed arc, approximately 70 percent of the light is emitted from the positive crater, and only 30 percent emitted by the *tail flame,* which is a combination of positive and negative outer flame. Since the edges of the tail flame are erratic and have a tendency to "flicker," baffles have been placed inside the housing toward the condenser to hide and prevent the flickering edges form interfering with the smooth center ray.

Underflame is "spill" from the negative tongue flame. Experienced studio arc operators use the shape of the underflame to indicate whether the positive is pushed too far into the housing, or more than 1½ inches (38.1 mm) from the baffle plate, or not far enough, less than 1⁷/₁₆ inches (36.5

mm) from the baffle plate. Too much protrusion of the positive will cause the underflame to billow beneath the positive; too little protrusion will cause the underflame to just about reach the edge of the crater. The ideal flame is shown in Figure 7–3.

7.2b Relight of Previously Burned Carbon

Once a carbon arc has been extinguished and is to be relit, it must be remembered that although the electrodes have been trimmed, i.e., finite adjustments have been made to the electrodes during its previous operating time, certain precautions are necessary. All instructions pertaining to *new* carbons apply to preburned carbons. Failure to regard preburned carbons as though they were new could result in a cracked and unusable positive electrode when the negative is brought up to restrike the arc. Therefore, when restriking an arc fixture containing preburned carbons, the positive must be cranked back, the striker lever depressed, and then the positive cranked forward *gently* to make contact with the negative *before* the unit is switched to "on." Then the normal procedure for striking and trimming is followed.

7.2c Polarity

The studio arc works on direct current (DC). In any DC circuit, the negative carbon must be connected to the negative side of the line and the positive connected to the positive side of the line. If these connections are the wrong polarity, the arc will sputter and hiss. If allowed to run in the wrong polarity, the core of the negative will burn out and the end of the positive will chip or split. Whenever sputter or hiss occurs, the arc should be switched off immediately and the lines from the grid to the housing reversed.

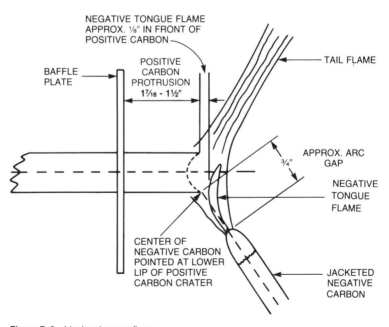

Figure 7–3 Ideal carbon-arc flame.

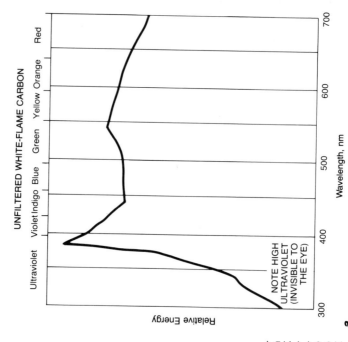

Figure 7–4 (a) Extended SED graph of unfiltered high-intensity white-flame carbon. Unfiltered white-flame carbon light has a continuous spectrum very high in ultraviolet and high in the visible "violet-indigo" areas. The light has a color temperature of approximately 6200K (±300K). (b) (facing page) Extended SED graph of the same white-flame carbon light intercepted by a Y-1 filter. Note how the ultraviolet is reduced. The filtered light has a color temperature of approximately 5700K (±300K). (c) (facing page) Extended SED graph of the same white-flame carbon light intercepted by a Y-1 plus MT-2 filter. Note the great reduction of the "blue" end of the spectrum. The filtered light has a color temperature of approximately 3100K (±300K).

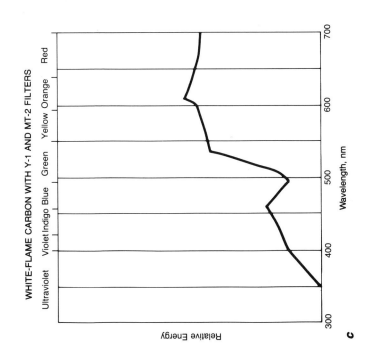

WHITE-FLAME CARBON WITH Y-1 AND MT-2 FILTERS

c

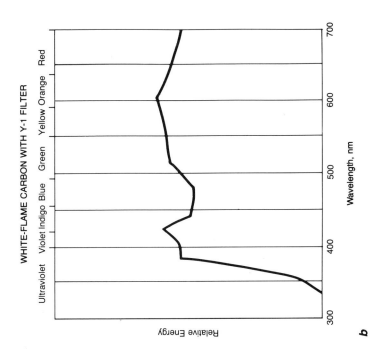

WHITE-FLAME CARBON WITH Y-1 FILTER

b

Figure 7-4 (continued)

79

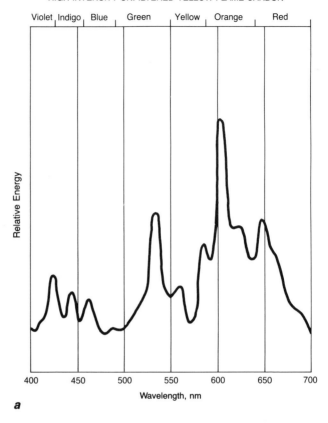

HIGH-INTENSITY UNFILTERED YELLOW-FLAME CARBON

Violet | Indigo | Blue | Green | Yellow | Orange | Red

Relative Energy

400   450   500   550   600   650   700

Wavelength, nm

a

Figure 7–5 (*a*) An SED graph of high-intensity unfiltered yellow-flame carbon. Unfiltered yellow-flame carbon light has a continuous spectrum with peaks in yellow and green. The light has a color temperature of approximately 4100K (±200K). (*b*) (facing page) An SED

A warning light at the rear of the housing glows when the polarity is reversed, but it should not be relied on as infallible. In case of failure of the warning light, the hiss and sputter are the only clues the Lamp Operator has that something is wrong.

7.3 THE GRID

The *grid* is a bank of resistors (coiled nichrome) that will not oxidize from heat. Input to the grid must be 120 volts (±10 volts DC) Therefore a 230-volt feeder cable must be "split" or the fixture's grid will be damaged. The grid reduces the 120-volt input to 73 volts across the electrode gap without reducing the amperage. Fins on the resistors serve to dissipate the great amount of heat generated by the high amperage.

More than 73 volts applied to the electrodes will cause excessive current to flow, and the carbons will burn away faster than normal. If high voltage is not adjusted for, the negative carbon will burn to a slender point. Less than 73 volts applied to the electrodes will cause a reduction in current, and

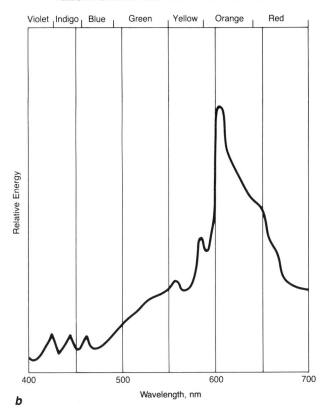

YELLOW-FLAME CARBON WITH YF OR YF-101 FILTER

Figure 7–5 (*continued*)
graph of yellow-flame carbon intercepted by a YF or YF-101 filter. Note how the peaks are reduced and the "red" end of the spectrum is enhanced. The light has a color temperature of approximately 3200K (±200K).

if the current is not corrected, the negative will burn to a blunt end. In either case, the arc flame becomes erratic and unusable.

Adjustment of the rheostat located at the rear of the housing and controlling the speed of the feed mechanism can, to a great degree, compensate for either excessive or insufficient voltage. If it is necessary to use the rheostat for this purpose, then finite adjustment can be made to the electrodes by using the handcranks to increase or decrease the gap between them, as pointed out in Feed Mechanism, earlier.

7.4 FILTERING THE ARC

Since all light emitted from carbon electrodes is high in ultraviolet, the light must be filtered to bring it into proper color balance. As noted previously, two types of electrodes are manufactured: white flame and yellow flame. Both can be used for black-and-white or color, and on either emulsion or target area. Regardless of the type electrode used, additional filters on the lamp are necessary in order to film/tape in color. Arc filters are listed in Ch. 14, Table 14–4.

7.4a White Flame

The SED graph in Figure 7–4*a* (page 78) indicates the relative values of "blues" to "reds" in a continuous spectrum and the Kelvin temperature of unfiltered white-flame carbon electrodes. The SED graph in Figure 7–4*b* (page 79) shows what happens to the relative values of the continuous spectrum and the Kelvin rating when a Y-1 filter is placed on the arc light. Use of a Y-1 filter alone converts the arc flame to a "daylight" balance. The SED graph in Figure 7–4*c* (page 79) reveals the changes that adding an MT-2 filter brings to the spectrum and color temperature of a white-flame arc. Use of an MT-2 with the Y-1 makes it possible to use the arc in an "interior" setting, with film balanced for 3200K to 3400K.

Use of the combined Y-1 and MT-2, while correcting the light to a color temperature of approximately 3100K, also drastically reduces the unit's light output (nearly half). When using arc light in the 3200K range, the yellow flame electrodes are recommended.

7.4b Yellow Flame

The SED graph in Figure 7–5*a* (page 80) indicates the relative values of "blues" and "greens" to "reds" and the Kelvin temperature of an unfiltered yellow-flame arc. The SED graph in Figure 7–5*b* (page 81) shows how the placement of a YF or YF101 filter on an arc light alters the relative values of the continuous spectrum and brings its Kelvin rating to 3200K.

chapter 8

The HMI Lamp

For a number of years, the HMI lamp, manufactured by Osram, in Germany, was the only such lamp in use in the lighting field. The HMI, as such, is trademarked; however, HMIs are now trademarked under several names.* The standards of quality are equally high on all lamps. (No endorsement is implied by the authors when the term *HMI* is used for all such lamps.)

The principle of the HMI was known for many years. In the mid-1960s, at the behest of the German television industry, who sought more efficient and less expensive lighting units, Osram GmbH (Munich) created the HMI lamp. Its use was introduced in 1972 for European television lighting. Filmmakers saw great possibilities for the lamp and began to use the units extensively. Use was hampered in the United States and other nations where 220-volt electric power and 50-Hertz (cycles) frequencies were not the norm. Modification of fixtures was refined, and adaptation to certain camera shutter angles and motor requirements, not previously in their respective film industries, had to be undertaken (detailed below).

The term *HMI* is used to specify a modified high-intensity discharge lamp, and is not to be confused with the Industiral High Intensity Discharge Lamp (see Industrial HID Lamps, Ch. 10). The modification for currents not 220 volts and 50 Herz involves the shortening of the arc, changes in bulb configuration, and addition of metal oxides and bromines. The letters *HMI* are an acronym for Hg, the symbol for mercury; M, for medium arc; and I, for iodides.

An SED graph (Fig. 8-1) shows that an HMI lamp has a multiline spectrum. Lamps, whether double-ended, single-ended, or PAR, are manufactured with three color temperatures: "daylight" of 5600K ($\pm$400K); "daylight" of 6000K ($\pm$500K), and "interior" of 3200K ($\pm$200K). When using HMI lamps, *always* verify the color temperature, since not all HMI "daylight" lamps are the same, e.g., a Britebeam** 1200 PAR has a C.T. of 5600K while a Metallogen† 1200 PAR is 6000K. At this writing the 3200K lamp is limited to a Britearc double-ended 1200W, although it can be made available in all sizes by *any* manufacturer on special order.

Many HMI lighting units have open-face housings with a heat-resistant, ultraviolet-absorbing glass placed at the front of the housing (see Safety

---

*HMI and Mettalogen, trademark of Osram Corp.; Brite-Arc, trademark of Sylvania GTE; Daymax, trademark of ILC Technology, Inc.

**Trademark Sylvania GTE

†®OSRAM Corporation.

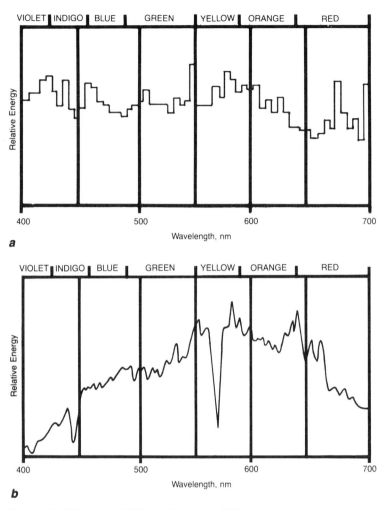

Figure 8–1 SED graphs of HMI lamp. Although the HMI lamp has a line spectrum, metallic oxides have been added to the bulb. These oxides emit individual lines at *each* wavelength and therefore impart to the lamp a *multiline* spectrum with each "spike" so close that the lamp emits wavelengths comparable to a continuous spectrum. (*a*) 5600K (daylight) type. Courtesy of Osram Corporation; (*b*) 3200K (interior) type. Courtesy of ILC Technology, Inc.

Precautions, below). The ultraviolet-absorbing glass is either clear, for maximum intensity, or stippled, to soften the projected rays. Open-face units are manufactured in both fixed-focus and variable-focus models. Manufacturers have also placed HMI lamps in enclosed housings fitted with fresnel lenses and focus controls. While the unit is focusable, its coverage and intensity (except at spot position) are less than those of an open-face unit of comparable wattage. With the exception of the 18K fixture with its modified parabolic reflector, much of the energy from the arc of an enclosed-type fixture is lost because the unit's reflector does not collect and distribute the HMI arc light properly: Most of the emitted energy is wasted because it is lighting up the interior of the housing. However, the focusable

HMI fixture is more versatile and more controllable than the open-face HMI, and therefore more popular.

8.1 THE LAMP

An HMI lamp requires an auxiliary ballast (see following) in order to operate, and is composed of three basic parts: bulb, electrodes, and base.

8.1a The Bulb

The HMI bulb is made of fused quartz, a high form of silica glass. The bulb shape varies to conform to the shape of the arc. At the time of manufacture, oxygen is withdrawn from the bulb and, along with mercury vapor and argon gases, metallic oxides, such as dysprosium, holmium, thalium, etc., plus a halogen (bromine), are injected into the bulb before it is sealed.

There are about ten different metal oxides that can be added to mercury vapor. Depending on the type, when it is added in proportional amounts, it is possible to increase response over the entire spectrum. The type and amount of added oxides determine if the final product will have a correlated color temperature of 5600K, 6000K, or 3200K.

The addition of the halogen (bromine) prevents the interior wall of the bulb from becoming blackened by tungsten evaporating from the electrodes (see Filament Lamps, The Bulb, Ch. 6, for details of the tungsten regenerative process). Therefore, no discoloration of the bulb occurs.

The physical dimensions of an HMI lamp vary according to its wattage. Figures 8–2 and 8–3 illustrate the configuration of the various types of defined lamps, and Tables 8–1 and 8–2 defines their measurements. The approximate "daylight" output of a 5600K and 6000K lamp are compared with an incandescent lamp in Table 8–3. HMI lamps have a higher lumen-per-watt efficacy of 80 to 102 percent. Note the following information carefully for best use of these lamps:

All single-ended lamps, which are primarily manufactured to work in a vertical axis, plus the 200-watt, 575-watt, and 1200-watt double-ended lamps, can be tilted up or down at any angle from their horizontal axis and still maintain a stable arc; the double-ended 2500-, 4000-, 6000-, 12,000-, and 18,000-watt lamps, however, will often show an unstable arc (flickering and color temperature change) when positioned at an angle of more than ±15 degrees from horizontal. However, *regardless of size,* the double-ended lamp must always remain on a horizontal axis. Placing the housing on its side, for instance, so that the lamp then burns vertically (or at a degree of axis other than horizontal) will affect the lamp's arc stability and color temperature.

The new HMI lamp is high in ultraviolet light (Fig. 8–4) and the fast films in use today are highly sensitive to ultraviolet. Therefore, when using HMI units with these fast films, a new lamp does not always emit the "best of all possible light." When an HMI lamp has less than 200 hours of use on it, an ultraviolet filter should be placed on the camera lens. After 200 hours of use, the filter is no longer needed.*

---

*It is always a good idea to check the amount of time on a lamp. Although an HMI fixture is fitted with a counter, it *is* possible that the unit has been relamped and the counter not changed. If so, the time recorded on the counter is of no value. When the unit is rented, the rentor should be able to supply the rentee with a record of the lamp's burning time.

Quite often the counter is checked before and after a job to determine how much burn time is on the lamp, because in some rental houses the lamp itself is rented separately from the fixture and paid for on a use-only basis, while the fixture is paid for on a daily basis. As the lamp burns the ultraviolet diminishes, but the film response remains the same.

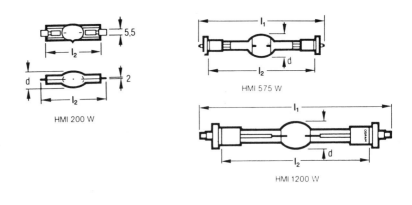

HMI 200 W

HMI 575 W

HMI 1200 W

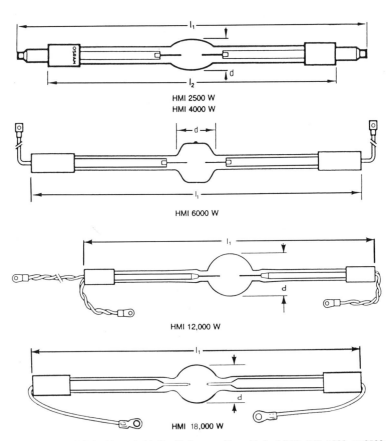

HMI 2500 W
HMI 4000 W

HMI 6000 W

HMI 12,000 W

HMI 18,000 W

Figure 8-2 HMI double-ended bulbs. Bulbs are either elliptical (200, 575, 1200, or 2500 watts) or tubular (4000, 6000, or 12,000 or 18,000 watts) depending on size. HMI bulbs are virtually "custom-made," and some are given serial numbers so that their history can be checked and recorded from date of manufacture to time of burnout. The 200-, 575-, and 1200-watt bulbs can be burned in *any* position; the 2500-, 4000-, 6000-, 12,000-, and 18,000-watt bulbs must be operated horizontally (within ±15 degrees), which limits their application. Disregarding these limitations will shorten the bulb's life considerably. Courtesy of ILC Technology, Inc.

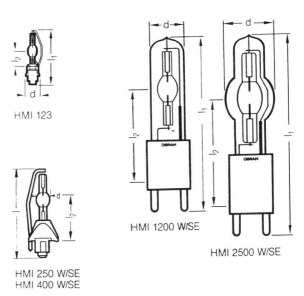

HMI 123

HMI 250 W/SE
HMI 400 W/SE

HMI 1200 W/SE

HMI 2500 W/SE

Figure 8–3 HMI single-ended bulbs The 123-, 250-, 400- and 575-watt (not shown) lamps are fitted with a nickel-plated copper support bar. The 1200- and 2500-watt lamps are double-jacketed, and the inner unit (the lamp's burner) is stabilized by a molybdenum pin. Courtesy of Osram Corporation.

Since an HMI has half the infrared emission energy of an incandescent lamp, it is self-defeating to use the HMI for such photography. The HMI is a comparatively "cool" source of light because of the low emission of infrared rays, and infrared film will not "pick up on it."

Safety precautions Since the arc in double-ended, single-ended, and HMI PAR lamps is high in ultraviolet radiation, damage can be done to the eyes when the bare bulb is viewed without a protective glass. Prolonged exposure to its unfiltered rays can also be harmful to the skin. Fixtures that house an HMI lamp are fitted with a protective heat-resistant glass (either clear, stippled, or fresnel lens) at the unit's face to absorb the emitted ultraviolet rays. The heat-resistant glass presses against a safety switch that automatically extinguishes the lamp if the glass is broken or the fresnel lens is swung away from the housing.

WARNING: Never attempt to use an HMI SE lamp in a fixture built to accept incandescent lamps. HMI lamps require a housing and circuitry capable of handling high voltages. Misuse of the lamp in the wrong type of fixture could cause electrical shock, fire, or damage to the fixture.

A heated HMI lamp builds up pressure within the bulb and is dangerous because it can explode if broken before it is completely cooled. Additionally, an HMI bulb contains mercury, and although the amount is small, one must remember that the mercury *can* be a lethal pollutant. We highly recommend that a burned-out or broken lamp be handled with protective gloves, wrapped in a plastic bag, and placed in a sealed metal drum for disposal to prevent mercury dispersal. The burned out and/or broken unit should be disposed of in an area designated for toxic wastes, not just thrown into the nearest trash bin in a city dump.

Table 8–1 Measurements of HMI Double-ended Lamps

Lamp		HMI 200 W	HMI 575 W	HMI 1200 W	HMI 2500 W	HMI 4000 W	HMI 6000 W	HMI 12,000 W	HMI 18,000 W
MOL	l_1 max (mm)	75	135	220	355	405	450	470	495
Diameter	d(mm)	14	21	27	30	38	55	65	75
Bulb length	l_2 max (mm)	60	115	180	290	340	–	–*	–*
Arc gap	(mm)	10	7	10	14	34	20	25	45

Source: Osram Corp.
*Varies slightly by manufacturer.

Table 8–2 Measurements of HMI Single-ended (SE) Lamps

Lamp		HMI 123W/SE	HMI 250W/SE	HMI 400W/ SE	HMI 575W/SE	HMI 1200W/SE	HMI 2500W/SE
MOL	l_1 max (mm)	64	84	84	145	195*	210**
Diameter	d (mm)	10	12.2	15.5	30	42	60
Bulb Length	l_2 max (mm)	26.7	35	35		107*	127**
Arc Gap	(mm)	4	5	5	7	10	14
Base		spec.	FaX	FaX	G22	G38	G38

*Available also as 1200W/SEL (Single-Ended Long) with l_1 of 215mm and l_2 of 127mm.
**Available also as 2500W/SEL (Single-Ended Long) with l_1 of 230mm and l_2 of 145mm.

8.1b Electrodes

The electrodes in an HMI lamp are made of tungsten-coated molybdenum. The gap between the electrodes varies according to the wattage of the lamp (Tables 8-1 and 8-2) and, depending upon the wattage, requires certain voltages to maintain the arc after the lamp has been activated (Table 8-3).

An ignitor is necessary to initiate the arc (see Ballast, below). When current is applied, the vapor in the bulb ionizes (this warmup time takes about 1 minute) as the initial arc discharge of high intensity occurs. The arc travels from one electrode to another, and, as it does, the electrons in the mercury are "jarred" between orbits. The intense speed at which the electrons transfer causes energy to be given off, producing light, but full color temperature is not reached until the lamp has been on and all gases within the bulb have ionized for about 3 minutes.

After working with HMI fixtures and accumulating expertise, one does not necessarily consult a timepiece to see if the lamp has warmed up, reached color temperature, or is operating at proper power. What one does is look at the illuminated lamp (through the ultraviolet shielding glass and using a Gaffer's glass or smoked glass) and check the position of the arc itself for clues as to "where the lamp is" in regard to its readiness for operation. One can see the arc go through changes. Immediately following

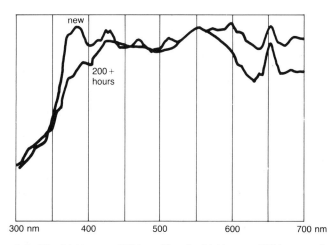

Figure 8–4 Ultraviolet in a new HMI lamp. The ultraviolet in a new HMI lamp remains high for at least 200 hours.

Table 8-3 Comparison of HMI Double-and Single-Ended Lamps with Incandescent/Carbon Arc Lamps

Lamp	HMI 123W/SE	HMI 200W*	HMI 250W/SE	HMI 400W/SE	HMI 575W**	HMI 1200W†	HMI 2500W††	HMI 4000W	HMI 6000	HMI 12000W§	HMI 18000W
Initial supply voltage	220	230	220	220	230	230	230	380	230	240	360
Lamp voltage	80	80	50	55	95	100	115	200	125	160	225
Amperage	1.7	3.1	5.4	7.3	7.0	13.8	25.6	24.0	55	83	88
Approximate incandescent equivalent	650W	1K	1K	1.5K	3K	5K	10K	2–10Ks	225 Carbon Arc	350 Carbon Arc	350 + 225 Carbon Arc +

*The HMI 200W (double-ended) and the HMI 200W PAR utilize the same initial Supply Voltage, Lamp Voltage, Amperage and approximate incandescent equivalent.

**The HMI 575W (double-ended), the HMI 575W/SE, and the HMI 575W PAR, utilize the same initial Supply Voltage, Lamp Voltage, Amperage and Approximate incandescent equivalent.

†The HMI 1200W (double-ended), the HMI 1200w/SE, and the HMI 1200W PAR, utilize the same initial Supply Voltage, Lamp Voltage, and Amperage.

††The HMI 2500W and HMI 2500W/SE utilize the same initial Supply Voltage, Lamp Voltage, and Amperage.

§Some double-ended 12,000W/HMI lamps (used in Europe) require an initial Supply Voltage of 380 v, have a Lamp Voltage of 224v, but only draw 62 amps. Their output is still equivalent to a 350 Carbon Arc.

ignition, the arc will often show tall "spikes" of mercury vapor riding the top. As the pressure increases in the bulb and the other gases ionize, the spikes slowly "flatten out" until they are very minute, or look like little pips. The spike (or pips) remaining on the arc after 3 minutes also provides a clue as to whether the proper voltage is reaching the electrodes. If there is an excess of voltage, the spike riding on the arc will often vibrate, become erratic and, in extreme instances, "bounce" around inside the globe. The vibrations will create "arc flicker," which may not necessarily be seen on the object being covered by the lamp's rays if the fixture is used in conjunction with other units. It will be apparent if the arc itself is viewed, and *will* be seen as a slight unsteady waver of light on the subject when the film is viewed later in the screening room.

Another factor to bear in mind is that when excessive voltage is applied, the electrodes erode more rapidly than normal. As the distance between the electrodes widens, it then becomes more difficult to reignite the arc. Poor control of voltage can cause lamps with less than 100 hours (which is one-third to one-seventh of the lamp's average life depending on bulb size) to be discarded as "unusable." When there is an *insufficient* amount of voltage to the electrodes, the spikes will disappear and the arc, instead of being a thin line, will appear to broaden out as a thick line. Serious attention must be given to proper control of voltage. It takes much time and practice to learn to evaluate the arc by eye. When this *is* mastered, the experience is invaluable on the job.

Color temperature   Even with proper voltage applied, electrodes do wear away, causing the lamp to draw more amperage and to lose one degree Kelvin in color temperature per hour of operation. The better-constructed HMI fixtures are fitted with counters calculated in hours and minutes so that time on the bulb can be readily checked. *Color temperature loss* of an HMI lamp can be compensated for by either filtering its rays or by altering the voltage. Rather than alter the voltage on a 5600K lamp as the color temperature decreases, a one-eighth or one-quarter booster blue filter can be placed on the fixture lens (see Fixture Filters, Ch. 14) to bring it back to "daylight" color temperature.

Lowering the voltage to an HMI will *increase* its color temperature; *raising* the voltage will *decrease* the color temperature. This occurs because as the current is decreased, less of the metallic oxides in the bulb are ionized and more mercury vapor (which is predominantly "blue") is emitted. Conversely, when the current is increased, the oxides ionize at a faster rate, overpowering the mercury vapor and thus emitting more "reds." This is contrary to the principle involved in incandescent tungsten standard or tungsten-halogen lamps.

Ambient temperature will also affect the Kelvin rating of an HMI lamp. Extreme cold, wind, or cool air will lessen the thermal emission from the connections and bulb and the color temperature will rise. Extreme heat, hot air, or enclosed spaces where convection is limited will cause an overheating of connections, a rise in bulb temperature, and a decrease in color temperature. Consideration must be given to the use of shields to protect the fixture from windchill factor, air conditioners, direct sun rays, or hot air vents.

Since the ambience of an area can alter the color temperature of an HMI anywhere from 4500K to 9500K, those who use HMIs should make it a practice to check the color temperature of each unit each time it is "fired and up to temp." Then, if found deficient or high, each unit can be fitted with either one of the booster blue, 1/4 or 1/2 series, or one of the 1/4, 1/2 85 series, or combination of both booster *and* 85 filters (see Fixture Filters, Ch. 14) to bring each lamp into the 5500K to 6500K range. Each housing is chalked with the type of filter pack to be used with that fixture and the pack placed on the unit each time it is used during the day's shoot. Many lighting people are content to check each unit's color temperature only at the start of a shoot, but careful people check color temperature set-up by set-up. It may take a few moments, but it will show up on the viewing screen — either way.

8.2 BASE
HMI lamps are fitted with double-ended and single-ended bases and differ depending on the lamp size.

8.2a Double-ended (see Fig. 8–2)
A 200-watt lamp has a knife-plug base (flat metal tab). The 575- and 1200-watt lamps have threaded-in bases. The 2500-, 4000-, 6000-, 12,000-, and the 18,000-watt lamps have plain-pin bases; the latter three lamps are also fitted with connection wires and clamps.

On some fixture sockets the knurled knobs on the 575-watt and 1200-watt lamps can be used to tighten the lamp in place after it has been inserted in the sockets. On other units the knurled knobs must be removed and discarded before the lamp can be inserted into its sockets. It is always good practice to inspect a fixture's socket carefully when replacing a lamp, especially if the lamp does not "fit" at the first try.

Manufacturers recommend that the base-lamp temperature of an HMI lamp should not exceed 230°C (446°F), the exception being the 18K (280°C or 536°F). The double ended, nickel-coated brass bases often provide a visual clue as to whether the socket is at its proper temperature or is overheating. The more extreme the temperature, the more the base darkens, electrical resistance increases, and lamp life is shortened. At excessive temperatures the metal will peel and chip. The most common causes for overheating are an improperly seated lamp in a socket and/or inadequate ventilation. When the lamp is properly seated, the addition of a heat sink to the socket to draw off thermal retention may cure the problem. External air cooling by fan or vacuum is not recommended unless the fixture is fitted for it by the manufacturer. For example, since heat inside an 18K lamp housing is excessive and can melt the interior of the housing and other components, the extended double-ended lamp sockets are fitted with foamed aluminum heat sinks (Fig. 2–1*b*). Additionally, an internal fan draws air from outside the housing, forces it through the bottom of the aluminum foam pores to help dissipate the high internal temperate, and removes the excess heat through convection, which keeps the lamp temperature below its maximum 280°C or 536°F.

There is a right way and a wrong way to insert a double-ended lamp into its sockets. First and foremost, the power should be off and the fixture should be cool, especially if an old or burned-out lamp is to be replaced (see Safety Precautions, above). All bulbs should be handled with clean cotton gloves or the padding the bulb is packed in. (Acid from the skin will mar and shorten the bulb's life). *Never* touch a lamp with the bare hands or fingers. If the bulb has been touched, the glass should be cleaned with alcohol and polished with soft cotton. Before inserting the lamp, all sockets, heat sinks, and electrical connections should be checked to determine that they are free from corrosion and dirt.

The lamp should be inserted with the ribbon horizontal and the nipple on the elliptical or tubular bulb pointed upward or toward the fixture lens, never down or toward the reflector. Finally, the lamp should be checked to see that it is tight in the sockets, that the pressure clamps are holding the lamp's base, and/or that the lamp is secured into the sockets by the threaded knobs on the lamp itself.

8.2b Single-ended (Fig. 8-3)
At this writing, the single-ended 123W Special base and the 250W/SE and 400W/SE Fax base are new and have been named by the manufacturer* who developed them. Once approved by the American National Standards Institute (ANSI), there is a possibility the bases may be re-named. The Special base and the Fax base fit small battery-powered portable lamps intended for newsreel camera use.

8.3 BALLAST
A *ballast* (Fig. 8-5) is a current-limiting device that controls the amount of voltage between the power buss or the generator and the lamp. A ballast varies in weight, depending on the wattage of the lamp it powers. Ballasts range from heavy-wheeled units weighing up to 159 kilos (350 lb) to hand-carried units weighing in at 1.7 kilos (3.5 lb). Manufacturers constantly work to lighten their ballasts. However, keep in mind that, because crew members prefer lighter loads (especially as the day wears on), the weight of a ballast rather than its technical excellence may unduly affect the crew's assessment of a piece of equipment. A few small ballasts are attached directly to a fixture's housing, but most are independent of the housing. When the igniter switch on the fixture is "fired" (activated), the initial volt-

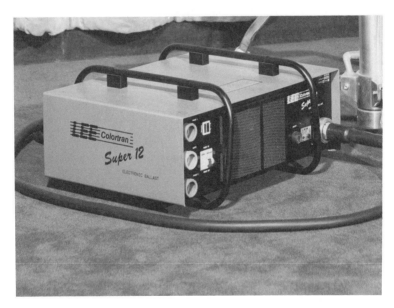

Figure 8–5 HMI Flickerless Ballast. Courtesy Colortran, Inc.

---

*OSRAM Corporation.

age to the ballast is increased 20 to 50 kilovolts (20,000 to 50,000 volts), which flows to the lamp's electrodes and creates the arc.

NOTE: Most people fear the peak voltage in the HMI ignitor circuit and believe that because the arc is fired in kilovolts it is a dangerous fixture to work with, and that *that* is the reason the unit should be grounded. Actually, the amperage in the ignitor circuit of a ballast amounts to approximately 0.25 to 1 amp and could cause a slight "tickle," depending on how well a person is grounded; it could, however, cause serious harm if the unit is shorted and the person is standing in water. The jolt from the 110-volt, 10-amp line leading to the fixture has more potential danger; *that* is why an HMI lighting unit should be grounded.

Some manufacturers of the 12w, 200w, 575w, 1200w, and 2500w ballasts have installed a ground-fault interruptor (GFI) in the unit. If an electrical leakage (short) should occur and draw more than 5 milliamps of power over its normal voltage, the ballast will shut down in 1/30th of a second. But, *never* assume that a unit is fitted with that safety factor! *Check it out* to see that it is *properly grounded.*

Once the lamp is fired, the coil in the ballast acts as a "choke"—it regulates the current (up or down) to maintain a steady rate of voltage flow to the lamp so that the lamp is neither over- nor under-powered (see Table 8–2). As the electrodes in the lamp burn away, the gap widens, the amperage drops, and the voltage to the lamp increases. The ballast compensates for this and serves to maintain a balance between amperage and voltage.

Ballasts are manufactured to operate in one of two modes: "constant power" or "constant current." The former delivers constant power to the lamp regardless of the lamp's voltage, but has a high start-up current, and more components; the latter delivers constant current on start-up, "fires" the lamp faster, has fewer components, and brings the lamp to its rated color temperature sooner. Even so, depending on who manufactures it, there are arguments favoring one over the other, not only by electronic engineers but also by users.

HMI ballasts are manufactured to accept an input of 220 volts, 50–60 Hz AC (actually they will operate with a voltage input ranging between 180 to 240 volts and a frequency ranging from 45 to 65 Hz) from the mains or a generator. Many ballasts intended for use in countries with electrical power that is less than 220 volts are manufactured so they can be plugged into 120 volt AC wall outlets, hooked up to 120-volt bussbars or to 120-volt generators. Such ballasts are fitted with an internal step-up (120 to 220 volts AC, 120 to 380 volts AC, or 120 to 360 volts AC, depending on type) transformer. There are also a few ballasts manufactured to accept either AC or DC (see DC Units, following). They will operate on inputs of 90–130 volts, 45–65 Hz AC—or 90–130 volts DC. All three types are available worldwide.

NOTE: While some ballasts can be plugged into and operated from a household outlet, in a studio they generally work off an AC bussbar supply from feeder cables; on location/remote, from an AC generator.

The 4K and the 18K each utilize a step-up transformer that boosts power from 120/220 volts to 380 volts and 120/220 volts to 360 volts, respectively. Once the lamp is "fired," the arc in the bulb is sustained (through the design of components, wiring, etc.) by bringing the voltage down to the lamp's operating level (see Lamp Voltage, Tables 8–2 and 8–3).

Ballasts manufactured for use in nations where 230 volts is standard power, do not use step-up transformers except in the 4K and 18K, which are fitted with step-up transformers to boost the initial voltage and fire the arc at 380 volts.

Regardless of its country of origin, it is important to ascertain the supply voltage of the input of the ballast.

When in operation, a non-solid-state ballast will sometimes emit an alternating current (AC) hum, which is caused by the magnetic components (reactor, transformer, etc.) and/or a frequency conversion. When this occurs, the ballast should be placed a suitable distance from the fixture (and action) to avoid noise pick-up by dialogue-recording microphones.

Concerning input plugs, polarity indicator, frequency meter, voltmeter safety lights, etc., each manufacturer differs in the fabrication and configuration of its specific models.

8.3a DC Units

Until recently a battery-powered unit, designed primarily for TV news, utilized a 200-watt double-ended lamp only. While that lamp is still in use, a typical recently manufactured battery-powered HMI fixture* with an integrated ballast utilizes a 250-watt single-ended (SE) lamp. The battery is a nickel-cadmium type and weighs 8.16 kilos (18 lb). It can be powered by 120 volts AC, 230 volts AC or 30 volts DC. The battery can supply approximately 30 minutes of power to 5600K (±400K) color temperature. A charger is available to recharge the battery.

To provide power to HMI "studio-type" fixtures 575 watts or larger, at this writing only one manufacturer's** solid-state units (the 575/1200 watt, 2500-watt, 4K, 6K, and 12K—no 18K—are fitted with a regulator that accepts as few as 90 volts or as much as 130 volts (AC or DC). If DC, the input voltage is inverted and stepped-up to 220 volts 50/60 Hz AC. If AC, the input voltage is stepped up to 220 volts 50/60 Hz AC.

8.4 DIMMING

HMI units can be dimmed either optically or electrically.

8.4a Optical Dimmer

Optical dimming of the HMI is accomplished by placing a shutter at the front of the fixture lens (see Lighting Controllers, Ch. 12). It does not alter the color temperature. It should be noted that closing the shutter too slowly, especially in low light levels, can create an effect that would be seen as "venetian blind" strata across the scene.

8.4b Electric Dimmer

While research and development continues to produce a workable unit, the only dimmer available at this writing is the common Variac (Variable AC) resistor. The dimmer reduces voltage to a lamp and has limitations.

When using a Variac with an incandescent lamp, the color temperature drops and the emitted light goes toward the red end of the spectrum. With its use with an HMI arc lamp, the color temperature (see above reference) increases, and the emitted light goes toward the blue end of the spectrum. At about 30 to 40 percent reduction of light (from 70 to 90 volts) the color temperature makes a sudden shift toward the blue-green, similar in hue to an unfiltered fluorescent lamp, and because the arc can no longer be sustained at that low voltage the lamp goes out. (The rheostat on the Variac must be turned up to maximum voltage before refiring the HMI, otherwise the arc will not ignite.) When done swiftly, in a high-light-level situation,

---

*LTM France/LTM Corporation of America's "Blue Torch."
**Lightmaker Company.

the color temperature shift may not be detectable except to the well-trained eye before the lamp extinguishes.

8.5 "FLICKER EFFECT"

Although recent technology has brought to market AC "flicker-free" ballasts, the fact remains that many older magnetic (choke-type) ballasts are still in use and still are *not* "flicker free." Therefore, a brief background and a few solutions to the problem of "flicker" are offered here in the event non–"flicker-free" (choke-type) ballasts are used. With the advent of the HMI lamp, film people realized the HMI was more efficient in light output and, regardless of its wattage, produced more light, emitted less heat, and used less energy than a comparative-sized incandescent lamp. But when the units were used with no regard for the variations and limitations of light, shutters, and camera speeds, the results were scenes that looked like the old-time movies of handcranking days. Back then, before the use of motors on cameras, the length of time a frame of film was exposed to light depended on the rhythm of the Camera Operator's turning the handle. When the frame was exposed too long, the film frame projected as too bright; when exposure was not long enough, the film frame projected as too dark. Handcranking had to be at a steady pace, exposing each frame equally. Thus a very long scene was tiring to the Operator. Density of the film was affected, depending on the length of time the frames were exposed to the light when the aperture was open.

The introduction of synchronous motors assured that the exposure of each frame was even, and "flicker" became a thing of the past. Or so it seemed until Directors of Photography used HMI lights and saw the results—there, on the screen, was flicker. Many film people turned away from the HMI, while others decided to work on the problem to determine why a modern lamp in wide use with *video* produced results without flicker, but did produce the flicker effect when used with *film.*

Numerous ways were discovered to overcome the "flicker-effect" problem. Based on recommendations from the lamp manufacturers, tests by photographic engineers, and working cinematographers, the following data were compiled. "Flicker" will result from uneven exposure (variation of density) on a frame of film:

1. When the film stock is limited in exposure latitude.
2. When a scene is underexposed.
3. In unlit areas predominantly covered by HMI fixtures.
4. When a scene is lit by a mix of incandescent fixtures and HMI units.

"Flicker*less*" cinematography will result from control of four factors:

1. Constant light pulsations from the lamps.
2. Constant frequency to the fixtures.
3. Compatible shutter setting of the camera.
4. Constant frame rate of the camera.

When any one of the preceding is ignored, "flicker" will be present.

NOTE: The use of a ballast fitted with a converter, which changes a typical sine-wave pulse to a square-wave pulse (see Fig. 8–9b), will reduce the possibility of "flicker." The square-wave ballast will pulse more light time than trough time. (See Square Wave Frequency, following.)

8.6 LIGHT PULSATION

All lamps, filament and arc discharge, that operate on alternating current (AC) will fluctuate—actually go off and on at twice the Hertz of the circuit at which they are operating. On a 50-Hz circuit, the fluctuation is 100 times per second, and on a 60-Hz circuit, the fluctuation is 120 times per second. When a circuit fluctuates 100 times per second, this means that there are two pulses of emitted light coming from the lamp per cycle (100 fluctuations divided by 50 Hz = 2 pulses), and the same applies to a circuit with 120 fluctuations (120 fluctuations divided by 60 Hz = 2 pulses).

The major difference between the filament lamp and the arc lamp, however, is the variation between the time the light goes on and then goes off, on and off, ad infinitum. The variations in light fluctuation of a filament lamp at twice its supply frequency, i.e., 50 Hz (100 times) or 60 Hz (120 times) is depicted in Figure 8-6. The variation in light fluctuation of an HMI gas-discharge lamp at twice its supply frequency is depicted by Figure 8-7. If the camera shutter is open when an HMI light pulse (1) is going out,

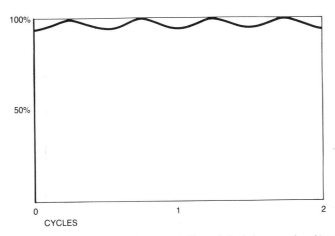

Figure 8-6 Typical filament-lamp intensity graph. The variation between peak and trough is slight and may only vary 10 or 20 percent because thermal retention in the filament does not permit the lamp to go out completely.

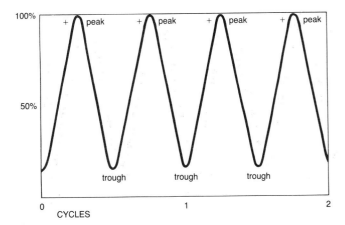

Figure 8-7 Typical HMI intensity graph. The variation between peak and trough may range between 60 and 85 percent because the arc is extinguished completely. The degree of variation depends on the size of the arc. The larger the lamp, the greater the variation.

(2) is out; or (3) is starting to come on (in a trough, see Fig. 8-7), the film frame will be unevenly exposed and the variation in density will appear on the screen as "flicker." When an HMI lamp is used as fill light (see Using the Fixture, Ch. 17) on a daytime exterior, however, this uneven exposure may not be discernible because the ambient daylight compensates for the loss of the lamp light. When an HMI is used on an interior as the *only* source of light and the camera speed, shutter, and lamp light pulses are not compatible, then "flicker" will be the result.

8.6a Constant Frequency

The supply frequency to the fixture *must* be constant so that pulses of light emitted from the fixture's lamp are of the same duration (see Light Pulses, following). A variation in the frequency will result in erratic light output; the frequency must be checked often. A frequency meter is essential when filming with HMI units, and they are built into some ballasts. When the ballast indicates that the frequency is constant, it is safe to assume that *all* the fixtures taking power from the same line are on the same frequency. However, the place to check the current frequency is anywhere in the line *before* the power gets to the fixtures (which should be fired up and already at color temperature).

8.6b Frequency/Light Pulsation Considerations and Options

Frequency from the electric utility services supplying the main power to a location or studio (outlets or bussbars) cannot be taken for granted. Surges and ebbs of voltage can change with the commencement and/or cessation of office/factory work nearby and can influence the voltage and frequency to the lamps considerably as power stations "switch over" and/or adjust for an increase or decrease of load. If, while filming, the lighting units appear to blink quickly or the units increase or decrease in intensity, a quick check of voltage and frequency is imperative.

An AC generator (see Generators, Ch. 16) that is used to supply power to HMI units requires a very sensitive frequency regulator. One cannot merely crank in a "guesstimate" on a generator's rheostat and walk away thinking that, since the unit has a voltage regulator and/or a governor, it will take care of itself. A generator must have a precision "frequency lock" and an operator to stay with it to make certain the frequency does not vary more than plus or minus one-quarter cycle. If there is more variation, light pulsations will be erratic; "flicker" is almost a certainty. Ideally, the unit should also have an alarm signal in the event of an over/under-modulation of frequency. In other words, one cannot merely call an equipment rental house and say, "Send me an AC generator." The type and its use with HMI lighting units must be explicitly stated. To utilize a generator that cannot be "fine-tuned" is asking for a visual catastrophe in the screening room.

8.6c Multiphased Frequency

This method utilizes a three-phase AC system whereby each lamp is connected to a different phase and "staggered" in frequency so that the emitted light pulses overlap. What this does is to provide peak or near-peak light from at least one of the lamps while the other two alternate between coming on and going off. There is never a trough where the light is actually out. Figure 8-8 illustrates the way the light pulses overlap. A three-phase AC system requires three times the number of lighting units to film a scene, one unit for each phase.

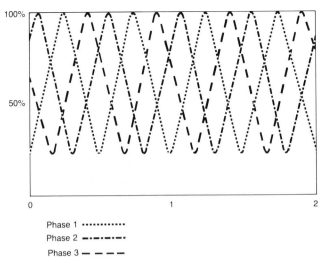

Phase 1 ············
Phase 2 ─·─·─·─·
Phase 3 ─ ─ ─ ─

Figure 8-8 Typical light-fluctuation pattern from a three-phase AC input. The "crossover" of peaks and troughs minimizes the uneven exposure time to the point that it is barely discernible.

8.6d Square-Wave Frequency

Most choke-type ballasts, when checked on an oscilloscope, display a typical sine-wave form (Fig. 8-9a). A few ballasts are constructed so that the AC input is converted to a square wave—is pulsed in such a manner that instead of the pulse rising to a rounded peak before it starts to fall, the top of the peak is "platformed" (Fig. 8-9b). With the rounded peak flattened out, the "hump" of the light pulse (the rise and fall aspect of it) moves horizontally instead. By "squaring the wave," the rise and fall duration of time is pulsed as steady light rather than the tailend of a rise and beginning of a falloff of light. And since the square-wave platforms are wider at the peak of a pulse, the trough is "squeezed" together (Fig. 8-10) the lamp is out less time than it is on.

A "flickerless" ballast usually shows a square wave in which the platform is almost a straight line with only a "glitch" (dip in the line) to indicate where the light goes "out" for only milliseconds (Fig. 8-11). Thus, the lamp emits an almost steady pulsation of light.

8.6e Increased Frequency

Most frequencies in the world are either 50 or 60 Hz. An HMI lamp does not necessarily have to be operated at these cycles. A special ballast is constructed that converts the 50- or 60-Hz input to other frequencies. When frequency is accelerated, the lighting unit emits more light pulses and the camera registers more light pulses per frame per shutter rotation (see Shutter, below).

Since the lamp goes off and on at twice the rate of the circuit at which it is operating (120 pulses at 60 Hz and 100 pulses at 50 Hz), when the frequency is increased to 200–250 Hz, the light will go off and on between 400 and 500 times per second. The more light pulses, the less likelihood there is that a density change will register on the film. Increased frequencies are generally limited to the 200–250 Hz range.

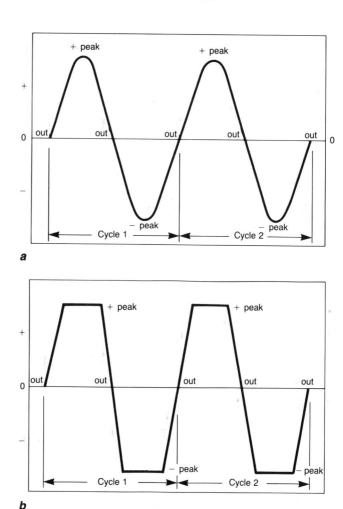

Figure 8–9 (a) Typical sine wave. A sine wave is used to indicate how the current alternates between plus and minus through its cycles. (b) Typical square wave. A square wave is a sine wave that has its plus and minus peaks flat instead of round.

It should be understood that this increased frequency will only eliminate "flicker" at 24 to 25 frames per second (fps) when the shutter angle is more than 100 degrees. At higher speeds and/or at shutter angles less than 100 degrees, the flicker risk is still there unless the increased frequency is multiphased (see above). In practice, at 200–250 Hz, the arc "sings" — resonates (toward the scene) with the noise, taking the path of least resistance, so that filming with sound is impossible.

8.6f Constant Frame Rate

Motor speeds vary from nation to nation. Some film standards call for motor speeds of 24 fps; others call for motor speeds of 25 fps. In the near future, with the practice of film being directly transferred to tape for postproduction editing, we will be seeing more productions being filmed and projected via video at 30 fps.

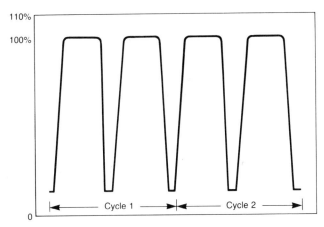

Figure 8–10 Typical square-wave intensity graph. The flat peak of a square wave expands the amount of time the light is on and narrows the gaps between the troughs.

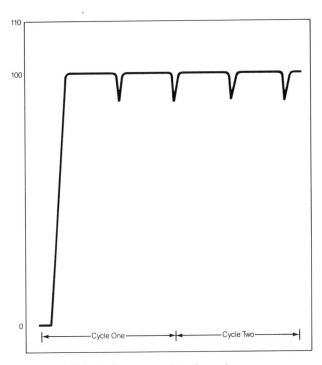

Figure 8–11 Typical "flickerless" square wave intensity graph.

Regardless of the frame rate (24 or 25 fps) or the frequency (50 Hz or 60 Hz), it is essential that the camera be fitted with a crystal-controlled motor, so that the shutter opens and closes at precise, nonvariant speed. For example, if a variable ("wild") motor were to be used on the camera, the frame rate could vary anywhere from 22 fps to 26 fps as the motor runs. The variation of speed would also vary the amount of light reaching the film frame—which would be viewed as "flicker."

A "constant-speed" motor does *not* ensure the user that the constant speed is *precisely* at 24 fps or 25 fps, although the motor markings may make that claim. Many constant-speed motors are found to be constant at speeds of 23, 23$^1/_2$, 23$^1/_4$, 24$^1/_4$, 24$^1/_2$, 24$^3/_4$ fps, etc., and the same applies to 25 fps constant-speed motors. This discrepancy is usually not noticeable where a constancy of motor speed is not critical, such as in daylight, or under tungsten lights, where frequency to the lamps is not subject to high peaks and deep troughs because of thermal retention of the filament, as noted in Figure 8-6.

A crystal-contolled motor can drive a camera for a length of 10,000 feet (3048 meters) with less than a one-frame variation. This precise frame rate ensures the exposure of the film to a specific number of light pulses each time the shutter rotates.

When the motor is crystal-controlled and the frequency to the HMI unit is 60 Hz, then at 24 fps the light will pulsate 5 times for every rotation of the shutter (120 pulses per second divided by 24 fps = 5 pulses per second; Fig. 8-12). With a 180-degree shutter on a reflex camera, this means that, at 24 fps, 2$^1/_2$ pulses will be utilized for exposure of the film and 2$^1/_2$ pulses will be utilized for viewing. Any variation in the motor speed and/or shutter will cause a variation in light reaching the film—which will be seen as "flicker."

When the motor is crystal-controlled and the frequency to the HMI unit is 50 Hz, then at 24 fps the light will pulsate at 4.17 times for every rotation

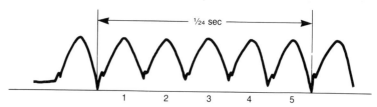

Figure 8-12 Light pulses at 60 Hz and 24 fps. With a crystal-controlled camera motor running at 24 fps and lamps with a frequency of 60 Hz, five light pulses will register every 1/24 second.

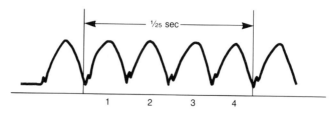

Figure 8-13 Light pulses at 50 Hz and 25 fps. With a crystal-controlled camera motor running at 25 fps and lamps with a frequency of 50 Hz, four light pulses will register every 1/25 second.

of the shutter (100 pulses divided by 24 fps = 4.17 pulses per second). With a 180-degree shutter on a reflex camera, this means that 2.09 pulses will be utilized for exposure of the film and 2.09 pulses will be utilized for viewing. At 25 fps, an HMI unit at 50 Hz will pulsate 4 times for every rotation of the shutter (100 pulses per second divided by 25 fps = 4), with 2 pulses utilized for exposure and 2 pulses utilized for viewing. (Fig. 8–13).

It should be noted that some camera manufacturers have developed crystal-controlled motors that run at 30, 60, 90, and 120 fps (e.g., Panavision Inc.'s Panastar model) which allows for "flickerless" slow-motion cinematography. More cameras with this capability are coming on-line almost daily.

8.7 SHUTTER

Frequencies vary with countries (and sometimes *within* countries) and are either 50 or 60 Hertz. The shutter angle on a camera must be altered to compensate for the results differing frequencies have in relation to "flicker," and specific motor speeds at given frequencies require specific shutter angles to eliminate the undesirable effect. The optimum combinations are

> 24 frames per second/60 Hertz/144 degree shutter
> 24 frames per second/50 Hertz/172.8 degree shutter
> 25 frames per second/50 Hertz/180 degree shutter

At these speeds, frequencies, and shutter openings, four pulses of light (two for registry on the film; two for viewing) are utilized and frequency variations of up to plus or minus 3 percent can be tolerated.

To contend with the problem of choke-type ballasts and their resultant "flicker," camera manufacturers resorted to fabricating new, or altering old, camera shutters to match the optimum combinations noted above. A number of cameras are fitted with adjustable shutters so that the cinematographer has a choice of selecting (1) 144 degrees so that the camera can be run at 24 fps with a crystal-controlled motor and HMI lamps burning at a frequency of 60 Hertz; (2) 172.8 degrees so that the camera can be run at 24 fps with a crystal-controlled motor and HMI lamps burning at a frequency of 50 Hertz; (3) 180 degrees so that the camera can be run at 25 fps with a crystal-controlled motor and HMI lamps burning at a frequency of 50 Hertz.

8.8 HMI PAR FIXTURE

The HMI PAR fixture houses a sealed-beam containing an HMI lamp (Fig. 8-14). At this writing, HMI PARS are available in three sizes: 200 watts, 575 watts, and 1200 watts. The basic HMI PAR lamp is manufactured in a very narrow spot (VNSP) only. To alter the beam of the unit, additional lenses are manufactured to fit into the front of the fixture's housing. These lenses—spot, medium, wide, and very wide—change the character of the light rays.

The rear of the HMI PAR housing rotates. As with all sealed-beam units, there is a definite rectangular shape to the beam that projects, according to the position of the lamp. If the lamp is horizontal, the light pattern will be wider than higher; if the lamp is rotated until the arc is vertical, the rectangular light pattern will be tall and narrow. Rotating the lamp between horizontal and vertical will produce a rectangular beam at an angle. Any one of the added lenses will disperse the pattern to a great extent, but the proportional pattern will still be there.

Figure 8–14 HMI PAR fixture and lenses. Courtesy of LTM Corporation of America.

To eliminate the beam pattern requires practice. It is accomplished by "feathering" the projected beam edges. For example, when a fixture is aimed and projects a rectangular beam pattern (wider than narrow) on the lower part of a wall, a second fixture is placed next to it, tilted up slightly, and the bottom of *its* wide beam is aimed just above the lower beam pattern. To achieve an even light-meter reading when "stacking" the beam patterns, the second fixture's beam is "feathered," i.e., adjusted slightly so that its bottom rays blend with the top edge of the first fixture's rays. Barndoors, scrims, flags, and so forth, are used to control the beam pattern, just as with other fixtures.

8.9 CSI/CID LIGHTS

The CSI/CID arc discharge lamp is a metal halide light source of British origin. The acceptance of either lamp in the United States has been slow as of this writing, although many outdoor sports arenas (football, baseball) are utilizing the units more and more.

The term CSI stands for compact source iodine; the term CID stands for compact indium discharge, although the CID is often referred to as a "tin-halide" because it incorporates the iodide of tin as well as indium.

All information pertaining to HMI lamps (Ch. 8) applies to the CSI/CID lamp as well. It is suggested that Chapter 8 be studied carefully when working with, or under, CSI/CID lamp sources.

The CSI/CID lamp is also subject to "flicker," but its light fluctuations exhibit less trough time—it is "out" less time than the HMI lamp.

The CSI lamp has a CCT of 4200K (±400K) and the CID lamp a CCT of 5500K (±400K). The CSI/CID is manufactured in bi-post (dual-pin base) "quartz configuration" (where the globe is smaller than a standard lamp) as well as encased in a sealed-beam PAR lamp (see Filament Lamps, Ch. 6, for PAR lamp shapes). These are the PAR-type lamps that are being installed in sports arenas.

The CID is an improvement over the CSI and is especially designed for film and video lighting. Both lamp types are designed to be operated on 120-volt (USA) or 230-volt (European) lines.

chapter 9

The Fluorescent Lamp

Sir George Stokes (1819–1903, England) proved in 1852 that certain substances would fluoresce when stimulated by ultraviolet light. Armed with this knowledge, physicist Alexandre Edmund Bequerel (1820–1891, France) built a fluorescent tube that worked; his basic method is still in use today. For years, the operation of a fluorescent tube required high voltage, then in 1938 the first practical hot-cathode low-voltage fluorescent lamp was offered to the public by General Electric; the lamps have been in commercial use since then. Fluorescent lamps are efficient and inexpensive to operate and are in wide usage today, particularly in factories and office buildings.

This chapter concerns itself with the standard fluorescent lamps that are predominant today before dealing with the newer continuous-spectrum fluorescent lamps.

There are problems that need to be dealt with by crews working with, and under, standard fluorescent lamps. It is very important that lamps already installed at a location/remote site be checked for their Correlated Color Temperature (CCT)* and Color Rendering Index (CRI).** These ratings appear on each lamp or on its packaging material.

Problems related to working under standard fluorescent lamps fall in two categories: (1) Faulty Color Rendition, and (2) Flicker.

Correlated Color Temperature (CCT) is rated: "Warm White" (3000K), "Cool White" (4800K), "Daylight" (6500K), etc. These classifications and their color temperature ratings refer to *how the light appears to the adaptive eye only.* CCT does not take into account how the emulsion and/or target area, both of which are non-adaptive, will react to the light. Emulsion and target will register standard fluorescent light as it really is: With a predominance of blue-green wavelength which, when viewed in a screening room or on a monitor, will be seen as green, since blue registers less than green.

**Color Rendering Index (CRI)* is a numbering system ranging from 1–100. The CRI indicates how near in fidelity colors will appear when exposed to the lamp's rays, as compared to those same colors when viewed in natural daylight (which has a CRI of 100).

The CRI of the most common standard fluorescent lamps are: "Warm White"—56, "Cool White"—67, and "Daylight"—75. The higher the number, the more the object being lit will reflect true colors. For example, a standard fluorescent with an index of 75 or higher is capable of rendering a color very close to the object's true color. Red will appear red, green as green, blue as blue; however, a standard fluorescent with a rating of say, 45, might register green as a gray, red as dark maroon, and blue as a deep purple or black. A high rating does *not* mean that the unit has a continuous spectrum, or that filtering is *not* required, or that it is impossible to work under a lamp rated less than 75. It simply means that the higher-numbered CRI lamp will render better colors to the eye—but not necessarily to the emulsion or target.

9.1 FAULTY COLOR RENDITION

Since standard fluorescent lamps emit high radiation in one or more wavelengths depending on the type of lamp, the "color" of the most dominant wavelength will register as an overall hue or cast on the emulsion or target and is usually a blue-green. The eye will, in general, compensate for this special discrepancy, but emulsion and/or target area will *not* compensate.

Use of a color temperature meter to read the Kelvin of a fluorescent lamp must be approached with caution; not just any meter will do. A *two-color meter* is only capable of measuring the reds and blues and *assumes* the "middles" (yellow-greens) are there. A *three-color meter*, however, measures reds, blues, *and* yellow-greens, and therefore is more accurate because it indicates which filters should be placed on the camera lens and/or the fixtures, in order to render colors "true." An SED graph of a typical standard fluorescent lamp is shown in Fig. 9–1.

The most common standard fluorescent lamps found on a location/remote are the "Daylight" (CCT 6500 CRI 7), "Cool White" (CCT 4800K CRI 67), and "Warm White" (CCT 3000K CRI 56), and/or their equivalents. "Daylight" and "Cool White" lamps, or their equivalents, are used in supermarkets, factories and office buildings where there are large windows and doors that permit daylight to enter. These lights tend to "even out" the difference between interior and exterior lighting, thus eliminating the need for adjustment of the eye to the difference.

Areas with small, or no, windows generally are equipped with "Warm White" fluorescent or its equivalent; this type approximates incandescent

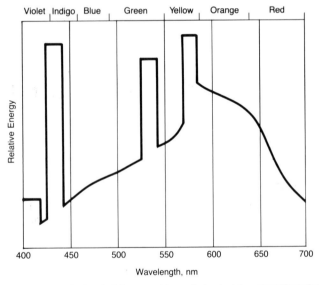

Figure 9–1 SED graph of typical fluorescent lamp. A standard fluorescent lamp has a hybrid spectrum. When activated, mercury vapor emits predominant wavelengths that "spike" (in this illustration at approximately 400, 435, 540, and 580 nanometers). At the same time, the activated phosphor radiates a continuous, but much weaker, spectra from 400 to 700 nanometers. Most colors will appear normal on an emulsion, or image plate, because of the continuous spectrum, but will have an overall hue of indigo, green, and yellow from the predominate wavelengths. When combined, the colors will appear on emulsion, or target, as blue-green. Fluorescent lamps "spike" as different wavelengths, depending on the type of vapor they have been filled with.

light and also eliminates the need for vision adjustment. In some instances a mixture of "Cool White" and "Warm White" will be found.

Working under standard fluorescent lamps is of more concern to those who are lighting for film, although those who are lighting for video cannot ignore the problems encountered in such areas in spite of the ability to "white balance" a video camera.

The following are a number of options available for filming/taping under fluorescent lamps *after determining the type of lamp installed at the location:*

1. Use fluorescent filters on the camera.
2. Treat the fluorescent lamps as "green daylight."
3. Filter the fluorescent lamps to daylight balance.
4. Filter the fluorescent lamps to 3200K.
5. Use a combination of color compensating (CC) filters and/or conversion filters (CF) and/or light balancing (LB) filters with an exposure increase on the lens.
6. Film/tape without filters and use fluorescent lamps.

1. *Use fluorescent filters on the camera.* Fluorescent filters (FLB/FLD)* remove the excess blue-green "spikes" from the standard fluorescent lamp's spectrum. By doing so, "Daylight" and "Cool White" standard fluorescent lamps are brought closer to daylight (Fig. 9–2). The FLB (Fluores-

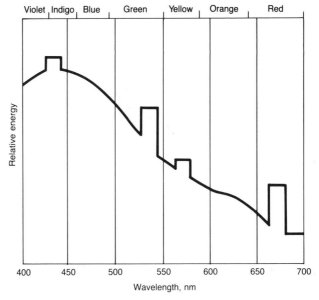

Figure 9–2 Typical effect of FL filter on fluorescent light. The FL filter reduces the predominate wavelength "spikes" of a hybrid spectrum and brings them closer to the phosphor wavelengths, which are a continuous spectrum. This illustrated reduction of the predominate wavelengths indicates that the filter would lower the "yellow-orange-red" end considerably and raise the "violet-indigo-blue" to a level close to daylight. A one-stop increase in exposure is necessary to compensate for the filter; a lightmeter is read as though exposing for daylight film.

*Manufactured by Tiffen Manufacturing Corporation, Hauppage, NY.

cent Type B film) is placed on a camera lens when film balanced for tungsten (3200–3400K) is being exposed. The FLD (Fluorescent Type–Daylight) is placed on a camera lens when film balanced for daylight (5500K +) is being exposed. An increase in exposure of one stop is required with either filter to compensate for light loss.

Although these filters work well, there are instances when a slight green hue will still be imparted to the emulsion or target, and this can be corrected in the film laboratory, or in the control room when transferring to tape.

However it must be remembered that use of the FL filters on the lens alone applies only when no daylight from windows or any supplemental lighting is used in the scene.

2. *Treat the fluorescent lamps as "green daylight."* When an FL filter is used on a camera lens and daylight comes through the windows or supplemental lighting (either 3200–3400K, or 5500K + light sources such as the arc, HMI, or dichroics) is used, one must bear in mind that, when the blue-green is deleted from the fluorescent lamps by the FL filter, the blue-green is *also* deleted from the daylight from the windows and/or the lamps used as supplemental lighting. When the loss of blue-green is not compensated for *at the time of filming or taping,* then later, when the scene is viewed in the screening room or tape monitor, the exterior seen through the windows will be pink in color, the light from the 3200–3400K lamps will turn everything red and the light from the 5500K + lamps will turn everything "rose color."

Therefore, to "put back" the green that the filter is deleting from the daylight and/or supplementary lighting, the windows *must* be covered with "Windowgreen"; 3200–3400K supplementary light sources will require filtering with "Plusgreen 50"; and the 5500K + supplementary lamps will require filtering with "Plusgreen" (see Table 9–1).

Table 9–1 Fluorescent Lamp Filter Purposes

Color	Purpose
GREEN	
Windowgreen*	Converts natural daylight from windows to fluorescent "green daylight"
Plusgreen*	Converts white flame arc and HMI lamps to fluorescent "green daylight"
MAGENTA	
Minusgreen**	Filters green cast from Cool White fluorescent lamps. Also on HMI lamps that read too "green." Will mix with daylight. Recommended use on Cool White fluorescents when HMI is primary source of light.
COMBINATIONS	
Plusgreen 50	Converts 3200–3400K incandescent light sources to fluorescent "green daylight."
Fluorofilter†	Converts fluorescent illumination to 3200K.

*Use with an FLB filter on camera if using "film balanced for light of 3200K to 3400K." Use with an FLD filter on camera if using "film balanced for daylight." Use either filter on video lens to correct for hue if camera is not equipped with a built-in fluorescent filter or "white balance" feature.
**Use 85A filter on camera lens.
†No filter required on camera.
NOTE: See Chapter 14, Table 14–5 for manufacturer equivalents of these filters.

Neutral Density (ND) filters may also be required on the windows to bring the light from the windows into balance with the light in the interior.
3. *Filter the fluorescent lamps to daylight balance.* This requires sliding a sleeve of the filter material "Minusgreen" onto *every* fluorescent tube except when the lamps are encased in a frame with either a grid or frosted glass panel. Then, it is easier to cut sheets of flat filter material to fit the fixture frame. "Minusgreen" absorbs the blue-green light that would appear on the emulsion or target if the fluorescent lamps were not filtered. A magenta-colored filter, it is intended for use on "Daylight" or "Cool White" fluorescent lamps or their equivalent. Any other type lamp found at the location/remote must be removed and replaced with the "Daylight" or "Cool White" type or equivalent.

Once filtered, however, the work area can be considered as a daylight balance, and will mix with daylight coming through the windows (see Table 9-1). Incandescent fixtures (fitted with dichroic or conversion to daylight filters—see Fixture Filters, Ch. 14, Table 14-1), and carbon arc and/or HMI fixtures (fitted with conversion filters—see Ch. 14, Table 14-4) can then be used on the supplementary units. The camera lens is filtered with an 85 filter if film stock balanced for light of 3200–3400K is being used, or is left unfiltered when using stock balanced for daylight. The use of these lamp filters can be applied quickly in small areas.

4. *Filter the fluorescent lamps to 3200K.* A "Fluorofilter" (see Table 9-1) corrects "Daylight" or "Cool White" fluorescent lamps to 3200K, and is manufactured to be applied as a sleeve over the tube or as a sheet from which the proper size can be cut to fit a fixture with either a grid or frosted glass panel. Windows that admit daylight must be covered with an 85-type filter.

A filter is not necessary on the camera lens when using film balanced for light of 3200K. Daylight-balanced film is *not* recommended. If a slight color discrepancy *should* occur, the laboratory can easily correct in printing.

5. *Use a combination of color compensating (CC) filters and/or conversion filters (CF) and/or light balancing (LB) filters with an exposure increase on the lens.* A CC Filter lessens certain colors of the spectrum while allowing other colors to transmit without alteration, and/or corrects for color deficiencies in emulsion batches as determined by in-plant tests by the manufacturer of the particular film in use. However, manufacturer's recommendations notwithstanding, personal and extensive tests at the site of filming are recommended.

A Conversion Filter (CF) (series 80 or 85) changes the spectral energy balance of light to match that of another. For example, the 80 series (80A, 80B, 80C, 80D, blue in color) converts light ranging between 3200K and 4200K to 5500K. The 85 series (85A, 85B, 85C, amber in color) converts light of 5500K+ to light ranging from 3200K to 3800K.

A Light Balancing Filter (LB) [series 81 (81, 81A, 81B, 81C, 81D, 81EF, yellow in color) and series 82 (82, 82A, 82B, 82C, blue in color)] allows for subtle adjustments in color temperature so as to either "warm" or "cool" a scene.

With most filters previously mentioned, an increase in exposure is necessary.

6. *Film/tape without filters and use fluorescent lamps.* A number of newer "continuous spectrum" fluorescent lamps are being used by many cinematographers and videographers. Actually, a "continuous spectrum" lamp is a fluorescent lamp that, although built the same as a standard fluo-

Table 9-2 "Continuous Spectrum" Fluorescent Lamps

Manufacturer	Type Name	CCT	CRI
Durotest	Optima 32 (O-32)	3200K	82
	Optima 50 (O-50)	5000K	91
	Vita-Life (V-L)	5500K	91
	Daylight 60 (D-60)	6000K	91
	Daylight 65 (D-65)	6500K	92
	Color Classer 75 (CC75)	7500K	93
GTE Sylvania	Design 50 (D-50)	5000K	91

rescent with the same wattage, diameter, length, base, and electrodes, differs in the blend of phosphor on the interior of the lamp. The phosphors increase response over the "blue" and "red" ends while leveling out the yellow-green "middles."

A "continuous spectrum" fluorescent lamp is lower in lumen output compared with a standard fluorescent lamp (approximately 35%), therefore a higher wattage of lamp should be used when replacing a standard unit in order to maintain the same footcandle measurement. The "continuous spectrum" lamps are shown in Table 9-2.

Either type (standard or "continuous spectrum") lamp emits a soft, even light. Quite often, when "continuous spectrum" lamps are placed in ceiling fixtures, they are also utilized on the floor as fill light (placed in fluorescent fixtures which are then mounted on rolling stands). Any other supplemental light (arc, HMI, incandescent) used for keylight or kicker or backlight, must of course be compatible with the CCT (3200K or 5500K) of the fluorescents.

Figures 9-3a through 9-3f show how two typical "continuous spectrum" fluorescent lamps compare to a filament lamp and standard "Warm White" fluorescent, as well as to skylight and to a standard "Daylight" fluorescent lamp.

9.2 "FLICKER"

The fluorescent lamp is a gas-discharge type of light source dependent on alternating current (detailed description follows). As with any AC lamp, the current reverses itself as it varies from plus to minus. The gas in a fluorescent lamp will discharge at a rate of twice the cycle of its frequency, so that a 50-Hz (cycle) light circuit will pulse light 100 times per second; a 60-Hz circuit will pulse light 120 times per second.

Unlike other gas-discharge lamps (see HMI, CSI/CID, HID) the fluorescent coating in the tube, when struck by an atom of gas (see Fig. 9-4) will remain fluoresced after the coating has been activated until it slowly fades. This action (the slow "dying" of the light) is called *decay time* and lasts only about one-half a cycle of the 50 or 60 cycles. Continuous bombardment of the coating and the natural retention factor of the human eye makes the lamp appear to give off constant light, although "flicker" can often be seen from the periphery of the eye; when one turns toward it, the "flicker" disappears.

Because of the opening and closing of a film camera shutter, however, the light pulses may not register on each exposed frame of film evenly: One frame of film may receive 4 light pulses while another frame might only receive 3 light pulses (a difference of about a half-stop in exposure), while another frame may register 3½ light pulses, still another 4 light pulses, etc. Then again, without the fluorescent coating, the phosphor, it is possible a

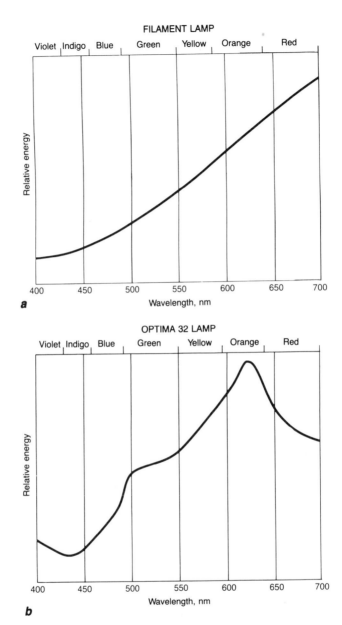

FILAMENT LAMP

Violet | Indigo | Blue | Green | Yellow | Orange | Red

Relative energy

400   450   500   550   600   650   700

a

Wavelength, nm

OPTIMA 32 LAMP

Violet | Indigo | Blue | Green | Yellow | Orange | Red

Relative energy

400   450   500   550   600   650   700

Wavelength, nm

b

Figure 9–3 *(a–f* above and on following pages) SED graphs of various types of light compared to fluorescent. These six SED graphs show how fluorescent lamps differ from each other as well as skylight, depending on their manufacture and intended use.

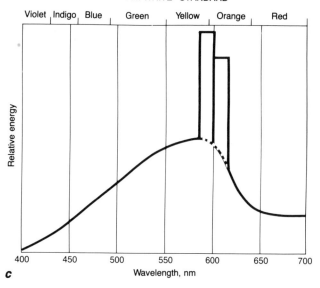

c

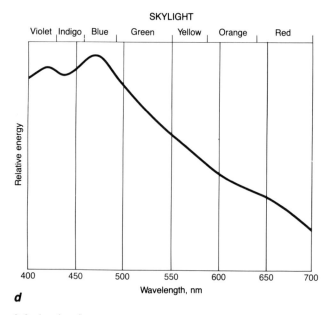

d

Figure 9-3 *(continued)*

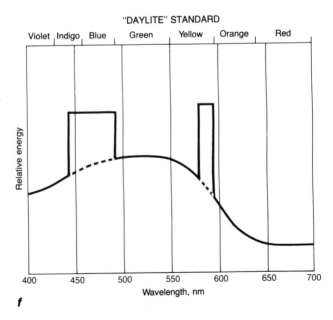

VITA-LITE LAMP

| Violet | Indigo | Blue | Green | Yellow | Orange | Red |

Relative energy

Wavelength, nm

e

"DAYLITE" STANDARD

| Violet | Indigo | Blue | Green | Yellow | Orange | Red |

Relative energy

Wavelength, nm

f

Figure 9–3 (*continued*)

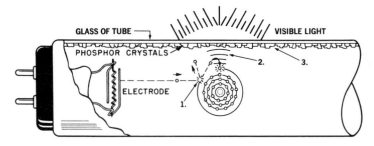

GLASS OF TUBE — VISIBLE LIGHT
PHOSPHOR CRYSTALS
ELECTRODE
1. 2. 3.

Figure 9–4 How light is produced in a fluorescent lamp. 1. Electrons emitted by the electrode at one end of fluorescent lamp travels at high speed through the tube until one collides with one of the electrons of a mercury atom. 2. The impact diverts the electron of the mercury atom out of its orbit. When it snaps back into place, ultraviolet radiations are produced. 3. When the ultra-violet radiations reach the phosphor crystal, the impulse travels to one of the active centers in the crystal and here an action similar to that described in step 2 takes place. This time, however, visible light is produced. Courtesy of North American Philips Lighting Corp.

film frame would not register light at all and be black (as happens with HMI, CSI/CID, and other gas-discharge lamps), but the decay time retains some of the light. Therefore with the frames exposed unevenly, when the film is later screened with a projector that has a constant light output, the variation in exposure will appear as "flicker."

"Flicker" under fluorescents most often occurs when filming with a camera that has spring-drive or a variable-speed ("wild") motor because the frame rate "drifts": The speed of the motor drifts between 22 and 26 frames per second. The drift factor can be easily controlled by using a crystal-controlled motor on the camera. This type of motor ensures that each film frame is exposed to the same number of light pulses.

The problem of exposure time still does exist. When the fluorescent lamps operate at a frequency of 50 Hz (100 pulses of light per second), the camera must be equipped with a shutter of not less than $1/50$th of a second; operating at a frequency of 60 Hz (120 light pulses per second), the camera must be equipped with a shutter of not less than $1/60$th of a second. In other words, the camera must have a shutter angle of at least 180 degrees ($1/48$th of a second). A camera (35 mm, 16 mm, or super-8) with a shutter angle of 200 degrees ($1/43$rd of a second) or 235 degrees ($1/37$th of a second) is best when filming under fluorescent lamps. A camera with less than a 180-degree shutter angle, such as 170-degrees ($1/51$st of a second), is borderline, 160-degrees ($1/58$th of a second) is risky, and a 120-degree shutter angle ($1/72$nd of a second) will definitely register "flicker." Where possible, cameras with these shutters should be avoided when filming under fluorescent lamps.

In addition, and because of the decay time of the interior coating of the lamp, a shutter angle of less than 180 degrees is likely to cause a variation in color, often within the same frame. The light pulses may only register on part of the frame, as explained, but the weaker decay time in the coating will also register on the remaining portion of the frame. The intensity of light on the subject being photographed will influence the hue recorded on the emulsion.

It should be remembered that when filming at high-speed (slow-motion), faster than normal frame rate, the time each film frame is exposed to light is different. A camera with a 180-degree shutter ($1/48$th of a second at 24 frames per second) only has an exposure time of $1/96$th of a second at 48 frames per second, $1/197$th of a second at 96 frames per second, and so on. The risk of registering "flicker" is very real. Fast action ("undercrank") is another matter. Exposure time is greater and will register more pulses and decay time than it would at normal speed.

9.3 THE LAMP

A tubular fluorescent lamp is made of lime glass; a bent or rounded fluorescent lamp is made of lead glass. The basic fluorescent lamp shape is tubular. A tube is formed by drawing molten glass over rollers and then through dies. A U-shaped, circular, or tubular-dented tube (some have the appearance of being twisted) is formed while the glass is still soft (Fig. 9–5).

A fluorescent lamp is comprised of three basic parts:

- Coated bulb (or tube)
- Electrodes
- Base

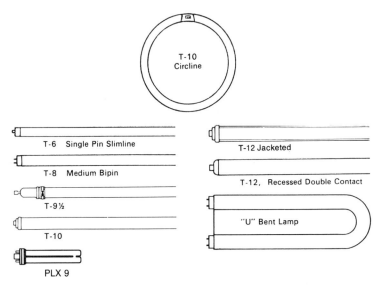

Figure 9–5 Fluorescents bulb shapes. Fluorescents are coded by wattage and overall length (including their pins and/or buttons), as well as bulb shape and color classification. For example: 48" T12 110w CW or 90w T17 60" WWX. Pre-heat lamps always indicate wattage first. Instant start lamps (including slimline) always indicate length first. Rapid-start lamps of 40 watts or less, as well as the circular and U-bent lamps, indicate wattage first. Jacketed lamps indicate length first.

Bulb shape is T for tubular, and its appended number designates the maximum diameter of a tube in eighths of an inch. Thus, a T-12 is a tubular bulb 12/8ths, or 11/2" in diameter.

Additional code letters are appended to the bulb shape: J—jacketed, C—circular, and B—U-bent. If the letter J follows (e.g., T12J) it indicates that a bulb 11/2" in diameter is surrounded (jacketed) by an additional clear glass tube and is therefore operable in low-temperature areas (exterior or cold storage). A T9C/12 indicates a circular bulb 9/8ths, or 11/8" in diameter, with the circle measuring 12" at its outside diameter. A T12B is a U-bent lamp with legs spaced 6" center-to-center and its length measured from the face of the base to the distance outside the U (unlike linear tubes, it does *not* include the pins).

The last letters indicate the lamp's color classification. Fluorescent lamps are color classified as D (Daylight), CW (Cool White), W (Warm), WWX (Warm White Deluxe), etc. Such terms refer to how the emitted light appears *to the adaptive eye* (cool or warm) and have no relationship to how the subject lighted by fluorescent will appear on the emulsion or image plate. Courtesy of North American Philips Lighting Corp.

9.3a Coated Bulb

The inner surface of a tube is coated with a phosphor crystal that is sensitive to ultraviolet radiation. The phosphor is inactive until the mercury atom snaps back into place (see Fig. 9–4). Various phosphor coatings have been developed for the purpose of achieving a different "atmospheric effect." Another way of stating the "atmospheric effect" radiated by the phosphor is to call it "Daylight," "Cool White," or "Warm White." These three named are the most common "atmospheric effects" encountered. Still other coatings are blue, gold, green, red, pink, and "black light" (ultraviolet); these colors are seldom filterable, which means they must either be changed or used for effect.

Oxygen is withdrawn before sealing the bulb and argon and mercury vapor is injected under low pressure. How the coating and gases work together is explained under Electrodes, below.

Tube discoloration   Blackening at the ends of the tube starts early in the lamp's life and gets progressively worse until it burns out. Gray at the end of the tube is merely a lack of mercury in the pressure chamber of a high-amperage lamp and appears only when the lamp is lighted; it has no effect on the lamp's efficiency. Dark spots in any part of a tube result from mercury condensation and generally disappear as the lamp burns. Banding (a circular discoloration inside the tube) is a phenomenon of a fluorescent lamp and has no effect on its efficiency.

9.3b Electrodes

At each end of a fluorescent tube is an electrode, a coiled-coil filament coated with an element (barium, calcium). The electrodes in a tube are often referred to as *cathodes* but, actually, because they operate in an alternating current, one end is a cathode (positive) and the other end is an anode (negative). This occurs only for a brief moment, then the positions are reversed — the anode becomes the cathode and vice versa. In a 60-Hz circuit, the positions are reversed 120 times each second. In a 50-Hz circuit, the positions are reversed 100 times each second. When voltage is applied sharply to an electrode, it arcs and an electron is "kicked" off the filament. What happens as it travels through the vapor is explained in Figure 9–4.

Types of electrodes   A fluorescent lamp is referred to as a "preheat," "instant-start," "rapid-start," etc., type of lamp. In a preheat lamp, a small amount of current flows through the filament before the arc takes place. After the switch has been turned on, the lamp glows slightly, and after a fractional delay, the rest of the lamp lights. In an instant-start lamp, the arc is immediate with no preheating of the filament. The ballast and filaments are designed to withstand initial voltage that strikes the arc immediately. A rapid-start lamp has continuously heated cathodes that reduce the amount of voltage necessary to start the lamp. Such a lamp is more suited to repeated on/off conditions such as a blinking sign.

Important items to remember about all fluorescent lamps are:

1. Electrodes are *not* the same, and lamps should not be interchanged indiscriminately (a preheat should never be placed in an instant-start circuit, and vice-versa).
2. Shock to the person, as well as damage to the electrodes, is possible if a lamp is replaced when the power is *on.*

9.3c Bases

Bases of fluorescent lamps are shown in Figure 9–6.

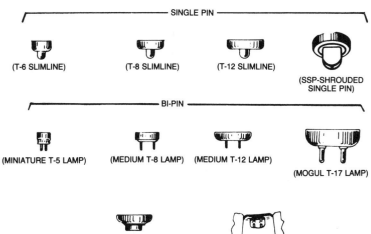

Figure 9-6 Base shapes of fluorescent lamps.
NOTE: The units that accept the bases of fluorescent lamps are called *lampholders,* not sockets. With a bipin base, each end of a lamp must be inserted into each lampholder and twisted to lock the lamp in place. Bipin bases are fitted with nubs that, when aligned to guidemarks on the lampholder, indicate the lamp is inserted correctly. For example, once the lamp is inserted the nub will point straight down at the floor, the same direction as the cutouts or similar guidemarks on the lampholder. With the singlepin and/or recessed double contact lamp, one base must be inserted into one lampholder and pushed against a spring before the opposite base is placed in the other holder. The spring in the first lampholder then pushes against the lamp and holds it in place. Courtesy of GTE Products Corp., Sylvania Lighting Division.

9.4 BALLAST

A fluorescent lamp requires a ballast in order for it to work. *Ballast* is the name given to the combination transformer/choke coil that is operated in series with a lamp. The transformer is necessary to increase the initial current to the electrodes so as to create an arc. In an arc lamp, the current will continue to increase until the lamp blows out, but the choke coil (a wire wrapped around a core of iron) creates an impedance that "chokes" the current if it exceeds a given rate of flow, thus acting as a regulator.

Most ballasts have an automatic circuit breaker (acb) that extinguishes the lamp in case of overheating. When an acb cools, the lamp will light again. Those units minus an acb are fitted with a manual reset switch.

Ballasts emit a noise similar to the AC hum heard when a fixture cable or a feeder cable falls across a microphone wire. The offending ballast can usually be located by turning off banks of fluorescents until the hum stops.

chapter 10

Industrial HID Lamps

In 1903, scientist and inventor Peter Cooper Hewitt (1861–1921, United States) devised the original mercury vapor lamp, which, after many refinements and improvements, is in wide use today in a variety of types. *High-intensity discharge* (HID) refers to any industrial lamp of the arc-discharge type that produces light through gas or vapor pressure. The most common of these lamps fall into three basic types: (1) mercury vapor, (2) metal halide, and (3) sodium vapor.

Brightly lighted areas are frequently encountered while filming on location or doing a remote telecast. With the new high-speed emulsions and sensitive pickup tubes available today, it would seem reasonable to utilize the illumination found on the site, i.e., in the factory, store, sports arena, etc. However, the existing illumination units must be checked out to determine the kinds of lamps (tungsten or arc-discharge) that are in use. When a lamp is of the arc-discharge type, it should be remembered that the HID lamp emits only certain wavelengths or, at best, emits the spectrum with certain "colors" predominating. In many instances, the spectral discrepancy can be seen with the naked eye, but there are circumstances under which this will not be easily discernible. Since camera film and video pickup tubes do not compensate for spectral discrepancy, the "color" of the predominate wavelength(s) will register as an overall hue on the emulsion or target.

HID light sources in the three major types that would most likely be on location/remotes are represented on an SED graph as having *line spectra;* i.e., the number of wavelengths that are present will appear on the graph as straight lines or blocks of varying widths called *spikes*. There may be other wavelengths present, but they are almost nil; therefore, they are not noted. Some graphs may show the full spectrum, indicating that the lamp appears as "white light," but contain one or two "spikes" that rise far and above the continuous spectrum. Typical SED graphs of industrial HID lamps are shown in Figure 10-1.

Although the HID lamps have many similarities, their differences will be pointed out first.

10.1 MERCURY VAPOR

In many industrial areas (factories, warehouses, etc.), the most common HID lamp in use is the mercury-vapor lamp. In the past few years, department stores and shopping malls have begun to install these lamps. The mercury-vapor lamp, lacking certain wavelengths, makes fabric and other reflecting materials appear richer than they really are.

A clear mercury-vapor lamp, whose SED is illustrated in Figure 10–1*a,* emits a bluish-white light with no red radiation. Under this light, blue, green, and yellow will appear to be brighter than they really are. However, orange and red will appear to be a muddy brown. Some lamps may have a phosphor coating on the interior of the bulb; the phosphor adds red, and these coated lamps are often referred to as "color improved." However, while they do impart some red, they still do not render a true tone.

The bluish-white of a mercury-vapor lamp is often immediately visible to the eye, but after being under them a while, there is a tendency for the eye to adapt, and the lamp will appear to be emitting "white light." Again, we emphasize that visual inspection is not enough.

In order to film or tape in areas already illuminated by mercury-vapor lamps, it is necessary that all additional lighting be done with incandescent or arc sources that have a continuous spectrum (white light). In huge areas it is not always possible to have enough lights to "cover" the entire area, in which case one should first measure the light emanating from the HID lamps and then light the foreground and other action areas with continuous-spectrum lamps with meter readings of at least one-to-two stops more than the readings taken on the mercury-vapor lamps.

The mercury-vapor lamp should appear somewhere in the scene (such as a ceiling light). Then, once established as a source of light, when and if the background walls reflect a bluish hue, the color will be acceptable to a viewing audience (although those walls should be "covered" by tungsten light if possible). People and action in the same scene *must* be lit with continuous-spectrum sources or they will take on a bluish hue.

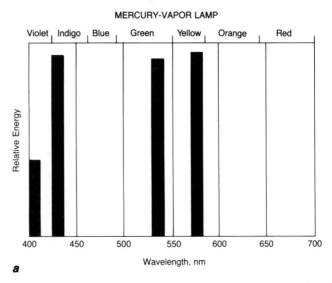

a

Figure 10–1 Typical SED graphs of industrial HID lamps. (*a*) The *mercury-vapor* lamp has a line spectrum. It emits wavelengths that spike at approximately 400, 435, 540, and 580 nanometers. These spikes impart a blue-green hue to emulsion or target. (*b*) (facing page) The *metal-halide* lamp has a hybrid spectrum which emits wavelengths across the entire spectrum, but which are subordinate to spikes that spike at approximately 410, 450, 540, 590, and 650 nanometers. These predominate spikes will impart a yellow-green hue to film emulsion and in many instances will be compatible with video, after minor adjustments. The addition of the iodides to mercury vapor subordinates the violet and indigo and shifts the yellow toward

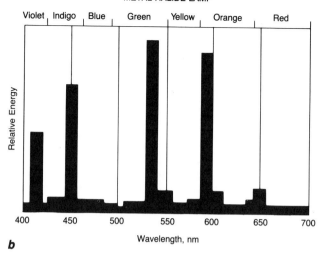

METAL-HALIDE LAMP

b

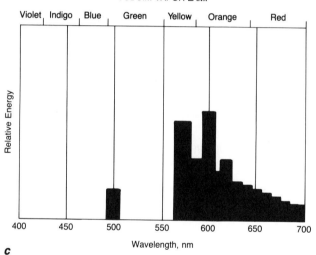

SODUIM-VAPOR LAMP

c

Figure 10-1 *(continued)*
the orange. *Note:* The spectrum will vary depending on the type of iodides added to the mercury vapor. The industrial HID metal-halide lamp is not to be confused with the type used in HMI fixtures (see Ch. 8). The HMI lamp has a multiline spectrum that closely resembles a continuous spectrum of either 5600K or 3200K with no predominant spikes. (*c*) The *sodium-vapor* lamp has a line spectrum. It emits wavelengths that spike at approximately 500, 570, 600, 615, and then trail off to 700 nanometers. These spikes impart a yellow hue to emulsion or target area. Before it reaches full brightness, however, the lamp may initially glow red, turn blue, then yellow, then golden.

10.2 METAL HALIDE

Most professional sports stadiums, aerospace facilities, and many public parks, malls, and stores are illuminated by metal-halide lamps. Externally, the metal-halide lamp is similar in appearance to a mercury-vapor lamp. Internally, it differs in construction as well as in the fact that metal halides have been added to the gases (see The Lamp, following). The added metal halides impart a continuous spectrum to the lamp, but this information should be used with caution. The lower the wattage of the lamp, the less red emission there is. To avoid a spectrum-deficient disaster it is wise to check a facility for size of lamps. The only two with sufficient overall spectra are the 1000-watt and 1500-watt lamps, but, as with all metal-halide lamps, they are extremely high in yellow-green wavelengths and will impart that hue to tape or film. When working with video, the color controller can usually take the unwanted hue out before it reaches the tape; with film, the emulsion will take on an overall yellow-green cast that is usually correctable in printing.

When telecasting or filming sports events the lighting person must, of necessity, "go" with the installed illumination. An 85A filter, or its equivalent, must be placed on the film camera lens. Any "hue" imparted to the film from the lighting can be corrected later in printing.

When working with video, interviews or close foreground actions can be taped with the *existing* light and a color controller will incorporate needed corrections in hue.

When filming close-ups and interviews, however, the addition of lamps with a continuous spectrum is required, preferably those balanced for daylight (5500K +). Whenever light from the installed illumination falls on any or all of the areas being filmed, it is necessary to measure the light emanating from the HID lamps and make certain that the areas "covered" by the supplementary continuous spectrum lamps are at least one stop more than the meter reading obtained from the metal halide lamps alone.

10.3 SODIUM VAPOR

Many roads and highways are illuminated by sodium-vapor lamps, as are parking lots and high school gymnasium interiors where film or video events are not a priority. Externally, the sodium vapor lamp is similar in appearance to a mercury-vapor and/or metal-halide lamp; internally it differs in construction as well as in the fact that sodium has been added to the gases (see The Lamp, following). The added sodium emits a yellow glow if it is a low-pressure type and a golden-white glow if it is a high-pressure type. In either lamp, ultraviolet is almost nil; therefore the light is greatly lacking in blue.

When telecasting or filming areas that are illuminated by sodium-vapor lamps, the foreground action must be lit with incandescent or arc light sources with a continuous spectrum to override the light emanating from the sodium lamps. It is necessary to measure the light emitted by the sodium lamps and then make certain that the areas "covered" by the continuous spectrum lamps are at least one-to-two stops more than the meter reading obtained from the sodium lamps alone.

10.4 SIMILARITIES

The similarities of all HID industrial lamps are:

Correlated Color Temperature and Color Rendering Index   Color temperature, as explained in Chapter 1, is measured on the Kelvin scale in regard to a lamp with a continuous spectrum, but it does *not* indicate whether certain wavelengths are more or less predominant in any one "color." HID lamps, because they have a "spiked spectrum," i.e., the wavelengths are either not continuous or predominate in one "color," are rated in *correlated temperatures* (CCT). CCT refers to *how the light appears to the adaptive eye* only. CCT does not take into account how nonadaptive emulsion or target area will react to the emitted light. Thus, although a mercury-vapor lamp is predominantly blue, it nevertheless has a CCT of 5900K; a metal-halide lamp, a CCT anywhere between 3400K to 4700K depending on its wattage; a sodium vapor lamp, a CCT between 1800K and 2100K.

A *color rendering index* is an arbitrary numbering system ranging from 1 to 100. The higher the number, the better an object will reflect standard colors. The CRI of a mercury-vapor lamp is 22. The CRI of a metal-halide lamp is between 65 and 70 depending on the lamp's size. The CRI of a sodium-vapor lamp is approximately 65.

10.5 FILTERS
There are no filters manufactured that will change the spectral energy of an HID lamp. When mercury-vapor and/or metal-halide lamps are phosphor coated, an FL filter (see The Fluorescent Lamp, Ch. 9) might work on a film camera. Tables depicting certain filter packs have been compiled. Manufacturers of the filters recommend tests and remind the lighting person that the table is merely a starting point. Table 10–1 is a typical example.

10.6 THE LAMP
HID lamps require a ballast to operate and are comprised of three basic parts: (1) bulb, (2) electrodes, and (3) base.

10.6a Bulb
Industrial HID lamps vary in size (Fig. 10–2). The BT bulb of a mercury-vapor and/or metal-halide lamp is a double bulb, i.e., an inner quartz "arc tube" surrounded by an outer "jacket." The inner tube, which contains the electrodes, is made of fused quartz; the outer bulb, which absorbs the ultraviolet given off by the arc, is made of borosilicate glass. The single E or BT bulb of a sodium-vapor lamp is also made of borosilicate glass and contains a ceramic "arc tube" that holds the electrodes.

Table 10–1 Typical Filter and Exposure Compensation for HID Lamps*

Manufacturer	Mercury Vapor	Metal Halide	Sodium Vapor
General Electric Co.			
Tungsten	70R + 10Y	60R + 20Y	50M + 20C
Open lens	1²/₃ stops	1²/₃ stops	1 stop
Daylight	60M + 30Y	40M + 20Y	80B + 20C
Open lens	1¹/₃ stops	1 stop	2¹/₃ stops
GTE Sylvania			
Tungsten	30M + 50Y	30M + 10Y	5G + 100B
Open lens	1¹/₂ stops	1¹/₃ stops	3 stops
Daylight	40M + 30B	30M + 10Y	10M + 50B
Open lens	1¹/₃ stops	1¹/₃ stops	1 stop
N.A. Philips	NA	NA	NA

*It should be noted that lamps vary in spectral output by manufacturer and by age. Extensive tests and close coordination with laboratories when working with film, and with the color controller when working with video, is recommended.

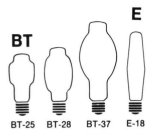

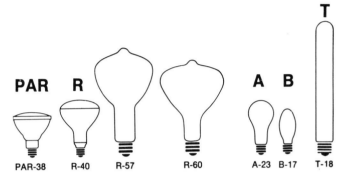

Figure 10–2 Industrial HID bulb shapes. HID lamps are manufactured in BT (bulging tube) and E (elliptical) as well as A, B, PAR, R, and T shapes. Manufacturers also append a number that designates the maximum diameter of the bulb in eighths of an inch. Thus a BT-56 is a bulging tube bulb 56 eighths or 7 inches in diameter; an E-18 is an elliptical lamp 18 eighths or 2¼ inches in diameter, etc. Courtesy of North American Philips Lighting Corp.

Oxygen is withdrawn before the manufacturer seals the inner bulb, and with the *mercury-vapor lamp,* argon and mercury vapor are injected under relatively high pressure. In the *metal-halide lamp,* mercury and some metallic iodide vapors (e.g., indium, thallium, sodium, scandium, etc., but lacking dysprosium) are injected under relatively high pressure. In the *sodium-vapor lamp,* mercury and sodium vapors are injected, either under high or low pressure, depending on the type.

As a rule, HID lamps of any kind are easily recognized by their bulging and elliptical shape, but it is a great mistake, when "scouting" a facility, to assume that lamps with the configuration of a PAR-38, R-40, R-57, R-60, A, B, and T are tungsten-filament types and compatible with continuous-spectrum lamps. Inspection of the units and discussion with a facility engineer at the location are essential in order to avoid this mistake. These latter-named lamp types are found not only where heavy dirt accumulates (foundries, oil rigs, railroad yards, and sheds), but in very clean areas as well, such as parking lots, airports and, in some instances, sports fields.

Coatings Mercury-vapor and metal-halide outer bulbs are sometimes phosphor-coated, similar to fluorescent lamps, to achieve "atmospheric effects" (see The Fluorescent Lamp, Ch. 9), but unlike the fluorescent, the phosphor coatings are not necessary to produce light in an HID lamp. The phosphors add red and "warm up" the "cold" blue green. The decay time is slow after the coating has been struck by the radiation from the arc.

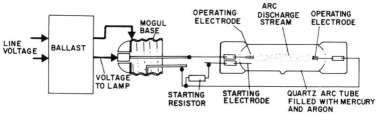

a

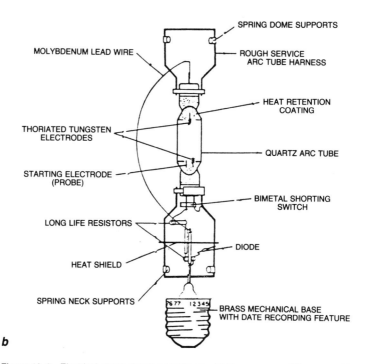

b

Figure 10-3 Electrical circuit of typical HID lamps. (*a*) Mercury vapor: When current is applied, the short gap between the starter and the first electrode ionizes the mercury vapor quickly. When the rest of the gases inside the bulb are ionized, an arc discharge of high intensity is struck. As the arc travels at high speed to the other electrode, the electrons in the mercury are "jarred" between orbits. The intense speed at which the electrons transfer causes energy to be given off that produces light. (*b*) Metal halide: The metal-halide lamp operates on the same principle, but requires a higher voltage between the starter and first

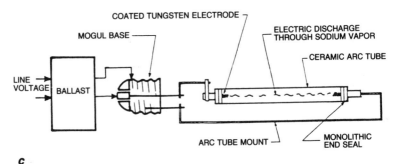

c

Figure 10–3 (*continued*)
electrode. (*c*) A sodium-vapor lamp operates the same as the other lamps except it has no starter. Instead, when voltage is applied and the xenon gas within the bulb is ionized, an arc discharge of high intensity is struck causing the arc to travel at high speed to the other electrode. Courtesy of GTE Products Corp., Sylvania Lighting Division.

Discoloration Unlike the HMI or tungsten-halogen lamp, there are no bromines in the HID lamp. Therefore, the inner bulb discolors as it ages. With clear outer bulbs this is easily seen; however, coated outer bulbs will appear dimmer, the only indication that the inner bulb is discoloring.

Safety precautions When the outer bulb is broken and the inner bulb continues to arc (remain lighted), the ultraviolet radiation normally absorbed by the outer bulb can be dangerous to the eyes and skin. Power to the lamp should be cut off immediately and the lamp changed.

All HID lamps contain mercury. While the amount is small, it should be remembered that mercury *can* be a lethal pollutant. Therefore, it is recommended that a burned-out or broken lamp be handled with protective gloves. The lamp should be put in a plastic bag and placed in a sealed metal drum to prevent mercury dispersal; then the burned out and/or broken unit should be disposed of in a toxic waste facility, not thrown into a trash bin.

10.6b Electrodes
At each end of the mercury-vapor or metal-halide inner bulb and at each end of the sodium-vapor ceramic tube is an electrode, a coiled-coil tungsten filament. The electric circuits of each of these lamps is shown in Figure 10–3*a–c*.

"Flicker" effect HID arc-discharge lamps operating on alternating current (AC) actually turn off and on at twice the Hertz of the circuit at which they are operating. On a 50-Hz circuit, the fluctuation is 100 times per second, and on a 60-Hz circuit, the fluctuation is 120 times per second. A video camera will not register this fluctuation, but a motion picture camera may record it on film as "flicker," as explained in Chapter 8.

10.6c Bases
Bases for HID Lamps are shown in Figure 10–4.

10.7 BALLAST
A *ballast* is a combination transformer/choke coil that increases the initial voltage so as to create the arc. The choke then regulates the current (up or down) to a given rate of flow. Industrial HID lamps use numerous types of ballast depending on the type of lamp. For example, the metal-halide lamp,

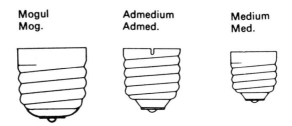

| Mogul | Admedium | Medium |
| Mog. | Admed. | Med. |

Figure 10-4 HID lamp bases. HID lamps have screw bases. The *mogul* base has a "code date" around its rim; i.e., the letters JFMAMJJASOND (representing months of the year) and the number 1234567890, so that an installer can record month and year of installation by scratching the appropriate letter and date. The *admedium* base is halfway between a medium and mogul screw in diameter. The odd size prohibits the use of the lamp in a circuit without a ballast. The *medium* screw base is found on HID lamps of 100 watts and less (75, 50, and 40 watts). Use of these lamps in a circuit without a ballast will blow them out. Courtesy of General Electric Co.

with its added iodides, requires a higher starting voltage to ignite its arc than does the mercury-vapor or sodium-vapor lamp. By making slight electrical changes in wiring, a ballast can be adapted for use with another type of lamp in the HID family.

An item all lighting persons should watch for when scouting a facility is the "self-ballasted" lamp. This is a lamp that contains a filament within the bulb itself that serves the same purpose as an outside ballast. These units have medium bases, and while the BT and E shapes are easily identifiable, the A, B, PAR, R, and T shapes are similar to incandescent lamps. In energy-conscious industries, replacement of incandescent lamps with self-ballasted HID lamps is becoming standard practice. It is easy to fool one's self into thinking that because no ballasts are evident, the lamp must be of the incandescent type. Always consult the company engineer (not the maintenance person) as to the type of lamp installed, or check it yourself. A self-ballasted lamp can be identified in one of two ways: The voltage is etched on the bulb (e.g., 120v to 240v), or the letters *SB* follow the type letter (e.g., HSB: mercury self-ballasted; MSB: metal-halide self-ballasted; SSB: sodium-vapor self-ballasted).

chapter 11

Reflector Boards

A *reflector board* (Fig. 11-1) is an important adjunct to lighting equipment. It can be used to supplement fixtures illuminating an exterior setting, or it can be used exclusively in place of exterior lighting units.

Reflectors came into being very early in the motion picture industry. Credit for creating them goes to Johann Gottleib Wilhelm "Billy" Bitzer (1872–1944, USA), cameraman to David Wark Griffith (1875–1948, USA).

Figure 11-1 Reflector boards. Reflector boards vary in size. The names of the boards are given according to shape and dimension: a "hand" reflector (not shown), also referred to as a "midget" board, measures *less than* 24 × 24 inches (610 × 610 millimeters); a "small" board measures 24 × 24 inches (610 × 610 millimeters); a "stationwagon" board measures 30 inches (762 millimeters) high by 36 inches (914 millimeters) wide; a "van" board measures 36 inches (914 millimeters) high by 30 inches (762 millimeters) wide; a "standard" board measures 42 × 42 inches (1.07 × 1.07 meters); and a "jumbo" board (not shown) measures 60 × 60 inches (1.52 × 1.52 meters). Reflector boards may be minus a few inches in one dimension or another. A few are "portable," i.e., can be folded into "suitcases" or rolled into circular boots for storage and/or shipping. Courtesy of Matthews Studio Equipment, Inc.

Billy used them to "punch" light into shadows that the high-contrast emulsion could not handle. They serve that purpose even to this day. A reflector board is surfaced on both sides with a silvered reflecting material (one "hard," the other "soft"). These silvered surfaces are used to catch the sun's rays and redirect the light into areas of shadow so as to reduce the contrast between the light and dark areas of a scene. They are extremely useful in getting light under broad-brimmed hats, beneath overhangs, into tunnels, and so forth.

A reflector board must be positioned properly in relation to the sun to catch its rays; a board (with the exception of the hand reflectors) is fitted with a yoke that allows for tilting to present its best angle to the sun. A spud on the yoke inserts into a stand and allows the board to be pivoted toward the sun so that maximum light will be reflected. The stand is usually built in telescoping sections to permit the board to be elevated as much as 10 feet (3.05 meters) in height. Special reflector stands, called "hi-rollers," have wheels that can be locked down. A "medium hi-roller" elevates to 14 feet (4.3 meters), and a "hi hi-roller" elevates to 18 feet (5.5 meters).

A board can be used to light an exterior scene much as a lighting unit is used — as a key, a fill, or a kicker. When used instead of a fixture, the same requirements for placement, height, and contrast ratio apply as with lighting an interior. Of course, reflector boards are not focusable (it has been tried, but with little success). Intensity of the reflected light from a board is controlled by moving the unit toward or away from the subject. Nets (single- and double-weave; see Light Modifiers, Ch. 13) *are* made to fit the board in order to inhibit the reflected rays when it is not feasible to move the board away from the subject.

The major problem associated with a reflector board is that the intensity will "die" temporarily if the sun is obscured by a passing cloud or permanently if the sky becomes overcast. In addition, although the sun may remain shining, it is constantly "moving," and this means frequent adjustment of the boards so as to catch the maximum rays. Then too, on windy days, the broad surface of the boards will act as a "sail" and tip the unit over.

A novice handling a reflector might have difficulty aiming the reflected beam toward the subject. With practice, however, use of the principles of reflectors and reflected surfaces can be mastered (see Fixture Reflectors, Ch. 4). The best method for picking up and redirecting the sun's rays is to:

1. Aim the reflector at the sun.
2. Tilt the reflector board down until the reflected beam can be seen on the ground.
3. Swivel the board until the reflected beam is in line with the subject.
4. Tilt the board up until the reflected beam illuminates the subject.

The four cardinal sins when using reflectors are:

1. To place the boards in such a position that the reflected beam forces the actor to squint, or interferes with his or her vision. This problem can be eliminated by shifting the boards slightly more to one side of the camera, removing the glare from the actor's direct line of sight.
2. Allowing the reflector board to bobble in the wind so that the light dances on the actor's face. This can be overcome by locking the reflector board down and adding extra sandbags to the base of the stand, as well as to the horizontal arm of the yoke.
3. To place the board so close to the performer that the actor's face looks sunburned, and/or the "fill" equals — or overpowers — the sunlight. This can be allevi-

ated by moving the reflector away from the actor, or placing a net on the board.
4. To leave the reflector aimed at the scene when the take is completed. When not in use, a reflector board should be tilted until one surface is parallel to the ground and the other surface (usually the one that has been lighting the scene) is pointed at the sky.

In windy weather each reflector must *always* be sandbagged and individually manned so the board does not tip over or get lifted by the wind and sail away, causing damage or injury to people and property.

11.1 SURFACE MATERIAL

Years ago, actual German silver leaf in 5-inch squares was used on boards. It required a great deal of skill and patience to apply, since each leaf was fragile and susceptible to wrinkling. If the applier literally breathed before the leaf adhered to the glued surface it was ruined.

Today, reflecting material comes in rolls, is much more durable, and can be easily applied. Surface material comes in many degrees of "hard" and "soft" finishes, depending on use. Surfaces are specular, diffuse, mixed, and scattered (see Fixture Reflectors, Ch. 4).

Reflector boards have either a mirror, hard, soft, or very soft surface.

1. A *mirror* surface is referred to as a "rifle" because it shoots an intense, concentrated beam. It is usually used for lighting a dark area from a great distance or for a "ricochet shot"—placing the rifle in the sun and concentrating its intense beam at a second board. The reflected beam from the second is then used to light the subject. This technique is used when the angle of the sun is such that the first reflector cannot light the subject. Redirecting the light from the first reflector onto a second reflector, at a better angle to the subject, makes the second reflector the new light source.
2. A *hard* surface produces a sharp, strong light, but does not have the intensity of the mirror surface. The majority of boards in use are covered with hard, rather than mirror, sides.
3. A *soft* surface is diffused so the light pattern is not harsh or too directional.
4. A board with a *very soft* (sometimes referred to as a *supersoft)* surface is scattered, and direction is almost undetectable by comparison to a soft surface.

A gold, blue, or cool surface is a soft material with a touch of color added to it.

1. A *gold* surface reflects very warm light and is often used to impart a sunset or sunrise warmth to a scene. It is also used when filming day-for-nite scenes (see Fixture Filters, Day-for-Nite, Chapter 14).
2. A *blue* surface can be used to reflect a tungsten lamp and convert the rays to daylight color temperature. Some lighting technicians line a tungsten-filament softlite with a sheet of blue material and use its indirect rays for a daylight fill.
3. A *cool* surface is one that reflects a slightly colder Kelvin than a regular soft (but nowhere near the blue above).
4. A *flex* surface is an extremely thin, very soft sheet that conforms to any configuration and does not tear easily. It is often used in interior automobile scenes to reflect light into faces. It has great value in such places as coal mines, closet ceilings, and/or small rooms to bounce light into areas where conditions restrict the number of lighting fixtures that can be used.

Lighting Unit Accessories and Fixture Use

Lighting unit accessories are classified as *controllers, modifiers,* and *filters.* Each is further classified according to its function.

Controllers
    Barndoors
    Snoot
    Shutter
    Gooseneck
    Gobo:
        Flag
        Cutter
        Blade
        Target, Dot
Modifiers
    Scrims and Nets
    Diffusion
    Cukaloris
    Frame
Filters
    Conversion
    Effect

Powerlines and *Generators,* while not technically fixture accessories, are obviously a necessary but distinct part of the lighting unit.

chapter 12

Lighting Controllers

Lighting controllers are pieces of equipment that are placed on the fixture itself or placed separately on a stand on the floor. Both types are used to control light rays emanating from the fixture.

12.1 FIXTURE-PLACED CONTROLLERS

A *barndoor* (Fig. 12–1) is a bracket fitted with either two or four adjustable opaque panels. Some panels can be rotated in their bracket. The bracket is designed to slide into a holder on the front of a lighting unit. Other types of barndoors are attached to fixture housings by springs and can be rotated; some are permanently attached horizontally.

A barndoor is used to prevent extraneous light from falling on given areas of a set; it controls the light by creating a "soft edge" where the panel intercepts the light beam. The difference in the margin of illumination between the light beam and the created shadow, while definite, contains a narrow region along its edge where the transition from light to shadow is gradual. That is why, in addition to barndoors, floor-placed controllers are necessary that can have a "hard" cutoff edge when placed properly (see following).

A barndoor can be utilized in a multitude of ways. The upper panel can be lowered into the beam to reduce the amount of light falling on an upper

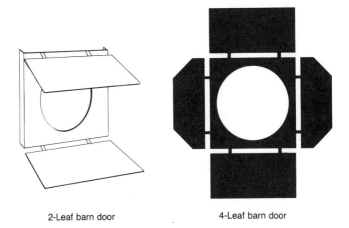

2-Leaf barn door   4-Leaf barn door

Figure 12–1 *Barndoors* control light rays that emanate from the fixture.

area of a wall so as to direct attention downward. Then too, when a fixture is used as a backlight, the lowering of the upper panel can prevent the light beam from striking the camera lens and causing flare. If required, the lower panel can be raised into the light beam rays to reduce or eliminate the amount of light falling on the set floor.

Barndoors are hinged, permitting the panels to be adjusted any given distance apart (between fully closed and fully open). The doors are often brought together to form a "slit" of light so that a sign or a particular piece of architecture can be emphasized. Barndoors can be played with to provide needed light in spots otherwise inaccessible to light.

There are times, when the key light is weak, that a lowered top barndoor can eliminate a boom-arm shadow, but this is rare. More often than not, a boom-arm shadow requires the insertion of a cutter into the key light beam to block it out (see Floor-Placed Controllers, following).

A *snoot* (Fig. 12–2) is a bracket fitted with a tube that eliminates spill light and concentrates the beam into a small round area without increasing its intensity. Tube diameters on a snoot vary, depending on the size of the lighting unit it is to fit, and may be anywhere from 3/4 inch (19.1 mm) to 10 inches (254 mm) in diameter.

Snoots are used to emphasize:

1. An area within a lighted scene; e.g., a grouping at a table in a crowded restaurant.
2. A wall fixture where the illumination is expected to appear hotter or more intense than the rest of the room.
3. An isolated beverage glass where only the contents are made to sparkle.

Sometimes a snoot fixture is used as a soft spotlite, as on a darkened stage where a performer entertains in a circle of light that has no hard edges. For this latter effect a snoot called a "Ted Lewis" is used. The snoot is made of soft copper that can be molded by hand into almost any shape conceivable for a soft-edge, concentrated effect. Its opening can be large, medium, or, as its smallest size is called a "penny." This particular snoot was named after Ted Lewis, a famous vaudeville comedian who wore a battered top hat and sang in a very soft spotlite.

A *shutter* (Fig. 12–3) is a bracket fitted with moveable horizontal blades similar to venetian blinds. Originally it was intended to control the intensity of a carbon arc, but in many studios and rental houses, a handle has been added to open the shutters much like a Navy signal light, and now it is mostly used for "lightning" effects. It also finds great use when other bright-light effects are desired; for example, a supposed opening of a door off-camera, an electrical short-circuit, or an explosion.

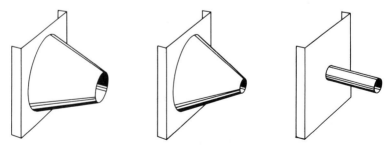

Figure 12–2 A *snoot* is used to add subtle effects to lighting.

Figure 12–3 A *shutter* is more for "effect light" than use as a regular controller. Courtesy of Mole-Richardson Co.

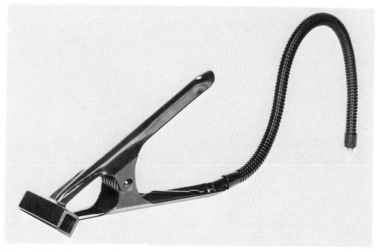

Figure 12–4 A *gooseneck* is so flexible it can be tied into a knot. Courtesy of Mole-Richardson Co.

A *gooseneck* (Fig. 12–4) is a flexible tube with a clamp at one end and a receptacle at the other. Spuds of tiny opaque blades or nets can be inserted into the receptacle and locked in place. The clamp is affixed to the yoke of the fixture, and the other end, with its blade or tiny net, is swung into the light beam to eliminate an unwanted flare or tone down a highlight.

12.2 FLOOR-PLACED CONTROLLERS

Floor-placed controllers consist of units that must be fitted to a gobo stand (Fig. 12–5) and then placed in front of a lighting unit to intercept a portion of the light. Although some of these units may at one time or another be hung from overhead scaffolding, they are still considered floor hardware.

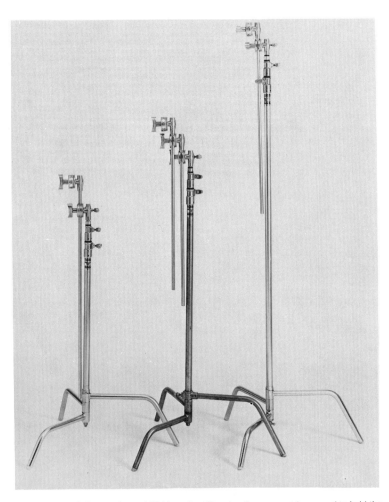

Figure 12–5 *Gobo stands* are foldable units with extension arms and are used to hold the floor-placed controllers (flag, cutter, target, dot, etc.) and modifiers (nets, butterflies, "cookies", etc.). They come in "short-," "regular-" and "hi-stand" sizes. Courtesy of Matthews Studio Equipment, Inc.

A *gobo* (Fig. 12–6), derived from the word *"go-between,"* is a term applied to any opaque unit used to eliminate light from a particular area in a scene. Gobos vary in size, depending on the intended use.

The most common gobo is the *flag,* a wire frame covered with a black duvateen or similar fabric that absorbs light. It is used to control light emanating from a single fixture; it can be inserted into a gobo head on a stand. Flags vary in size, the most common being 12 × 18 inches (30.48 × 45.72 cm); 18 × 24 inches (45.72 × 60.96 cm); 24 × 30 inches (60.96 × 76.20 cm); 24 × 36 inches (60.96 cm × 0.91 m); and 30 × 36 inches (76.20 cm × 0.91 m).

A *cutter,* a long narrow flag, is used when light from more than one side-by-side lighting unit is to be controlled, or the shadow of a microphone boom-arm must be eliminated. When lowered into the key light beam, the shadow of the cutter becomes more obvious than the shadow of the boom-arm. This is easily remedied by bringing in a secondary fixture *behind* the boom-arm (and out of scene, of course) to light the shadow caused by the cutter. The light from the secondary fixture should be of the same intensity as the light from the key, so that they blend. Thus it appears that the illumination on the set is from one light source (the key), and the boom shadow is

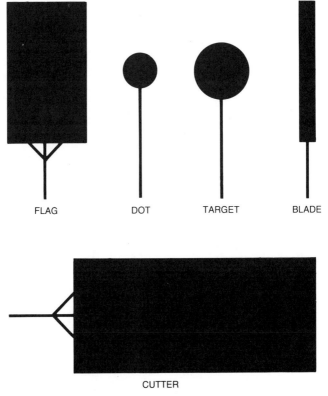

FLAG   DOT   TARGET   BLADE

CUTTER

Figure 12–6 A *gobo* can eliminate light completely or just be "tipped in" to take out a small point of light.

eliminated. If a cutter is made of plywood instead of wire and cloth, it is referred to as a *meataxe*.

The most common cutter sizes in use are 10×42 inches (25.40 cm × 1.06 m); 18×48 inches (45.72 cm × 1.22 m); and 24×72 inches (60.96 cm × 1.83 m).

A *blade* is a small narrow flag. Blades are also made of translucent and/or clear plexiglass so as to vary the amount of light falling on the area they are intended to control. Clear plexiglass blades are often spray-painted with varying degrees of thickness and pattern to create different densities of light control. Actually, a translucent or plexiglass blade modifies a light beam (see Light Modifiers, Ch. 13). The most common cloth sizes in use are 2×12 (5.08 cm × 30.48 cm) and 4×14 inches (10.16 cm × 35.36 cm).

A *target* and a *dot* are circular flags that can be inserted into a light

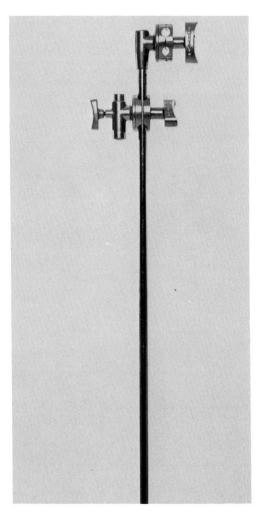

Figure 12–7 A *gobo head* adds to the versatility of an already versatile gobo stand. Courtesy of Matthews Studio Equipment, Inc.

Figure 12–8 A table-top set-up for a commercial showing the utilization of gobo stands to a) hold the umbrella light, and b) hold a flag which is preventing the light rays from spilling onto the background. Courtesy of Matthews Studio Equipment, Inc.

beam to cover a minute area (especially offending highlights) without having a great effect on the rest of the beam. The difference between a target and a dot is size. Targets are 3 inches (76.2 mm) or larger in diameter. Dots are, of course, smaller. The circles may be solid or of varying layers of net and diffusion (see Light Modifiers, Ch. 13) so as to vary the amount of light falling on the area they are to control.

A *gobo head* (Fig. 12–7) is fitted to a stand and accepts gobo rod extension arms of various diameters that can be rotated in any position. When a stand has a gobo head with extension arms added to those already on the stand, an infinite number of positions can be found in which to place the gobo.

Gobo stands that hold the flags, cutters, targets, and dots are of three types. When fitted with double-risers, they measure as follows:

Type	Folded	Extended
Lo-boy	26 in. (66.04 cm)	4½ ft. (1.37 m)
Standard	52 in. (1.29 m)	10½ ft. (3.15 m)
Hi-boy	72 in. (1.83 m)	14 ft. (4.26 m)

Figure 12–8 shows the utilization of some of the equipment mentioned above.

chapter 13

Light Modifiers

When an object in a scene reflects too brightly, or an area is overlit, or the lighting is in opposition to the mood of the scene, it become necessary to intercept and/or alter the light rays falling on the object or area. The materials used to intercept the *intensity,* and/or alter the *character* of the light are called *modifiers.*

13.1 INTENSITY MODIFIERS

Scrim and *net* are terms often used interchangeably to describe woven screen materials that reduce the amount of light falling on a subject. However, to be technically correct, a *scrim* is made of metal, and a *net* is made of cloth.

The term *scrim* is applied to those circular units sized to fit into the same front brackets of a lighting unit that hold the barndoor. The screen, in various thicknesses, is used to cover any portion, or all of the circle (Fig. 13–1). Open-face lighting units especially, because of the intense heat they generate, require scrims made of stainless steel mesh.

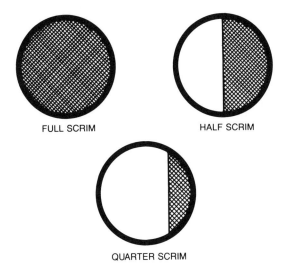

FULL SCRIM

HALF SCRIM

QUARTER SCRIM

Figure 13–1 Scrims. *Full scrims* reduce all the light emanating from the fixture. *Half-scrims* or *quarter-scrims* reduce light on a segment of the field. By rotating these partial scrims, light can be partly reduced at any angle.

Net is a shortened form of the word "bobbinet" and is used to identify cloth-mesh material fitted into a holder that is placed into a gobo stand (Fig. 13–2). Cloth nets can be used close to the fresnel lens of an enclosed-type lighting unit when it is at "full flood" because the lens protects the bobbinet from the heat generated by the fixture's light source. However, when "spotted down," the transmitted heat (because the light source rays are more concentrated; see Fixture Lenses, Ch. 3) may cause shriveling and distortion of the weave.

The degree to which a scrim/net material reduces the intensity of a light depends on four things; (1) its weave shape, (2) the size of the net opening, (3) the color of the material, and (4) how many layers the light must penetrate.

Weave shapes are square, rectangular, diamond, and hexagonal. Each design has a different effect on the light that passes through it. Although the dispersion is quite subtle and hardly noticeable to the untrained eye, the shape most preferred in film and TV production is the hexagonal weave. It is the closest shape to a "round hole" and it "breaks up" the light evenly.

The net opening — the distance between the threads of the net — also has an effect on how the light is modified. The more threads and fewer openings there are, the more the interference with the light rays, therefore, the less light that can get through. The weave openings of some scrim/net materials are so fine the material looks almost solid; others, such as the type used on a carbon arc, have such large openings they resemble huge fish nets.

Black is the color of most scrim/net material; blue material of the same weave will reduce light less than black, while white of the same material and weave will reduce light even less than blue. The reason for this is that black will absorb as much as 90 percent of the light that strikes it, blue will absorb about 50 percent and reflect 50 percent, while white will absorb about 30 percent and reflect 70 percent.

These delicate shades of scrim/net colors are utilized to achieve the fine subtleties of quality lighting — exteriors as well as interiors. For example, a net material that is as much as 10 feet (3.05 meters) high and 20 feet (6.10

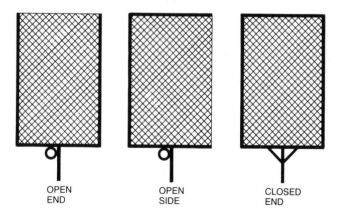

OPEN   OPEN   CLOSED
END   SIDE   END

Figure 13–2 Net holders. Holders are constructed of ⅜-inch diameter rods and are called *open-end, open-side,* and *closed-end* nets, depending on whether the frame is solid or incomplete at one end or side. A stud, which permits the unit to be inserted and clamped onto a gobo head, is welded to the frame and supported by either a circular ring or two crutches, which are used to hang the unit on a net rack.

meters) long is rolled on small-diameter poles and can be unfurled and stretched behind actors in an exterior medium shot or close-up. The various shades and densities of material impart different effects to a background: Black tones down any bright areas that would draw the eye away from the foreground, blue adds haze, and white adds a diffusion similar to fog.

Although there are various net openings and colors available, most manufacturers of scrim/net holders have found it economical to settle on a single weave size. This has brought about somewhat of a "standardization." In order to reduce the light more than a single piece of net is capable of, the manufacturer simply has added another layer of the same weave size. The additional layer has been placed slightly offcenter or at an angle to the primary layer so that it will interfere with the rays and lessen their intensity. While there is only one weave size, one frame may contain many layers. When sandwiching two or more nets in one holder, sometimes a moiré (wavelike) effect is created: The shadow of the net becomes visible instead of invisible. This effect can often be eliminated by rotating one net 90 degrees to the other in the frame. In order to readily identify these layered weaves, manufacturers color-code both scrims and nets for instant identification and name them appropriately according to the number of layers of weave in the holder.

In the early days of motion picture production, color codes varied from studio to studio, but with the advent of television, there has been a trend to uniformity in the entire industry.

One layer of mesh is called a *single*. It is color-coded green.
Two layers of mesh are called a *double*. It is color-coded red.
Three layers of mesh are called a *triple*. It is coded yellow.
Four layers of mesh are called a *four'ble*. It is coded blue.
Five layers of mesh are called a *fi'ble*. It is coded white.

The single and double are the most commonly used, and it is possible, with combinations of singles and doubles, to make a triple, four'ble, or a fi'ble.

A *butterfly* (Fig. 13-3) is a large net, single or double, used to reduce the amount of sunlight falling on a subject. A butterfly is large enough to cover a medium shot or a two-shot. It reduces contrast and the "harsh" look that sunlight often imparts to an actor's complexion. It is also extremely useful in hiding wrinkles on actors should the need arise.

When a translucent material is used on a butterfly frame to diffuse the light, it is called a *silk* (see Diffusion, following). A large silk can be used when the angle of the sun is such that unflattering or unwanted light falls on the actors. The silk between the sun and actors creates a soft fill light. The key light is reintroduced at a more flattering angle by means of a Brute, HMI, modules, or a reflector.

When a butterfly frame is fitted with a black duvateen material, it is called a *solid*. In actuality, a solid is a controller (see Lighting Controllers, Ch. 12), blocking out unwanted light rays. In shaded areas where a shaft of sunlight cuts across a foreground scene or illuminates an area in the background, setting the solid to intercept the offending rays is faster than having to reset the shot, change angle, or bring the light level up.

Miniature nets with various layers such as single, double, and triple are often used in gooseneck flexible tubes to reduce light falling in specific areas within an otherwise evenly lighted area. Highlights and flares on shiny objects can be reduced considerably, or completely, by miniature nets without interfering with the main source or rim light.

Figure 13–3 Butterfly. A *butterfly* fits in an assembled frame never less than 4′ × 4′ (1.22m × 1.22m) and sometimes as large as 10′ × 12′ (3.05m × 3.66m). At some studios when large frames are suspended between two gobo stands, the large butterfly is then called a *combination.* A butterfly scrim is fitted with either two sleeves for the rods to slide through, or grommets around its border, enabling it to be lashed to the frame. Courtesy of Mole-Richardson Co.

Blade and dot shapes of net with various layers are also quite common and serve the same purpose as the miniature nets.

13.2 CHARACTER MODIFIERS

Diffusion, as with scrim, reduces light intensity. Additionally, diffusion changes the character of the light; it breaks up and scatters the light beam so that it appears to be: (1) larger than its original source, or (2) "softer," so that the shadows are less distinct or at times virtually nonexistent.

A diffused fixture beam is difficult to barndoor, flag, or cut because of the scattered light. The degree to which diffusion material reduces light and alters its character depends on the density of the material used: silk, gelatine, acetate, polyester, vinyl, etc.

Silk is a term used for a material that has a bright translucence, a hangover from the days when actual silk was the only diffusion available. Silk is fragile and must be used in holders that fit into gobo stands because the proximity to heat from a fixture will destroy it. Many silks in use today are made of nylon or lustrous cotton.

Frosted gelatine, as a material, is fragile and will either fade or discolor with use. It is gradually being replaced by plastics.

Plastic (acetate, polyester, vinyl, etc.) is the most durable of all diffusion materials. There are a number of names used by manufacturers to designate their product, and while it is not our intention to endorse the product of a specific manufacturer, certain terms, names, and/or numbers will be mentioned.

Some plastic acetate is very dense, has a tendency to warm the light 200K, and is of stiff sheeting. It must be used on a gobo frame placed in *front* of a light fixture. Another material — *polyester mat* — is less dense, soft and stretchable, but it also must be used in a frame in *front* of a lighting unit, *not on it,* because the material melts easily.

"Shower curtain" is a vinyl material that is pliable and frosted, and is hung in front of a fixture; its resistance to heat is very low. Therefore, care must be taken that it does not touch the unit.

A clear polyester sheet that is scratched will transmit light much as a silk does and is quite popular because it has good resistance to heat and can be placed on the fixture.

Another type of polyester mat in use is similar to spun glass. Polyester mat, however, can be used with safety on lighting units because it has none of the disadvantages spun glass had (darkening, irritating fibers, and loss of color temperature).

It is advisable, prior to filming or telecasting, to spend a few moments testing the transmission factor of each piece of diffusion to be used. This is done in order to ascertain its density in the event that reduction of light intensity becomes necessary. To make a test, simply hold a light meter in the beam of a light, note the reading in footcandles, and then place the diffusion material between the fixture beam and the meter. The amount of light that is reduced should be noted in the event it is needed later.

A word of caution, however. When too much diffusion is used on the fixture, the scene can become flat and uninteresting. This often happens on a multicamera show where the person doing the lighting, in an effort to reduce shadows in each camera angle, diffuses every fixture on the set. Scattered light rays have no source that a viewer can relate to; therefore, the light — and the scene — has a tendency to lose its "sparkle."

A *cukaloris* (Fig. 13–4), sometimes spelled *kukaloris,* is a unit made of fine-mesh hardware cloth (window screen) painted with a translucent plastic and cut with irregular holes. Some are made from solid plywood. The solid material will project a harder shadow than a translucent one.

Commonly referred to as a "cookie," this unit is used mostly to intercept a light beam and project a mottled shadow effect on a highly reflectant surface, thus breaking up the flatness and glare that often attracts the eye away from a foreground action. The density of the shadow pattern varies depending on the distance the cookie is placed from the light source. For subtle mottling, the cookie is placed nearer to the face of the fixture; for heavy mottling, the cookie is moved away from the face of the lighting unit.

No two cookies are alike in design. The units are generally the creation of a Grip (a film or video Stagehand) and there seems to be an unspoken rivalry among the crew members as to who can come up with the most creative (and weirdest) cutouts. Diplomatic lighting people see to it that all cookies on a set are used at least once.

Incidentally, there are a number of Hollywood "old-timers" who claim to have known Charlie Gobo and George Cukaloris, the inventors of these particular units bearing their names. However, upon investigation, it seems

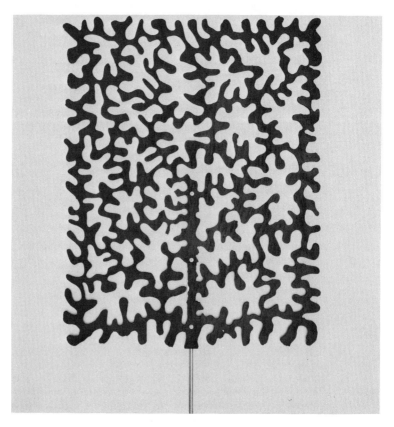

Figure 13–4 *Cukaloris.* This intricate design of plywood is considered to be a "perfect cookie;" it has no square corners on its perimeter or within the cutout sections. A small straight-edge where the unit attaches to the stud is necessary for strength. However, a "purist" (often called a "nit-picker") would insist that the small piece be rounded before the cookie could be called "perfect." Courtesy of Mole-Richardson Co.

that these claims are equivalent to the old lumberjack who swears he knew Paul Bunyon. Every field has its legends.

A *frame* (not shown) is a unit cut from plywood and designed so that when placed in front of a light fixture, it throws a shadow of prison bars, paned windows, venetian blinds, or any other desired silhouette across a set.

chapter 14

Fixture Filters

Most filters designed for use on film or video fixtures are made of gelatine, plastic, or glass.

Gelatine is a thin, fragile material that must be supported in a frame; "melting" occurs when water is splashed on the gelatine surface. Although heat from the fixture's light source causes colors to fade, the reds and ambers hold up longer than the blues and greens.

Plastic filter material is categorized as "thin" or "heavy." Thin plastic, such as vinyl or mylar, requires a support frame. It is much more fade-resistant to heat than gelatine and is waterproof. Heavy plastic, such as acetate or polyester, seldom requires a support frame and is almost completely fade-resistant to heat. It can be submerged in water, wiped dry, and reused; there will have been no change in color or deterioration of material.

Glass filters are manufactured with limited color selection and are used infrequently in film and video; they are more often in permanent installations for lighting on legitimate theater stages.

All filters, regardless of material, are flame-resistant; when subjected to fire, they will shrivel or break, but they will not ignite.

In the manufacture of filters, formulas and procedures are rigidly followed. However, because of the nature of dyes, the possibility of a minute color shift from batch to batch does occasionally occur, although manufacturers assure consumers that only a slight variation of color is permitted. The type of filters most often used in theaters, TV, and motion picture soundstages in the United States and British Commonwealth are listed in this chapter. Since manufacturers provide proprietary names and numbers to their many types of filters, Tables 14–1, through 14–14 provide data regarding filters of various manufacturers, as well as equivalent or near cross-references to numbers and colors of other manufacturers' filters. Manufacturers are listed alphabetically and not according to preference.

The authors wish to thank the majority of manufacturers for supplying cross-reference data and information that is normally kept "in house." In a few instances, the authors chose to make their own comparisons and have altered some data. Such variations from the manufacturer's recommendation are based on side-by-side comparison tests conducted privately. Since most equivalent selection is, in the final analysis, subjective, it is possible that a slight dye variation or shift in voltage on the test lamps influenced the authors' decision; we hereby acknowledge mistakes as our own. In the tables, an asterisk (*) indicates a hue that would, in the authors' opinion, be close (slightly lighter or darker) to the color desired. Near-equivalents are included in the event the exact match is not available.

Fixture filters fall into two classifications: (1) conversion, and (2) color enhancement. Some *conversion filters* change the spectral balance so that emitted light will be compatible with different color temperatures; other conversion filters are intended to reduce the light intensity.

14.1 3200K TO DAYLIGHT

Many lighting people utilize fixtures fitted with 3200–3400K incandescent lamps and add blue filters to convert the rays to so-called daylight color temperature (nominally 5500K). The filters used to convert 3200–3400K to various daylight color temperatures are listed by equivalent manufacturer's product number in Table 14–1.

The *MacBeth* filter, made of glass impregnated with blue dye, has largely been replaced by the dichroic filter as a method of converting incandescent light to daylight balance. The *dichroic* filter converts incandescent light to daylight balance (3200K to 5600K). It is made of heat-resistant glass with a number of extremely thin coatings that have been vacuum-applied to either the inside or outside of the glass. Each coating is either one-quarter or one-half the thickness of the wavelength of light that is to be absorbed and creates interreflections that interfere with and cancel out the wavelength entirely, which is why a dichroic filter is called an *interference filter.* Many glass-coated dichroic filters are placed in clip-on frames so that the filter can be attached to a fixture containing a 3200K lamp and thus convert the light source to "daylight" color temperature.

In the early days of dichroic manufacture there was a tendency for the coatings to fade, and as they did, their color temperature was affected. As a result, blue filter sheets of acetate and polyester, dubbed *boosters,* came into use. Placed in front of a fixture, these boosters raised the color temperature of coated lamps an additional 400K (half-booster) to 800K (full-booster). Today, dichroic coatings are much more stable and durable, but many lighting people still use the full- and half-boosters on coated glass or coated lamps, depending on the measure of "blue" they desire.

It should be noted here that the term *dichroic* is often used by people in the film and video fields to designate a filter that interferes with the "reds" so that only the "blues" are transmitted. However, another type of dichroic filter is one that interferes with "blues" and lets only the "reds" come through. An infrared heat lamp is an example. Another example of a dichroic is a lamp that transmits the entire visible spectrum but either cancels out the ultraviolet (to protect the eyes) or the infrared (so that the lamp burns cool). About the only time this information might be necessary is

Table 14–1   3200K-to-Daylight Conversion Filters and Equivalents

Type of Filter	GAM	Converts 3200K to	Lee	Converts 3200K to	ROSCO Cinegel	Converts 3200K to
Extra Blue CTB	1520	6050K				
Full Blue CTB	1523	5000K	201	5700K	3202	5500K
3/4 Blue CTB	1526	4200K				
1/2 Blue CTB	1529	3800K	202	4300K	3204	4100K
1/3 Blue CTB					3206	3800K
1/4 Blue CTB	1532	3450K	203	3600K	3208	3500K
1/8 Blue CTB	1535	3300K	218	3400K	3216	3300

when ordering lamps from a manufacturer or distributor who is unfamiliar with video or motion picture lighting.

Lamps coated for use as daylight supplements have color temperatures ranging from 4800K to 5200K (±200K). There is a tendency to call all dichroic daylight supplement lamps FAY lights, but this is a bad habit to get into. The American National Standards Institute (ANSI) designates lamps of various wattages by a three-letter code, and most manufacturers conform to the code. Under the code, FAY refers to a 650-watt PAR-36 5000K lamp that has a spot beam and *ferrule contacts*. The same 650-watt PAR-36 5000K lamp with *screw terminals* is coded FBE/FGK, and this difference should be understood thoroughly, especially if the lamps have to be ordered or are to be taken on a job as spares. The correct type to use would depend on the sockets in the fixture housing. In addition, a 1000-watt PAR-64 5200K daylight supplement lamp with extended mogul end prong is coded either FGM (wide flood), FGN (medium flood), or FGP (narrow spot). The danger of referring to these lamps as FAY is the difference in wattage, bulb size, and base.

14.2 DAYLIGHT TO 3200K

Converting daylight to 3200K is accomplished by placing an 85A filter in such a manner as to interfere with the source of incoming daylight. On exteriors, this is accomplished by placing a filter on the film or video camera lens. On a location interior, large sheets of 85A filter are placed on a window or doorway. In some instances, and especially when time is a factor, large 4 × 8-foot (1.22 × 2.44 meter) rigid panels are utilized. They cover windows easily and are invaluable when an entrance through a doorway must be made from the outside. The panels can be placed several feet behind the door, joined with transparent tape, and positioned so that, from the camera's point of view, the joints are aligned with the door frame. This allows an actor maximum freedom of movement in and out without the background "flaring blue" when the door is opened.

Thin, flexible 85A filter material can be applied to a wet window, smoothed out to eliminate wrinkles and bubbles, and then trimmed to fit. It can be easily removed by peeling it from the glass surface. Other 85A materials are of acetate and polyester, which can be fitted to frames larger than the windows they are to cover. In tall buildings, these frames are often lowered into place from the roof by two ropes at each corner of the top rail, with the bottom rail of the frame heavily weighted. The most common daylight-to-3200K filters, combination filters, and their variations are listed in Table 14-2.

14.3 NEUTRAL DENSITY

Neutral-density (ND) filters reduce the light intensity without affecting colors in the scene. While gelatine neutral density comes in all grades, from a 0.10 (80 percent transmission) to a 4.00 (0.010 percent transmission), ND filters of acetate or polyester come in only five densities: 0.15, 0.30, 0.60, 0.90, and 1.2. These densities are referred to simply as N1.5 ("en one and a half", or "point fifteen"), N3, N6, N9, and N1.2 ("en twelve"). Their transmission values are shown in Table 14-3. ND filters, just like the 85A filter material, can be applied to wet windows, placed on frames, or used as panels outside doorways.

14.4 COMBINATION

When an 85 filter is added to a neutral-density filter, the unit converts daylight to 3200K and at the same time reduces the light intensity. At this writ-

Table 14–2 Daylight (5500K) to 3200K Conversion Filters and Equivalents

Type of Filter	GAM	Converts 5500K to	Lee	Converts 5500K to	M-R	Converts 5500K to	ROSCO Cinegel*	Converts 5500K to
Extra CTO	1540	2250K					3401	3200K
Full CTO	1543	2950K	204	3200K	85	3200K	3407	2900K
3/4 CTO	1546	3200K						
1/2 CTO	1549	3750K	205	3800K			3408	3800K
1/4 CTO	1552	4500K	206	4600K			3409	4500K
1/8 CTO	1555	4900K	223	4900K			3401	4900K
85N3			207	3200[a1]			3405	3200K[b1]
85N6			208	3200[a2]			3406	3200K[b2]
85N9							3404	3200K[b3]

*Also called Roscosun
[a1] A combined Lee 204 and 209.
[a2] A combined Lee 204 and 209.
[b1] A combined Roscosun 3405 and 3402.
[b2] A combined Roscosun 3405 and 3403.
[b3] A combined Roscosun 3405 and 3404.

Table 14–3 Neutral Density Filters and Equivalents

Type of Filter	GAM	Lee	M-R	ROSCO Cinegel	Reduces Light
ND 1.2			73T		1/2 stop
ND 1.5	1514				1/2 stop
ND 3	1515	209	74T	3402	1 stop
ND 6	1516	210	76T	3403	2 stops
ND 9	1517	211		3404	3 stops
N 10			77T		3 1/4 stops
N 12	1518				4 stops

ing, 85 filters are only combined with three densities: 0.3, 0.6, and 0.9. These combination filters are referred to as 85N3 (one stop), 85N6 (two stops), and 85N9 (three stops). Thin, flexible combination filters can be applied to wet windows or framed. Rigid panels only come in 85N3 and 85N6 panels.

14.5 CARBON ARC AND HMI FILTERS

As stated previously, the type of external filter used on a carbon arc (see Carbon Arc, Ch. 7) varies, depending on the type of carbon electrode (white-flame or yellow-flame) used inside the fixture. The external filter will either reduce the emitted ultraviolet on exteriors or convert the color temperature to 3200K ($\pm$200K) on interiors. Since the HMI (see The HMI Lamp, Ch. 8) is also high in ultraviolet, the same types of filters are utilized on that fixture as well. Equivalent filters are listed in Table 14–4.

14.6 FLUORESCENT FILTERS

Equivalent fixture filters intended for use when working with film or video under fluorescent lamps are listed in Table 14–5. Additional data, plus information regarding fluorescent filters intended for placement on a camera lens are discussed in Ch. 9.

Table 14–4 Carbon Arc/HMI/CID/CSI Conversion Filters and Equivalents

Type of Filter	GAM	Lee	M-R	ROSCO Cinegel
Y1[a]	1560	212	Y1	3107
MTY[b]	1565	236		3106
MT2[c]	1570	104		3102
1/2 MT2[d]	1575			3115
1/4 MT2[e]				
MT-54[f]				3134
WF Green[g]		213		3110
UY[h]	1510	226		3114
YF[i]		230		
WF[j]		232		
HMI/T[k]		236		
CID/T[l]		237		
CSI/T[m]		238		

[a]Reduces Kelvin of white flame carbons and HMI to daylight balance, and inhibits UV transmission.
[b]A Combined Y1 and MT2; corrects white-flame carbons and/or HMI to 3200K.
[c]Use with Y1 filter to correct color temperature of white-flame carbon arcs and HMI to 3200K.
[d]Half the reduction of an MT2 (approx. 4600K).
[e]One-fourth the reduction of an MT2 (approx. 5200K).
[f]Warms white flame arcs and HMI.
[g]Same application as Y1; preferred in Europe; can be used as substitute for Y1 but has 7% less transmission.
[h]Absorbs ultraviolet of white-flame carbon arc and HMI; has slight warming effect.
[i]Corrects yellow-flame carbons to 3200K.
[j]Corrects white-flame carbons to 3200K.
[k]Corrects HMI to 3200K.
[l]Corrects CID to 3200K.
[m]Corrects CSI to 3200K.

Table 14–5 Fluorescent Conversion Filters and Equivalents

Type of Filter	GAM	Lee	ROSCO Cinegel	ROSCO Cinecolor	Roscolene	Roscolux
Plusgreen	1585	138	3304	671		88
1/2 Plusgreen	1587		3315			
1/4 Plusgreen			3316			
Plusgreen 50		219	3306	675		
Minusgreen	1580		3308	625		37
1/2 Minusgreen	1582		3313	623		
1/4 Minusgreen			3314	622		
Flurofilter			3310	611		
Windowgreen	1585	138	3304	671		88
Tung/Fluor 5700K[a]		241				
Tung/Fluor 4300K[b]		242				
Tung/Fluor 3600K[c]		243				

[a] Converts 3200K tungsten to fluorescent 5700K; requires FLB filter on camera lens.
[b] Converts 3200K tungsten to fluorescent 4300K; requires FLB filter on camera lens.
[c] Converts 3200K tungsten to fluorescent 3600K; requires FLB filter on camera lens.

14.7 LIGHT LOSS

Light loss is a factor to consider when a filter (conversion or effect) interferes with a light source, especially when calculating footcandles. Table 14–6 shows light-loss factors of the most commonly used fixture filters in video and film.

14.8 COLOR-ENHANCEMENT FILTERS

The use of color for effect is being widely employed in film and video by imaginative lighting people. The psychology of color is an immense subject and beyond the scope of this book, but its use for mood will increase in the future. Familiarity with color-enhancement filters will enable a lighting person to be increasingly creative in the art of lighting.

Tables 14–7 through 14–15 (pages 165–178) list color-enhancement filters of various manufacturers as well as other manufacturers' equivalent or near-equivalent filters.

14.9 FILTER EFFECTS

A very important aspect of a lighting person's job is working with filters to create effects — to convince the audience with the use of filters and fixtures that the object/scene being viewed is the "real thing" even though what is being seen has been expertly faked. There are a number of ways to achieve

Table 14–6 Light Loss

Filter	Color	Approximate Light Loss
Y-1	Pale Yellow	1/4 stop
MT-2	Orange	3/4 stop
MT-2 (1/2 density)	Pale Orange	1/2 stop
MT-54	Pale straw	1/4 stop
MTY	Amber	1/2 stop
Y-1 + MT-2	(Sandwich)	1 stop
YF or YF-101	Pale Yellow-Green	1/4 stop
WF	Green	1/4 stop
MacBeth Glass	Deep Blue	1 3/4 stops
Dichroic Coating	Blue	1 1/2 stops
Extra C.T. Blue	Dark Blue	1 3/4 stops
"Moonlight" Green	Pale Yellow-Green	1/4 stop
Plusgreen	Light Green	3/4 stop
Plusgreen 50	Blue-Green	2 stops
Windowgreen	Light Green	3/4 stop
Minusgreen	Salmon	3/4 stop
Fluorofilter	Orange	1 stop
Full C.T. Blue	Medium Blue	1 stop
1/4 C.T. Blue	Pale Blue	1/2 stop
1/8 C.T. Blue	Blue Tint	1/4 stop
Extra CTO	Dark Amber	1 stop
Full CTO	Amber	2/3 stop
3/4 CTO	Amber	2/3 stop
1/2 CTO	Medium Amber	1/2 stop
1/4 CTO	Light Amber	1/3 stop
1/8 CTO	Pale Amber	1/4 stop
85N3	Amber/Grey	1 2/3 stops
85N6	Amber/Medium Grey	2 2/3 stops
85N9	Amber/Dark Grey	3 2/3 stops

effects; however, it takes much experimenting and study—the more the better. As in every other phase of this book, the basics will be presented and suggestions offered—the imagination and/or choice is left to the individual. The "workhorses" of the filter family are the straw and amber filters. One use for them is to de-emphasize a highlight. For example, a backlight on a bald actor may cause a shine that makeup cannot cure. The placement of a straw or amber filter on the fixture causing the highlight will intercept the fixture's rays. Very often this will entirely eliminate the problem or at least make it possible to live with. Glossy surfaces of fabric, or set material, can also be toned down with the use of a straw or amber filter.

14.9a Day-for-Nite

A *day-for-nite* shot is an exterior scene actually shot in daylight, but which, when viewed, appears to have been shot at night. Day-for-nite demands advance planning, because certain requirements must be met in order to accomplish the sought-for effect, which is to make the sunlight appear to be moonlight and the shadow areas to go black, as they would at night. The location site must be chosen carefully, since most of the action must take place in strong backlight, three-quarter backlight, and/or sidelight. The effect will be lost if the scene is front-lit.

When the subject is favored with backlight/sidelight, a good portion of the action is then in full darkness or semidarkness. The camera should favor the shadow side of the subject so as to obscure some of the subject's features. This adds to the illusion of night.

When shooting at a site that has windows, doors, bare globes, etc., in the background, these openings should be strongly lit with incandescent fixtures, which also add to the effect of night. Perhaps the most important thing in shooting day-for-nite is the *avoidance of sky*. Sky will always show as daylight blue and destroy the illusion.

In addition to the preceding requirements for a day-for-nite scene, the camera lens (for both video and film) must be stopped down anywhere from 1 1/2 to 3 stops to achieve the degree of darkness desired, depending on the script or action. Early evening will call for one kind of darkness; midnight is darker and predawn has an ambience all its own.

Normally, when shooting daylight exteriors, an orange-colored 85A filter is placed on the camera lens. In day-for-nite shooting, the 85A is not used. Instead, an Aero-1 (Wratten no. 3) or a Harrison and Harrison GY-1 (both yellow filters) is placed on the lens, and the lens is stopped down 1 1/2 to 3 stops. The yellow filter takes the harshness out of blue that will be registered on the emulsion or target area, and stopping down the lens will impart the darkness desired. A 2-B UV (ultraviolet) filter will also serve the same purpose.

In instances where the Aero-1 or GY-1 are not available (no filter used), the lens should be stopped down 1 1/2 to 3 stops. The saturated blue hue (due to the unfiltered ultraviolet) that is imparted to skin tones when a filter is not used can be corrected slightly by the laboratory in printing. Another option is to leave the 85A filter on the camera lens, stop the lens down 1 1/2 to 3 stops, and let the laboratory add the blue; this has its drawbacks in that the entire scene, including faces, will have an overall blue cast.

When an 85A filter is not used on the lens, gold reflectors and/or tungsten lamps are used to light the *sunny* side of an actor or set. This serves to render skin tones and colors near normal. In the absence of a gold reflector, a large sheet of 85A filter can be draped over a silvered reflector board and its reflected rays directed at the subject. Either type of reflector will transmit white light with an appropriate color temperature rating of 3400K. Therefore, when reading a meter to determine the proper exposure, the light from the reflector should be read as though for an interior, with appropriate ASA/DIN indexes. Thus, face tones will be properly exposed, while the rest of the scene will have a "moonlight blue" cast.

A few years ago Harrison and Harrison introduced a set of three Day-For-Nite filters. Reddish-blue in color, the no. 1 filter controls the color only; i.e., the "red" holds the skin tones and the "blue" provides the "night" color. Filter no. 2, while providing the same effect as no. 1, also lowers the contrast of a scene. Filter no. 3 also retains the same effect as no. 1 but lowers the contrast even more than no. 2. Regardless of which filter is used, exposure is cut by two stops. When using the new high-speed films and/or highly sensitive video cameras, neutral-density filters may be necessary on the camera lens to reduce the quantity of light reaching the aperture or target area.

14.9b Nite-for-Nite

Nite-for-nite is a term used for location exterior shooting to differentiate it from the term *night shooting,* which simply means working at night in a studio sound stage. The areas used in nite-for-nite shooting are lit with fixtures. Sidelight is used extensively, either from one or both sides of the camera (often alternately), and backlight is utilized to create highlights and convey depth. Fill light is *not* used, so that the deep shadows created by the lighting will be in evidence and will add to the notion that the action is indeed taking place at night. Front lighting is only used on the immediate foreground action.

When there is a location interior/exterior to be shot, the *interior* is lit with white (that is, unfiltered) light, and the *exterior* is differentiated from the interior by the addition of "moonlight blue" filters on the fixtures illuminating the exterior area.

14.9c Moonlight

On a soundstage, filters and back and cross lights are used to simulate moonlight. The most common filters in use are the ³/₄ blue and the pale green. These two filters are sandwiched before placing them on a fixture. The blue conveys a feeling of moonlight, the pale green serving to color the highlights; the combination is kinder to skin tones and tends to subdue the blue, especially on foliage. Blue used alone exposes skin blemishes and can turn foliage a dull black. *Warning:* The use of any green other than pale green will destroy the moonlight effect.

When windows, doors, lighted globes, or other props on a set are visible in a moonlight scene, the moonlight and "feeling of night" effect is emphasized by adding straw or amber filters to the fixtures used to light those openings or practicals.

14.9d Fires

Firelight playing on objects, or faces, can convey charm, romance, danger, or mystery, depending on one's intent and the circumstances. Real fires, unaided, are incapable of projecting the desired effect. Filters placed on fixtures used to simulate the fire add the proper dimensions and color to make the reflection appear more real.

Amber filters are used to convey the color of small fires; a mix of amber and straw filters is used for medium-sized fires; a straw filter by itself is used to color the light from a large-sized fire; a red filter is used to represent the color of glowing coals; and a mixture of straw *and* red is used to represent the embers of a wood fire. The fixtures used to direct the lighting on a subject that is supposedly from coals or embers are focused at full flood and diffused to impart the softness to the scene that light from a dying fire truly has.

The "dancing" of flames on a subject and the surrounding area is accomplished by different means, depending on the size and type of fire. These methods are outlined below by type of fire.

Campfire A campfire scene shot at night requires the use of small fixtures, such as inkies or midgets, that can be tucked behind an object or person(s) sitting beside a fire. There must be enough bodies or objects in the scene to hide the units. All light must appear to be coming from the fire itself, and the objective also is to simulate the blaze playing on the faces and surrounding area. Flame color is achieved by placing an amber or orange filter on the fixture. To create a flicker, a "wick" effect is employed: A heavy cord or rag is saturated with oil, placed in a saucer, then set on fire, and the flames are blown out. The smoldering wick in its saucer is then placed between the light source and the actor. The smoke interferes with the light beam, causing a realistic-looking flicker.

Offscreen fires Experienced camerapersons are occasionally called on to shoot footage of reactions of bystanders watching an offscreen fire—footage that will be cut into scenes from stock or was shot some months or years previously. Intensive study of the previous footage must be made to determine such things as direction of light, action, and weather elements. Once again, filters can be very helpful in the recreation of the original atmosphere, since the filter will convey the color of the original fire and differing filters will be used to depict the various stages of the fire or holocaust as it progresses.

The "dancing" quality of the light coming from the simulated flames is achieved by the use of a "flicker stick," which is a slender length of wood to which multicolor strips of gelatine filter material have been attached. The color of the strips are predominantly straw, amber, orange, and red, and should also include greens and purples. The thinly cut strips vary in width ($1/4$ to $3/4$ inch), are about 2 feet in length, and are placed on the stick in alternating colors. A crew member dangles the strips in front of the fixture and jiggles them; the heat from the rays of the fixture causes the strips to flutter; and that, added to the movement of the stick, creates the flicker effect. This is quite an art, and there always seems to be one person in the crew who is a better "flicker-sticker" than anyone else and more than eager to go for the "flicker stick" when the lighting person turns to him or her and says, "Be a fire."

Another exceptionally good offscreen fire effect is the use of a "space blanket," a fabric that is covered with a soft, silvered reflecting surface. The perimeter of the fabric is fitted with grommets. The blanket is suspended by rubber bands looped through the grommets and attached to hooks on a wooden frame with an inside measurement about 8 inches larger than the reflective blanket. A fixture fitted with an orange, amber, or red filter (or all three, depending on one's preference) is set to the side or just below the wooden frame and beamed onto the blanket. Once the silvered blanket is aimed at the subject, the flicker is obtained by lightly tapping the center of the blanket from the rear. The blanket can be low on the ground or high in the air—it throws excellent "flame" shadows at either level.

Offscreen flame that grows in intensity is obtained by placing the fixture on a dimmer. When its intensity is brought "up," flame can be two to three stops over the key light if the subject is side- or back-lit, providing it is done quickly and is a short scene. The overexposure adds to the effect of searing heat.

When the scene is front-lit or intended to be a slow buildup of flame, the normal key-light exposure should be determined and the lens set one stop *darker* than the reading. Then when the "firelight" is brought "up" two or three stops, the footcandle level will appear much "hotter" than the lighting really is. The visual impact will be greater than the side- or back-lit effect.

14.9e Candlelight

A candle has a color temperature of about 1900K and throws a very warm, soft light. Illumination that is supposed to be coming from the candle must be diffused or *bounced*—that is, indirectly reflected from a white card or silvered umbrella—and it must be filtered. A medium or dark amber seems to convey the proper degree of warmth.

The fixture to use should have a map that is frosted (RFL, PS, etc.) or one can use a small unit fitted with a fresnel lens. Low light level, which calls for a wide aperture on the camera lens, helps soften the scene. With a wide aperture, much of the glow and halo that a candle flame radiates can be retained.

Wall-mounted candles When shooting Gothic or costume scripts, candle-holders must be emphasized by a halo against the wall to give the illusion that they are actually holding the candles that are creating the light within the scene. The halo is achieved by placing an offscreen fixture (fitted with a snoot) high and at such an angle that the shadow of the holder created by the fixture's rays is forced downward, thus minimized.

To throw light into the set and make it appear the illumination is coming from the candles, fixtures are placed on top of the set wall above each holder and aimed into the set. A filter is fitted to each fixture to help create a warm glow and to act as a kicker or backlight when the actor is between the candleholder and the camera. Front light is diffused and filtered as well.

Walking with a lighted candle There are two methods used to simulate walking with a lighted candle depending on the circumstances. First, when a camera is revealing a wide area of a set and an actor must walk through it carrying a candle, a large number of fixtures are connected to separate dimmers. As the actor moves along, each units is "powered up," and as the actor continues on his way, the initial units are then "faded down" as the next units are "powered up," etc. This method requires considerable rehearsal, many fixtures, and lots of manpower. Second, when the camera trucks with an actor, three lamp operators walk alongside and close to the dolly. They carry fixtures with filtered snoots. Lamp operator 1 aims his or her fixture, which will simulate light from the candle, at the actor. Lamp operator 2 aims at the area preceding the actor; operator 3 aims his or her fixture at the area behind the actor. The fixtures being carried by lamp operators 2 and 3 are diffused to approximately half the intensity of that held by lamp operator 1. In both methods, a peanut lamp is placed so that its light will fall on the actor's face only; wires run up the sleeve to a belt battery or extension cable.

14.9f Lantern

Lantern light is virtually the same effect as candlelight except that it is more confined within a base and top and has a slightly harder intensity. Modern lanterns have a degree of straw or very light amber color. Old-fashioned lanterns exhibit an amber hue.

Lanterns can be used as a source light in a scene. When an actor lights the lantern, the illumination on the walls is brought up on dimmers and left there. The light of a lantern does not "umbrella" or halo like a candle (i.e., does not include the higher walls and ceiling); therefore, it requires the use of cutters or barndoors instead of snoots on the fixtures to create the effect that the lantern's top and bottom are cutting off light to the higher walls and ceiling as well as the floor.

When the lantern is being carried, a peanut lamp helps create the illusion that the actor is being lit by the lantern. These tiny lamps are attached to the side nearest the actor and must be hidden from view. They are wired the same as a candle. A *bull's-eye lantern,* with only one opening, calls for a set-up similar to a flashlight.

14.9g Flashlight

Special "dummy" flashlights are manufactured for film or video use in two voltages: 30 and 110 volts. The color temperature of the lamps is 3200K, and the case is equipped with wiring that is run up the sleeve and attached to either a battery or extension cable. Although 3200K is compatible with the rest of the fixtures on a set, a very light amber can be placed on the flashlight lens to lower the color temperature so that the beam will more closely resemble that of an actual flashlight.

When a dummy flashlight is not available, a flashlight beam is simulated by the use of a small off-camera ellipsoidal fixture fitted with a snoot and handheld, which will convey more natural movement, i.e., when "searching" out an object. "Dimness" is obtained by adding various shades of straw or amber filters to the unit.

14.9h Water Reflections

When working on a sound stage on sets that have a nautical motif, the creation of water reflections enhances the scene and adds credibility as well. Whether it is an interior of a cabin with water reflections coming through a porthole and shining on the ceiling or actors at the rail of a ship at night, the procedure is the same.

To create overhead reflections: The lighting person stands on a ladder and positions his or her head at the area on the ceiling where the reflections will fall. (At a rail, the lighting person stands where he or she wants the reflection to fall.) A direct line of site is taken from the spot on the ceiling through the porthole to the offstage floor (or from the rail to the offstage floor). When that degree of angle is determined, a pan of water is placed on the stage floor at the end of the line of site. Then an offstage fixture is placed at the spot an exact number of feet away from the pan of water, as the reflection will be from the pan. Once placed, the fixture head is elevated to the same height as the ceiling (or rail) and pointed downward at the pan of water and at the same degree of angle as the line of site.

Since real water will *not reflect* rays evenly and the water in the pan *will,* broken bits of mirror or mylar are scattered along the bottom of the pan. The mirror will "kick" hard rays upward and fracture the evenness of the reflection, adding to the illusion. When the water pan is rocked or tipped or the contents stirred, the reflected light will "break up," creating the illusion of rolling water or sea. The degree to which the reflection is broken up depends on the desired mood of the scene—slow movement generally depicts a romantic mood, medium movement conveys mystery, and quick movement, excitement.

When creating reflections for a nautical scene, filters placed on the fixtures help indicate time—pale blue for night and yellow-red for sunrise or sunset. Filters are not used on fixtures in daylight scenes.

14.9i Lightning

In the early days of film, studios used bundles of carbon-arc electrodes to create lighting by applying high voltage and touching the bundles together. When sound was introduced, a silent unit that emitted bright light was created that is still in use today in many studios. It is a reflective pan with approximately 24 no. 4 photofloods; its depth is at least that of the height of the lamps. The unit is fitted with a knife-switch contact to create the flashes.

The fixture does not register a lightning blue. This lack of color is compensated for by adding a quarter-booster or half-booster blue filter to the fixture. Since the filter lowers the intensity, more than one unit is necessary to create the overpowering flash of light that would depict lightning.

The best lightning effect is an unfiltered white-flame carbon arc with a shutter mounted on the lens. The unit is quiet, and the resultant color, blue-white, is very close to actual lightning. The shutters, fitted with either a knob or handle, much like a Navy signal lamp, can be controlled easily. Subtle changes in the intensity can also be had by varying the shutter openings.

There are two good methods used to depict lightning. Some lighting people prefer the use of side or back light on actors or as an effect coming through windows, so that the intensity of the light will not wash out the scene. Others contend that lightning comes from anywhere, anytime, and if it should frontlight a scene and wash it out, that is how life is. The director, doubtless, would make that decision.

14.9j Rain

Rain can be seen only when it is strongly back lit from two sides, which gives the raindrops a roundness. When back lit from one side only, rain has a tendency to show up as short light streaks. Great care must be taken to prevent back lights from shining into the lens, thus causing flare. When working with dolly shots, more than two back lights have to be set.

A half-booster blue on back lights will add to the coldness of rain. However, the loss of light caused by the filter may be a determining factor regarding the visibility of the rain. A larger fixture will solve the light-loss problem.

Water must go up before it can come down as rain. There are pipes, called "birds," fitted with sprinkler heads that spew water upward and at the same time fracture the stream so that, like real rain, the drops are of differing sizes. The birds should be rigged high above and out of camera range. Rows of these units can vary the amount of rainfall by a change of heads for drizzle, patter, or downpour and can be controlled by a single shutoff valve that allows rain to fall on cue.

In the absence of birds, simple garden hoses can be used to spew water into the air while whipping the nozzle so that the drops do not come down uniformly; it requires a number of hoses to equal the effectiveness of a sprinkler head. Care should always be taken to see that water does not splatter the camera lens, fall on the camera itself, or drip off the front of the camera cover—the rain would show up as vertical blurs dropping through the frame.

It is important that *no* area be in bright sunshine when shooting a rain scene in daylight. Sunlight will erase the illusion completely. And day or night, visible or in shadow, everything the camera "looks at" should be hosed down. It is amazing and pleasantly surprising how many unknown highlights will pop into the hosed-down scene and enhance the rain effect as well as add to the illusion that it is raining *all* over, not just near the camera.

Rain rarely falls in an absolutely vertical direction. The use of wind machines is highly recommended. The machines will give anywhere from a gentle slant to a hurricane incline to the drops and add realism to the effect. A FOG-1 filter on the camera lens adds realism to the effect, which has the look of real rain. When a front-light fixture is used to light foreground action, it must *always* be diffused.

14.9k Fog

As with rain, fog also calls for heavy back light. Fog is created by a machine called, appropriately enough, a *fogmaker*. Those used in a studio will plug into 110-volt outlets; those used on location are equipped with tiny gasoline engines. When liquid "fogjuice" is injected into a hot exhaust tube on the machine, it is vaporized, then condensed, and then becomes a thick white cloud as it mixes with the cooler atmosphere. When an attached container is filled with dry ice, the fog will lie low in quiet air, like a ground mist, and can be easily blown away by fans.

It is essential that everything within a fog scene is covered with moisture to enhance the illusion of mist. This can be easily accomplished with the use of spray nozzles. Again, a subtle quarter-booster or half-booster blue filter placed on the back lights can add to the "coldness" of a fog scene; however, too much blue will create a moonlight effect and destroy the illusion. Shafts of warm light emanating from windows or doorways, when filtered with straw or light amber, will also contribute to the coldness of the fog.

Front light is always diffused, as with a rain scene. Anything from a FOG-1 to a FOG-5 on the camera lens also adds to the diffusion that is typical of fog. The degree of filtering depends on the halo effect desired from street lights, window lights, etc., within the scene.

14.9l Smoke

Smoke is created by a combination of "smoke fluid" and compressed air under heat and pressure. The newer smoke makers burn clean. When older-type smoke makers are used, the units produce smoke by spreading mineral oil over hot coils and vaporizing it or by burning beeswax in a "bee smoker," a small unit fitted with bellows and a nozzle. Squeezing the bellows causes the unit to puff billows of smoke. Mineral oil and beeswax are heavy and tend to coat and stain everything—actors, set, crew and equipment—with an oily film.

In actuality, smoke from a fire is more gray-brown in color than fog, and it can be made more realistic by an occasional weak back light of red or orange, especially if flame is supposed to be in the scene.

When filming in a crowded, smoky bar, however, cigarette smoke, being a white smoke should be back lit with an occasional half-booster blue mixed with a nonfiltered back light. When back lighting both fog and smoke, care must be taken not to reveal unnatural shafts of light without a source.

Fog and smoke have a tendency to reduce highlights and flatten out a scene; therefore, a little more contrast than normal can be tolerated. Exposure should be determined when the fog and smoke are present.

14.9m Snow

Years ago, bleached cornflakes were used for snow. They worked very well until someone crunched across the set and almost deafened the soundman. Today, plastic is used. It does not crunch. (Sound people are now as happy as they ever get!)

Artificial snowflakes are *never* to be back lit; they must be front lit. Otherwise, they register as black pieces when they fall. Shadows in real snow show up blue in sunshine because a lot of sky reflection is present. On a sound stage, snow on the ground must be lit to match the look of real snow. A snow scene should be keyed with hard incandescent light and the shadow areas filled in by a snooted or barndoored fixture with a half-booster blue to achieve the "outdoor look."

Artificial snowflakes are thrown by the handful into a slow-turning wind machine and allowed to float to the stage floor to achieve a gentle snowfall effect. They are thrown by the shovelful into high-speed wind machines for a blizzard effect.

In the action area, artificial snow is used for ground cover. For the areas slightly beyond the camera, ground cover is mostly absorbent cotton. Far way from camera, sheets of white plastic are used. Distinguishable overlaps or butted joints are hidden by covering them with strips of cotton and artificial snowflakes. In snow scenes where the sun is shining brightly, glitter should be sprinkled loosely on all surfaces to pick up highlights.

Icicles, like the window glass that stuntpersons crash through, are made of plastic (sometimes candy) and shown to best advantage by back lighting with a half-booster blue. When sun is present, "melting" icicles should be dripping water. This is accomplished by pumping water through tiny hidden plastic tubes to the top of each icicle and letting gravity take it from there.

Heavy overcast on a soundstage snow set is created with heavy diffusion on the front lights and no back light. Some cross light may be used if depth is necessary to separate foreground and background.

14.9n Sunset or Sunrise

At early morning or late afternoon the sun is low on the horizon, long shadows are cast by its rays, and fill light will be minimal. Exterior scenes calling for action at either time of day are handled with wide-angle shots to establish time and locale and are usually shot quickly before the sun is either too high or too low to continue the scene. It is not necessary to wait for an entire day to intercut small group shots of close-ups to match the lighting of the establishing shot; the intercut lighting can be created at any time of day.

First, the actors must be shaded from the sun with a double- or triple-scrimmed butterfly (see Light Modifiers, Ch. 13). This allows ambient light to fall on the scene, yet cuts the directional light considerably.

Second, gold reflectors or silvered reflectors draped with 85A filter material or the warmer MT-2 filter are then set at about eye level and aimed at the actors from the same direction as the real sun in the long shot. In combination with an 85A on the camera, the light on the actors will take on the warm glow of sunrise or sunset. Getting light to the filtered reflectors is accomplished by using "rifles" to obtain a ricochet shot (see Reflector Boards, Ch. 11).

Table 14–7 Dura 60/70[†] Filters and Equivalents

Dura	GAM	Lee	M-R	ROSCO Cinegel	ROSCO Cinecolor	Roscolene	Roscolux
02 F Frost		129	01	3008		801*	103
03 LY Light Yellow							07
05 Y Yellow							
07 L Lemon							
08 DL Dark Lemon	460	102					11
09 LS Light Straw	510	159			604	804	06
10 S Straw	440	103*		3134	605		08
14 GA Golden Amber	385*	104*	57	3102	613	813*	16
17 LA Light Amber	375	147		3106	614	811	18
18 A Amber	350	105			615	815	21
19 DA Dark Amber	290		60			817*	22
21 FR Fire Red	235*					819	24
24 R Red	245	106					26
25 DR Dark Red						823	
26 BA Bastard Amber							03*
27 PA Pink Amber	305	152*				802	01*
30 LFP Light Flesh Pink						825	
31 FP Flesh Pink		109					
33 P Pink							
35 BRP Bright Rose Pink						829	
37 RP Rose Pink							
38 LM Light Magenta	220	113					42
39 M Magenta	995	126				838	49
43 SP Surprise Pink							51*
44 SL Special Lavender							52*
45 L Lavender	960	194					57
47 SB Steel Blue							62*
48 LB Light Blue	850	132			657		80
49 B Blue	890	119			661	863	83
51 VDB Very Dark Blue	890*	119*	37			866	85
53 LDB Light Daylight Blue	740	118				855*	72
54 DB Daylight Blue	815	165				851	67
55 EB Evening Blue		141*				856	
56 MB Moonlight Blue	810	183			659	859	77
57 GB Green Blue							
61 LT Light Turquoise	780*		117			849	70
63 DT Dark Turquoise							854
65 PB Peacock Blue		116*				877	95
67 LYG Light Yellow-Green							
68 YG Yellow Green						878	
70 LG Light Green	660*	122*	47			871	89
71 G Green	655	139				874	90
73 LN Light Neutral	1515	209		3402	680		97

[†]60 series: acetate/70 series: polyester.
*Denotes nearest equivalent.

A sunrise or sunset effect can be extended far into midmorning in medium shots by adding a graduated 85A filter to the 85A already on the camera lens. This will impart an extremely warm golden glow to the sky in an overall scene.

A *graduated filter* is one that is partly clear optical glass and partly filter. The line of demarcation between the two is usually a wavy line, or blending area, and the filter part is adjusted in the camera matte box so that it covers only the sky. No compensation is made on the lens for the added filter. The graduated filter cannot be used for anything other than a lockdown shot or pan across a flat horizon, but the glow in the sky is rich and golden and worth the effort.

Unfiltered 3200K to 3400K light sources cannot be used in close-ups to create a sunrise or sunset glow outdoors when there is an 85A filter on the camera because skin tones will turn extremely red and "bleed."

Table 14–8   GAM Filters and Equivalents

GAM #	Dura	Lee	M-R	ROSCO Cinegel	ROSCO Cinecolor	Roscolene	Roscolux
110 Dark Rose							44
120 Bright Pink		128					39
130 Rose					631*	828*	44*
140 Dark Magenta							
155 Light Pink					624	825	33
160 Chorus Pink	30*	110					36
170 Dark Flesh Pink		111					44*
180 Cherry		148					
190 Cold Pink	31	107	03		626	826	31
195 Nymph Pink	31*	107*					31*
220 Pink Magenta	38	113			620		42
235 Pink Red							
245 Light Red	24	106			621		26
250 Medium Red XT							27
260 Rosy Amber		107					30*
270 Red Orange		182*				819	25
280 Fire Red		164				818	19
290 Fire Orange	19		60			817*	22
305 French Rose	27*	151					01
315 Autumn Glory					618	817	23
320 Peach					617		40*
325 Bastard Amber	26*	152					02
330 Sepia		156			682		99
340 Light Bastard Amber		162			602	802	02
345 Deep Amber		158					23*
350 Dark Amber	18*	105			615	815	21
365 Warm Straw				3115	608		09
375 Flame	17	147		3106	614	811	18
385 Light Amber	14*	104*	57*	3102	613*	813*	15
420 Medium Amber	14	104*	57			810	15
440 Very Light Straw	10	103		3134	605		08
460 Mellow Yellow	08	102					11
480 Medium Lemon		101			609		12

Table 14–8 GAM Filters and Equivalents (*cont.*)

GAM #	Dura	Lee	M-R	ROSCO Cinegel	ROSCO Cinecolor	Roscolene	Roscolux
510 No-Color Straw	09	159			604	804	06
520 New Straw	67*	189					87*
540 Pale Green	67*	138		3304	671		88
570 Light Green Yellow		121					87
650 Grass Green					674		91
655 Rich Green	71	139				874	90
660 Medium Green		122			672		89
680 Kelly Green					673		92
710 Blue Green		115*					73*
720 Light Steel Blue		117					66
730 Azure Blue							70
740 Off Blue	53*	118*			658		72
750 Nile Blue							69
760 Aqua Blue							
770 Christel Blue							
780 Shark Blue		117*			652	849*	70*
790 Electric Blue		202*			647		62*
810 Moon Blue	55	132			609		68
815 Moody Blue	54	165				851	67
820 Full Light Blue							63*
830 North Sky Blue							61
840 Steel Blue		161					64*
850 Blue (Primary)	48	132			657		80
860 Sky Blue		174			651		64
880 Daylight Blue		174*					64*
890 Dark Sky Blue	49*	119			661	863	83
905 Dark Blue		120				866	85
910 Alice Blue							
920 Pale Lavender							53
930 Real Congo Blue		181			645		59
940 Light Purple		142					
945 Royal Purple		181			645		59
950 Purple					644		58
960 Medium Lavender	44						57
970 Special Lavender		170*				840*	52*
980 Surprise Pink	44*	136			642		51
990 Dark Lavender					638		47
995 Orchid	39	126				838	49
1505 Clear		130					00
1510 UV		226		3114			
1514 0.15ND							
1515 0.3ND	73	209	74T	3402	680		97
1516 0.6ND		210	76T	3403	681		98
1517 0.9ND		211		3404			
1518 1.2ND			77T*				
1520 Extra Blue CTB							
1523 Full Blue CTB		201		3202	655		
1526 3/4 Blue							

Table 14–8   GAM Filters and Equivalents (*cont.*)

GAM #	Dura	Lee	M-R	ROSCO Cinegel	ROSCO Cinecolor	Roscolene	Roscolux
1529 ½ Blue CTB		202		3204	647		
1532 ¼ Blue CTB		203		3208			
1535 ⅛ Blue CTB		218		3216			
1540 Extra CTO							
1543 Full CTO				3407			
1546 ¾ CTO		204	85	3401			
1549 ½ CTO		205		3408			
1552 ¼ CTO		206		3409			
1555 ⅛ CTO		223		3410			
1560 Y-1 LCT Yellow		212		3107			
1565 MTY	17	236		3106			
1570 MT2		104		3102			
1575 ½ MT2				3115			
1580 Minusgreen				3308	625		37
1582 ½ Minusgreen				3313	623		
1585 Plusgreen		138		3304	671		88
1587 ½ Plusgreen				3315			

*Denotes nearest equivalent.

Table 14–9   Lee Filters and Equivalents

LEE	Dura	GAM	M-R	ROSCO Cinegel	ROSCO Cinecolor	Roscolene	Roscolux
101 Yellow		480				609	12
102 Light Amber	08	460					11
103 Straw	10	440		3134	605		08
104 Deep Amber	14*	420				810	15
105 Orange	18	350			615	815	21
106 Primary Red	24	245			621		26
107 Light Rose	31*	190	03		626	826	31
109 Light Salmon	31						
110 Middle Rose	30*	160					36
111 Dark Pink		170					44*
113 Magenta	38	220					42
115 Peacock Blue		710*					73*
116 Medium Green Blue						877*	95*
117 Steel Blue	61*	780*				849*	66
118 Light Blue	53*	740					72
119 Dark Blue	49	890			661	863	83
120 Deep Blue		905				866	85
121 Lee Green		570					86
122 Fern Green	70*	660	37*		672		89
124 Dark Green	70*		47*				
126 Mauve	39	995				838	49
127 Smoky Pink							50
128 Bright Pink		120					39
129 Heavy Frost	02		01	3008		801*	103

Table 14-9 Lee Filters and Equivalents (*cont.*)

LEE	Dura	GAM	M-R	ROSCO Cinegel	ROSCO Cinecolor	Roscolene	Roscolux
130 Clear		1505					00
132 Medium Blue	55	810					68
134 Golden Amber							321
135 Deep Golden Amber							321*
136 Pale Lavender	44*	980			642		51
137 Special Lavender							
138 Pale Green	67*	540		3304	671		88
139 Primary Green	71	655				874	90
141 Bright Blue							
142 Pale Violet		940					
143 Pale Navy Blue							
144 No-Colour Blue							
147 Apricot	17	375		3106	614	811	18
148 Bright Rose		180					
151 Gold Tint	27*	305					03
152 Pale Gold	26*	325					02
153 Pale Salmon	27*						
154 Pale Rose							05
156 Chocolate		330			682		99
157 Pink							
158 Deep Orange		315			618	817	23
159 No-Colour Straw	09	510			604	804	06
161 Slate Blue		840					64*
162 Bastard Amber		340			602		02
164 Flame Red	21	280				818	19
165 Daylight Blue	54	815				851	67
166 Pale Red							32
170 Deep Lavender		970*				840*	52
174 Dark Steel Blue		860			651		64
176 Loving Amber	27*						01
179 Chrome Orange							
180 Dark Lavender							
181 Congo Blue		945			645		59
182 Light Red							
183 Moonlight Blue	56	810			659	859	77
184 Cosmetic Peach							
185 Cosmetic Burgundy							
186 Cosmetic Silver Rose							
187 Cosmetic Rouge							
188 Cosmetic Highlight							
189 Cosmetic Silver Moss		520*					87*
190 Cosmetic Emerald							
191 Cosmetic Aqua Blue							
192 Flesh Pink							
193 Rosy Amber							
194 Surprise Pink	44	960*					57
195 Zenith Blue		890					74
196 True Blue					654		65
197 Alice Blue					653		84
201 Full CTB		1523		3202	655		

Table 14–9 Lee Filters and Equivalents (*cont.*)

LEE	Dura	GAM	M-R	ROSCO Cinegel	ROSCO Cinecolor	Roscolene	Roscolux
202 ½ CTB		1529		3204			
203 ¼ CTB		1532		3208			
204 Full CTO		1546	85	3401			
205 ½ CTO		1549		3408			
206 ¼ CTO		1552		3409			
207 CTO-N3				3405			
208 CTO-N6				3406			
209 ND3	73	1515		3402	680		97
210 ND6		1516		3403			
211 ND9		1517		3404			
212 LCT-Y		1560	Y-1	3107			
213 White Flame Green				3110	669		87
214 Full Tough Spun				3006			105
215 Half Tough				3007			106
216 White Diffusion				3026			116
217 Blue Diffusion							
218 ⅛ CTB		1535		3216			
219 Fluorescent Green				3306	675		88
220 White Frost							
221 Blue Frost							
223 ⅛ CTO		1555		3410			
224 Daylight Blue Frost							
225 ND Frost							
226 UV		1510		3114			
228 Brushed Silk							
229 Quarter Tough Spun				3022			
230 Super Correction LCT-Y							
232 Super White Flame				3110*			
236 HMI/Tungsten							
237 CID/Tungsten							
238 CSI/Tungsten							
239 Polariser				8073			
241 Tung/Fluor 5700K							
242 Tung/Fluor 4300K							
243 Tung/Fluor 3600K							
250 Half-White Diffusion				3027			117
251 Quarter-White Diffusion				3028			118
253 Hampshire Frost							119
261 Tough Spun Frost-Full							
262 Tough Spun Frost-¾							
263 Tough Spun Frost-½							
264 Tough Spun Frost-⅜							
265 Tough Spun Frost-¼							
270 Scrim				3809			
271 Mirror Silver				3801			
272 Soft Gold Reflector				3805			
273 Soft Silver Reflector				3803			
280 Black Foil		Blackwrap		Cinefoil			

*Denotes nearest equivalent.

Table 14–10 Mole-Richardson Filters and Equivalents

Mole-Richardson #	Dura	GAM	Lee	ROSCO Cinegel	ROSCO Cinecolor	ROSCO Cinelene	Roscolux
01 Frost	02		129	3008		801*	103
03 Flesh Pink	31*	190	107		626	826	31
09 DuBarry Pink							
17 Special Lavender							
37 Dark Blue	51	890	119			866	85
47 Light Green	70						
48 Medium Green							
54 Light Straw							
55 Medium Straw							
57 Light Amber	14	385*	104*	3102	613		16
60 Dark Amber	19	290				817*	22
63 Special Light Red							
67.5 Medium Red							

*Denotes nearest Equivalent.

Table 14–11 ROSCO Cinegal Filters and Manufacturers' Equivalents

ROSCO Cinegel #	Dura	GAM	Lee	M-R	ROSCO Cinecolor	Roscolene	Roscolux
3000 Tough Rolux							111
3001 Light Rolux							115
3002 Soft Frost							
3004 Half-Density Soft Frost							
3006 Tough Spun			214				105
3007 Light Tough Spun			215				106
3008 Tough Frost	02	129				801*	103
3009 Light Tough Frost							102
3010 Opal Tough Frost							112
3011 Tough Silk							104
3012 Tough Booster Silk							109
3013 Tough Booster Frost							107
3014 Hilite							
3017 Full Blue Frost							108
3022 Quarter Tough Spun			229				
3026 Tough White Diffusion			216				116
3027 Tough 1/2 White Diffusion			250				117
3028 Tough 1/4 White Diffusion			251				118
3029 Silent Frost							
3030 Grid Cloth							
3032 Light Grid Cloth							
3102 Tough MT2		1570	104		613		16
3106 Tough MTY	17	1565	147		614	811	18
3107 Tough Y-1		1560	212	Y-1			
3110 Tough WF Green			213		669		87
3114 UV		1510	226				
3115 Tough 1/2 MT2		1575			608		
3134 Tough MT 54	10	440	103		605		08
3202 Dull Blue (CTB)		1523	201		655		

Table 14–11   ROSCO Cinegal Filters and Manufacturers' Equivalents (*cont.*)

ROSCO Cinegel #	Dura	GAM	Lee	M-R	ROSCO Cinecolor	Roscolene	Roscolux
3204 Half Blue (1/2 CTB)		1529	202		647		
3206 Third Blue (1/3 CTB)							
3208 Quarter Blue (1/4 CTB)		1532	203				
3216 Eighth Blue (1/8 CTB)		1535	218				
3304 Plusgreen/Windowgreen		1585	138				88
3306 Plusgreen 50			219		675		93*
3308 Tough Minusgreen		1580			625		37
3310 Fluorofilter					611		
3313 Tough 1/2 Minusgreen		1582			623		
3314 Tough 1/4 Minusgreen					622		
3315 Tough 1/2 Plusgreen		1587	138				88
3316 Tough 1/4 Plusgreen							
3401 Roscosun 85		1546	204	85			
3402 Rosco N3		1515	209		680		97
3403 Rosco N6		1516	210		681		98
3404 Rosco N9		1517	211				
3405 Roscosun 85N3			207				
3406 Roscosun 85N6			208				
3407 Roscosun CTO		1543					
3408 Roscosun 1/2 CTO		1549	205				
3409 Roscosun 1/4 CTO		1552	206				
3410 Roscosun 1/8 CTO		1555	223				
3421 Black Scrim							
3801 Roscoflex M (Mirror)			271				
3802 Roscoflex H (Hard)							
3803 Roscoflex S (Soft)			273				
3804 Roscoflex SS (Supersoft)							
3805 Roscoflex G (Gold)			272				
3808 Roscoflex F (Flex)							
3809 Roscoscrim (Scrim)			270				
3810 Roscoflex W (White)							
8073 Polarizer			239				

*Denotes nearest equivalent.

Table 14–12   ROSCO Cinecolor Filters and Equivalents

ROSCO Cinecolor #	Dura	GAM	Lee	M-R	Roscogel	Roscolene	Roscolux
602 Bastard Amber		340	162				02
603 Warm Rose							
604 No Color Straw	09	510	159			804	06
605 Pale Gold	10	440	103		3134		08
608 Warm Straw		365			3115		09*
609 Straw		480	101				12
610 Light Flame							17
611 Rose Amber		320*			3310		
612 Golden Amber		375*					

Table 14–12 ROSCO Cinecolor Filters and Equivalents (*cont.*)

ROSCO Cinecolor #	Dura	GAM	Lee	M-R	Roscogel	Roscolene	Roscolux
613 Light Amber	14	385*		57	3102	813	16
614 Flame	47	375	147		3106	811	18
615 Deep Straw	18	350	105	60		815	21
617 Peach		320					
618 Orange		315				817*	23
619 Fire		280	164			818	19
620 Deep Salmon		235*	113				42
621 Light Red	21	245	106				26
622 Pink Tint					3314		
623 Light Pink					3313		
624 Pink		155				825	33
625 Pale Rose Pink		1580			3308		37
626 Flesh Pink	31	190	107			826	31
627 Rose Pink		170	111*				44*
631 Middle Rose		130*				828	44
632 Salmon							41
638 Light Rose Purple		990					47
639 Lilac		950*				841*	58*
641 Lavender						857*	57
642 Surprise Pink		980	136				51
644 Deep Lilac		950					58
645 Indigo		945	181				59
647 Pale Blue		790	202		3204		62*
648 No Color Blue		830*	203*				60
649 Booster Blue		820*	202*				62
650 Light Blue							
651 Light Steel Blue		860	174				64
652 Azure Blue		780	117*				70
653 Zephyr Blue			197				84
654 Daylight Blue			196				65
655 Steel Blue		1529	202			3202	6
56 Slate Blue			161*				
657 Primary Blue	48	850	132				80
658 Medium Green Blue	53*	740					72
659 Green Blue	56		183			859	77
661 Medium Blue	49	890	119			863	83
669 Pale Yellow Green			213		3110		87
671 Light Green	67*	540	138		3304		88
672 Moss Green		660	122*				89
673 Turquoise		680					92
674 Primary Green		650					91
675 Light Blue Green			219		3306		93*
676 Blue Green			219*				93
677 Medium Blue Green		680					92
680 Light Grey		1515	209		3402		97
681 Medium Grey		1516	210		3403		98
682 Chocolate		330	156				99

*Denotes nearest equivalent.

Table 14–13 Roscolene and Equivalents

Roscolene #	Dura	GAM	Lee	M-R	ROSCO Cinegel	ROSCO Cinecolor	Roscolux
801 Frost				01	3008		101
802 Bastard Amber	27*	305	151				01
803 Pale Gold		340	162			602	02
804 No Color Straw	09	510	159			604	06
805 Light Straw							
806 Medium Lemon							
807 Dark Lemon							
809 Straw			102*				14*
810 No Color Amber	14*	420	104*	57*			15
811 Flame	17	375	147		3106	614	18
813 Light Amber		385*	104	57	3102	613	16
815 Golden Amber	18	350	105			615	21
817 Dark Amber		315	158			618	23
818 Orange		270	182*				25
819 Orange-Amber		235*					24
821 Light Red							
823 Medium Red	25						
825 No Color Pink		155				624	33
826 Flesh Pink	31	190	107	03		626	31
827 Bright Pink							
828 Follies Pink		130*				631	44
832 Rose Pink							
834 Salmon Pink							
836 Plush Pink							
837 Medium Magenta							
838 Dark Magenta	39	995	126				49
839 Rose Purple							
840 Surprise Lavender		970*	170*				52*
841 Surprise Pink							
842 Special Lavender							57*
843 Medium Lavender							
844 Violet							
846 Medium Purple							
848 Water Blue							
849 Pale Blue	61						
850 No Color Blue							
851 Daylight Blue	54	815	165				67
853 Middle Blue							
854 Middle Blue	63						
855 Azure Blue	53*	740*	118*				72*
856 Light Blue	55		141*				
857 Medium Blue							79
859 Green-Blue Moonlight	56		183			659	77
861 Surprise Blue							
862 True Blue		890*	119*			661*	83*
863 Medium Blue	49	890	119			661	83
866 Dark Urban Blue	51	890*	119*			661*	85
871 Light Green	70	660*	122*	47			89

Table 14–13 Roscolene and Equivalents (*cont.*)

Roscolene #	Dura	GAM	Lee	M-R	ROSCO Cinegel	ROSCO Cinecolor	Roscolux
874 Medium Green	71	655	139				90
877 Medium Blue-Green			116*				95
878 Yellow Green	68						
880 Light Grey	73*	1515	209*		3402	680*	97*
882 Light Chocolate		330*	156			682*	99*
883 Medium Grey			210*		3403	681*	98*

*Denotes nearest equivalent.

Table 14–14 Roscolux Filters and Equivalents

Roscolux #	Dura	GAM	Lee	M-R	ROSCO Cinegel	ROSCO Cinecolor	Roscolene
00 Clear		1505	130				
01 Light Bastard Amber	27*		176				802
02 Bastard Amber	26*	340	162			602	
03 Dark Bastard Amber							
04 Medium Bastard Amber		325	152				
05 Rose Tint			154				
06 No Color Straw	09	510	159			604	804
07 Pale Yellow	03						
08 Pale Gold	10	440	103		3134	605	
09 Pale Amber Gold							
10 Medium Yellow							
11 Light Straw	08	460	102				
12 Straw		480					
312 Canary			101				
13 Straw Tint							
14 Medium Straw	08		102*				809*
15 Deep Straw	14*	420	104				810
16 Light Amber	14	385*	104*	57	3102	613	813*
17 Light Flame						610	
18 Flame	17	375	147		3106	614	811
19 Fire	21	280	164				
20 Medium Amber							
21 Golden Amber	18	350	105			615	815
321 Soft Golden Amber			134				
22 Deep Amber	19	290		60			
23 Orange		315	158			618	817
24 Scarlet	21	235*					819*
25 Orange Red		270	182*				819
26 Light Red	24	245	106				
27 Medium Red		250					
30 Light Salmon Pink							
31 Salmon Pink	31	190	107	03		626	826
32 Medium Salmon Pink			166				
33 No Color Pink		155				624	825

Table 14–14 Roscolux Filters and Equivalents (*cont.*)

Roscolux #	Dura	GAM	Lee	M-R	ROSCO Cinegel	ROSCO Cinecolor	Roscolene
34 Flesh Pink							
35 Light Pink		160*	110*				
36 Medium Pink	30*	160	110				
37 Pale Rose Pink		1580			3308	625	
337 True Pink			110*				
38 Light Rose							
339 Broadway Pink		120	128				
40 Light Salmon							
41 Salmon						632	
42 Deep Salmon	28	220	113			620	
43 Deep Pink		120*	128*				
44 Middle Rose		130*				631	828
45 Rose			128*				
46 Magenta	38						836*
47 Light Rose Purple		990				638	
48 Rose Purple							
49 Medium Purple	39	995	126				838
50 Mauve			127				
51 Surprise Pink		980	136			642	
52 Light Lavender			170				840*
53 Pale Lavender							
54 Special Lavender							
55 Lilac			137*				
56 Gypsy Lavender		945*					
356 Middle Lavender							
57 Lavender	44	960					
58 Deep Lavender		950				644	
358 Rose Indigo							
59 Indigo		945	181			645	
60 No Color Blue		830*	203*			648	
61 Mist Blue		830					
62 Booster Blue		820*	202			649	
63 Pale Blue							
64 Light Steel Blue		860	174			651	
65 Daylight Blue			196			654	
66 Cool Blue	61*	720	117				
67 Light Sky Blue	54	815	165				851
68 Sky Blue	55	810	132				
69 Brilliant Blue		750					
70 Nile Blue		730					
71 Sea Blue							
72 Azure Blue	53	740	118*			658	
73 Peacock Blue		710*	115*				
74 Night Blue		890	195				
77 Green Blue	56		183			659	859
78 Trudy Blue							
79 Bright Blue							857
80 Primary Blue	48	850	132			657	

Table 14–14 Roscolux Filters and Equivalents (*cont.*)

Roscolux #	Dura	GAM	Lee	M-R	ROSCO Cinegel	ROSCO Cinecolor	Roscolene
81 Urban Blue							
82 Surprise Blue							
83 Medium Blue	49	890	119			661	863
383 Sapphire Blue							
84 Zephyr Blue			197			653	
85 Deep Blue	51	890*	120*	37			866
385 Royal Blue							
86 Pea Green		570	121				
87 Pale Yellow Green			213		3110	669	
88 Light Green	38	540	138		3304	671	
388 Gaslight Green			138				
89 Moss Green	70*	660	122			672	
389 Chrome Green							
90 Dark Yellow Green	71	655	139				874
91 Primary Green		650				674	
92 Turquoise		680				677	
93 Blue Green			219*			676	
94 Kelly Green							
95 Medium Blue Green	65			116*			877
96 Lime							
97 Light Grey	73	1515	209		3402	680	880*
98 Medium Grey			210		3403	681	
99 Chocolate		330	156			682	
100 Frost							
101 Light Frost							
102 Light Tough Frost					3009		
103 Tough Frost	02		129	01	3008		
104 Tough Silk					3011		
105 Tough Spun			214		3006		
106 Light Tough Spun			215		3007		
107 Cool Frost					3013		
108 Daylight Frost					3017		
109 Cool Silk					3012		
111 Tough Rolux					3000		
112 Opal Tough Frost					3010		
113 Matte Silk							
114 Hamburg Frost							
115 Light Rolux					3001		
116 Tough White Diffusion			216		3026		
117 Tough 1/2 White Diffusion			250		3027		
118 Tough 1/4 White Diffusion			251		3028		
119 Light Hamburg Frost			253				
120 Red Diffusion							
121 Blue Diffusion							
122 Green Diffusion							
123 Amber Diffusion							
124 Red Cyc Silk							
125 Blue Cyc Silk							

Table 14–14   Roscolux Filters and Equivalents (*cont.*)

Roscolux #	Dura	GAM	Lee	M-R	ROSCO Cinegel	ROSCO Cinecolor	Roscolene
126 Green Cyc Silk							
127 Amber Cyc Silk							
128 Magenta Silk							
129 Sky Blue Silk							
130 Medium Blue Green Silk							
131 Medium Amber Silk							
150 Hamburg Rose							
151 Hamburg Lavender							
152 Hamburg Steel Blue							

*Denotes nearest equivalent.

chapter 15

The Powerline

The term *powerline,* as used in this text, refers to (1) the electrical parts and connections that are attached to a fixture housing and carry current to its light source, and (2) the cables that transmit electric current from the main power source (bussbar or generator) to the fixture's connector.

1. The powerline of a fixture consists of:
   On/off switch(es)
   Cable
   Wiring
   Connector
2. The powerline that brings current from the main power source to the area that is to be lit consists of:
   Feeder cables
   Extensions
   Adaptors
   Splicers

15.1 FIXTURE POWERLINE

15.1a On/Off Switch

The on/off switch is manufactured in one of three types: tumbler, rocker, or toggle (see Fig. 15–1) and is either single- or double-pole. It can be an integral part of the housing (attached to the fixture) or part of the cable (in-line) between the connector and the housing. Regardless of type, a switch must be capable of withstanding given voltages and amperages for lengthy periods. Each switch has its specific rating stamped on it by the manufacturer. Applying voltage and amperage greater than the rating will cause the contacts of the switch to oxidize and will shorten its life; far more important, the resultant short in the circuity becomes an extreme fire hazard, the most dreaded catastrophe on stages.

To avoid a short, a fixture must be fitted with a switch that has a rating greater than that of the output voltage and amperage of the power supply to be used. In practice, a switch should not be subjected to voltage or amperage more than 85 percent of its rating.

NOTE: For example, a switch with a rating of 270 volts and 10 amperes should never be subjected to more than 230 volts and 8.5 amperes (270 volts × 85% = 229.5 volts, 10 amp × 85% = 8.5 amp).

The voltage and amperage *can* be exceeded for a *short* period of time up to its full rated value; this often results inadvertently from voltage and current surges that occur in power lines.

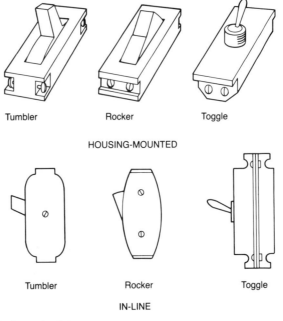

Tumbler Rocker Toggle

HOUSING-MOUNTED

Tumbler Rocker Toggle

IN-LINE

Figure 15–1 Types of switches.

Single-pole switches are used on fixtures fitted with a light source of less than 2000 watts (2K). Double-pole switches are used on fixtures fitted with a light source of 2000 watts (2K) or more.

15.1b Cable

A fixture's cable is made up of one or more insulated wires and is classified as single-conductor, two-wire, three-wire, etc. (Fig. 15–2). The covering is called the *sleeve* and is either rubber or neoprene.

Single-conductor cable Two single-conductor cables must be used with large fixtures such as carbon arcs or teners; the cables have matching plugs for the receptacles on the fixture.

Two-wire cable The two-wire cable currently in use on motion picture, theater, and video stages came into existence when all electricity was direct current (DC) — current that flows in one direction only; it is not grounded. With a two-wire DC cable, electricity flows from the power source (bussbar or generator) through one wire to the fixture and returns through the other wire to the power source. The insulation on the wires is color-coded; the black wire is the "hot" leg and is the wire to be broken when being run through a switch. The white wire is called the "neutral."

Should a broken wire touch the fixture housing, direct current will "short" until it burns away and breaks contact; the electricity will then cease to flow. If the housing is touched by a person while the "shorting" is in progress, the flowing current will "kick" the individual away from the housing.

Since January 1990, the Occupational Safety and Health Administration (OSHA) has issued a directive stating that all two-wire cable used in the motion picture and television industries must carry a warning affixed to

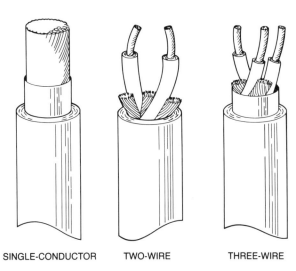

SINGLE-CONDUCTOR   TWO-WIRE   THREE-WIRE

Figure 15–2 Types of cable.

the plug and/or receptacle that two-wire cable should be used on DC only. If it is so-labeled, and a person uses it as a carrier of AC and is injured, then, under contributory negligence rulings, the individual has little if any resort to legal or medical action.

Equipment rental houses or studios that *don't* label two-wire cables with the warning leave themselves open to personal-injury litigation.

The reason for OSHA's directive is basic: In the event a two-wire cable carrying alternating current (AC) breaks and the fixture is not grounded, the current in the wire that touches the housing will seek the path of least resistance. Should an individual be unfortunate enough to touch the fixture, his or her body would become the past of easiest flow, and the current would "grab and hold" the person to the housing indefinitely. A steady flow of electricity through a body can set up a fibrillation of the heart until it stops beating. *Exercise caution!*

Three-wire cable Three-wire cable was designed as a safety factor for handling alternating current (AC), and its use in the motion picture and television industries is now the law. Alternating current carries itself in a sine waveform; half the time the current is positive, and the other half it is negative. The alternating takes place at the rate of 50 times per second in a 50-Hz line and 60 times per second in a 60-Hz line.

The insulation on the wires is color-coded. The black wire is the "hot" leg; this is the wire to be broken when the wires are run through a switch. The white wire is called the "neutral," and the green wire is the one connected to "ground."

In the event one of the current-carrying lines in a three-wire cable breaks and touches the fixture housing, the third (ground) wire will "siphon off" the current and carry it to earth, much in the manner a lightning rod will carry a bolt of electricity away from a building, expending it harmlessly into the earth. It must be carefully noted, however, that the bussbar and/or generator supplying the current must also be grounded; otherwise there will be no protection when a fixture with a broken cable is touched.

15.1c Wiring

External wiring refers to sleeved wire that is *outside* the fixture housing; it is connected from one end of the on/off switch to a connector at the feed, or plug, end. The term may also refer to the sleeved wire connected to the housing that passes through an in-line switch and then to a plug.

When a fixture is hung, more or less permanently, from an overhead pipe, the wiring should be sleeved with heat-resistant neoprene covered with a jacket of fiberglass. Jacketed fiberglass sleeves can withstand rising heat, which often bursts weaker material.

Internal wiring refers to the wiring that is *inside* the fixture housing, connected from one end of the on/off switch — or a splicing block — to the light source socket.

When an incandescent fixture is properly vented and/or the ambient temperature within the housing does not exceed 50°C (122°F), the internal wiring need not be fiberglass-jacketed. An HMI, which creates intense heat within the housing, *must* contain wiring that is fiberglass-jacketed. Asbestos-sleeved wiring, often found in older fixtures, contains carcenogenic fibers, and is illegal. Asbestos wires found in a fixture should be replaced. Wear a face mask and protective gloves, wrap the asbestos in a plastic bag, and place it in a sealed metal drum until ready for disposal. It should be disposed of in a toxic waste facility, not just thrown into the nearest trash bin for carting to a city dump. Note that asbestos is an excellent insulator, except when it is wet — then it becomes the opposite, a conductor. Handling wet asbestos-sleeved wire while current is flowing through it is equivalent to handling a bare wire.

15.1d Wire Size and Amperage

Wire size is designated by number: the lower the number, the larger the diameter of the wire. The largest size used in motion picture, video, and theater lighting is no. 0000, called "four-ought." The smallest size is no. 18 (Table 15–1). As a rule, the larger the diameter of a wire, the more amperage it can carry.

NOTE: Various materials are used for wiring. Most common are copper and aluminum. Copper is a better conductor than aluminum, but it is heavier in weight and less resistant to current. For example, a no. 000 ("three-ought") copper wire is approximately equivalent to a no. 0000 ("four-ought") aluminum wire, so that the smaller-diameter wire, in this instance, is almost equivalent to the larger in conductivity.

The length of time a wire is to be in use is of equal importance and is categorized in two ways: (1) less than 20 minutes, *intermittent,* and (2) 20 minutes or longer, *continuous.* When wire is for continuous use, the smallest size for safety on a stage is no. 14; for intermittent use, the smallest size for safety is no. 18.

It must always be borne in mind that current (amperage) generates heat, and the amount of amperage a wire can withstand safely is determined by (1) the type of material used as insulation (it must be able to maintain a temperature without breaking down), and (2) the temperature of the area surrounding the wire (the ambient temperature).

Wire is rated at a given amperage capacity (*ampacity*) when it is to be used in an open area such as a studio floor, because the surrounding air can readily absorb the heat dissipated through the insulation. However, that same wire placed in a raceway or conduit will be rated at a lesser ampacity because the heat dissipated through the insulation builds up quickly and has no place to go in a confined space. Excessive ambient temperature will

Table 15–1 Amperage Capacity (Ampacity) of Fixture Powerlines, Feeder and Extension Cables, and Fiberglass-Jacketed Wiring in Free Air. Based on an ambient temperature of 30°C (86°F) and intermittant use.

Wire Size (no.)	Diameter (mils)	Fixture Powerline with S, SO, SJO, ST, STO Type Insulation (Ampacity) Multiconductor		Feeder and Extension Cable with RH, RHW, RUH, THW Type Insulation (Ampacity) Continuous		Intermittant		Fiberglass-Jacketed Insulation (Ampacity)
		(3-Wire)	(2-Wire)	Single Conductor	Multiconductor (2-Wire)	Single Conductor	Multiconductor (2-Wire)	Single Conductor
18	40	7	10					
16	51	10	13					
14	64	15	18		15		20	45
12	81	20	25		20		30	55
10	102	25	30		30		40	75
8	128	35	40		45		60	100
6	162	45	55		65		85	135
4	204	60	70		85		115	180
2	258	80	95		115		155	240
0	325			230		280		325
00	365			265		330		370
000	410			310		385		430
0000	460			360		450		510

NOTE: All wire is first referred to by its wire size number except for 0 gauge. 0 gauge is called "ought", i.e., 0 = "one-ought"; 00 = "two-ought"; 000 = "three ought"; 0000 = "four-ought". It is then referred to by the number of wires in the sleeve; e.g., a cable with two no. 8 gauge wires is 8/2 (pronounced "eight-two"), and a cable with three no. 16 wires in a sleeve is 16/3 ("sixteen-three"), etc. Lastly, the type insulation is mentioned: S, RH, etc.

contribute to the deterioration of the wiring and insulation, causing it to become brittle, soften, burn, and short out. That is why caution should be taken in a studio. One must drape overhead wiring on hangers. Moreover, as far as possible, the wiring should be kept apart by spacers so that air can circulate around the wires. In video-control areas, the equipment is kept cool by air-conditioning and strict temperature control.

15.1e Fixture Cables

Manufacturers of fixtures in the United States follow strict standards wherein fixture wiring and its insulation must be able to resist a reasonable amount of abrasion, have flexibility (for example, be capable of being coiled for storage), and must be able to withstand a given degree of heat. Table 15–1 shows the permissible ampacity of various types of insulated wire commonly used in film, video, and theater.

Most fixture cables are stamped with code letters along the length of the cable. The manufacturer can supply the code letter if the cable is not stamped. Knowing the letters can provide information regarding the type of material used as insulation in and on the cable. For example,

S	= sleeved rubber	T	= thermoplastic
J	= junior service	O	= neoprene
P	= plastic	V	= varnished cambric

Thus, an S alone would indicate the wires are sleeved in rubber; an SJ would indicate a sleeved-rubber junior service (J indicating wiring no larger than no. 14); an STO would be a sleeved thermoplastic neoprene; and so forth. Combinations of material are possible, such as SO, ST, SJ, SJO.

15.1f Connectors

Standardization of connectors will continue to go on in the industry over the next several years. Until the transition is completed, some older connectors will still be in use.

A fixture connector varies in shape and size (Figs. 15–3 and 15–4); the male end of a connector is the *plug;* the female end is the *receptacle.* On very modern film and video stages, a polarized plug (sometimes called a *three-pin* or *union connector)* is used, and it has one wider blade on the plug and inserts into a matching receptacle. This prevents the insertion of the connector backwards and avoids the possibility of reversed polarity and electrical shock.

In less modern studios, large fixtures will still be found that are fitted with *stage plugs* and medium units fitted with *paddles* (half-stage plugs). A paddle is half the thickness of a stage plug; otherwise they are identical. Stage plugs and paddles fit into outlet boxes that contain one or more pockets. Each pocket in the box is the width of one stage plug and will accommodate either one stage plug or two paddles side by side. Outlet boxes are referred to by the number of pockets in each box: a one-hole box, two-hole box, three-hole box, and so forth.

In the past, stage plugs, paddles, and the outlet boxes that accommodate them were mainly used when all electricity was direct current. An in-line fuse, either in the plug or outlet box, was sufficient to protect an overloaded circuit. Today, with the use of AC current, the boxes must be grounded.

Pin connector A *pin connector* is a wooden or plastic block fitted with either two (for DC) or three (for AC) copper circular studs on the plug end and matching holes on the receptacle end. Attaching a small cord to each

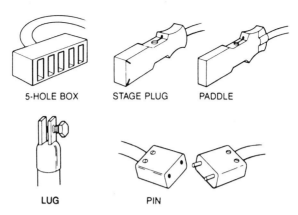

5-HOLE BOX   STAGE PLUG   PADDLE

LUG   PIN

Figure 15–3 Types of DC connectors.

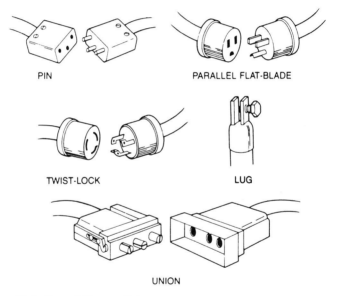

PIN   PARALLEL FLAT-BLADE

TWIST-LOCK   LUG

UNION

Figure 15–4 Types of AC connectors.

end serves to hold the plug and receptacle together after they have been joined, alleviating the tendency for these two parts to loosen and pull apart. Some pin connectors are notched so they can be hooked together but have a button to release the joining; this type does not need the cord to hold them together.

Twistlock connector A *twistlock,* also called a *Hubbel,* is self-locking when joined and given a turn. A three-wire connector, it has either a slight projection on its ground-wire blade or its ground-wire blade is larger than the other two blades. The blades fit into matching keyways in the receptacle.

Flat-blade connector A three-wire flat-blade plug, often called a *tri-Edison,* comes in two styles: parallel and Y. The parallel type is fitted with two blades side-by-side and the ground is a U-shaped key. The Y type is fitted with the two blades at 45° angles, and the ground is a straight center blade that is the key. With either style, the blades on the plug fit matching keyways in the receptacle.

15.2 CURRENT POWERLINE

15.2a Feeder Cable

Feeder cable is the term applied to the heaviest wire that brings the electricity, or "juice," from the main power to the area to be lit. Feeder cable falls into two categories: main and secondary.

Main feeder cable Main feeder cable is generally single-conductor and is reserved for carrying power loads from the generator or main bussbar to a distribution box. Three lines of single conductor are run — a positive, a negative, and a neutral. The three single-conductor set-up carries the "juice" on the negative leg to the lighting area and returns it on the positive leg to complete the circuit; then it reverses itself. The neutral conductor acts as a safety valve — it carries the extra current when the load is unevenly balanced or one leg shorts out.

A main feeder cable is fitted with *lug connectors* at each end. A lug is clamped to one of the three main power bussbars, and the lug at the other end is clamped to a *distribution box.*

A distribution box (often called a "spider") contains three bussbars of copper to accommodate the positive, negative, or neutral cables. AC bussbars are encased in a see-through solid plastic frame. (Older DC styles are built of three copper bussbars encased in a wood frame that is open at two sides and covered with rubber sheets).

Secondary feeder cable A secondary feeder cable is a two-wire or three-wire cable that is clamped to the distribution box bussbars and terminates with a number of fused receptacles: stage plug pockets, Edison, or twist lock.

15.2b Extensions

Extension cables, with a plug at one end and a receptacle at the other, are run from the distribution boxes to provide power directly to a fixture or to still smaller distribution boxes fitted with even more receptacles.

15.2c Cable Codes

Feeder and extension cables are also coded. The most commonly used are

- RH   = heat-resistant rubber
- RHW = heat- and moisture- (W = wet) resistant rubber
- RUH = heat-resistant latex rubber (U = latex)
- THW = thermoplastic heat- and moisture- (W = wet) resistant

Reference to Table 15–1 shows that, because of the composition of their insulation, the feeder and extension cables are equal to or have a greater amperage capacity (ampacity) than a fixture powerline. When used intermittently for less than 20 minutes, the ampacity is even greater.

15.1d Adaptors and Splicers

An *adaptor* is a short length of cable that has one style of plug and a different style of receptacle (such as an Edison plug at one end and a twistlock receptacle at the other, or a stage plug at one end and an Edison at the other). The possible combinations can be seen by referring to Figures 15–3 and 15–4. With the proper adaptors, a variety of connections can be made, thus enabling the use of cables with differing plugs and receptacles.

A *splicer* is a single piece of cable that has one plug with two receptacles (called a "Y-splice") or three receptacles (called a "W-splice"). A splicer allows two or three small fixtures to be fed from one extension cable. Care should be taken not to overload a splicer.

15.3 LOAD CALCULATIONS

When lighting a set, it is necessary first to determine the amount of current the fixtures will draw when they are illuminated. Only then can the size of feeder cables be calculated.

Most fixtures intended for use in the United States operate at 110 to 130 volts. Although the voltage may be referred to as "one-ten" (110 volts), for safety purposes in calculating loads, the voltage is figured at "one-twenty" (120 volts).

In countries outside the United States, where fixtures are manufactured to operate with power sources of 210 to 240 volts, the voltage may be referred to as "two-twenty" (220 volts), but once more, in load calculations the voltage is figured at 230 volts.

The following formula is used to determine incandescent load calculation:

$$\frac{\text{Wattage total of all fixtures}}{\text{Voltage supply}} = \text{Amperage}$$

The result will be the amount of amperage the feeder cables can safely carry. For example, if the lighting units on a set were

Two Seniors (two 5K's)	=	10,000 watts *or* 83.2 amps
Three Juniors (three 2K's)	=	6000 watts *or* 50.1 amps
Two 1000-watt Babys (two 1K's)	=	2000 watts *or* 16.6 amps
Five Lite Babys (five 750's)	=	3750 watts *or* 31.5 amps
One-Gallon Softlite (four 1000's)	=	4000 watts *or* 33.2 amps
		25,750 watts *or* 214.6 (approx. 215) amps

Table 15–1 demonstrates that in order to carry the actual continuous-load supply from the power source to the feeder block *safely,* the minimum cable size should be a no. 0 ("one-ought") cable capable of carrying 230 amps. This leaves a safety allowance factor of only 15 actual amperes, so that only *one* additional 1.5K fixture could be added (a 2K would overload the circuit):

$$\begin{array}{r} 230 \text{ amperes capacity of no. 0 cable} \\ -215 \text{ amperes actual load} \\ \hline 15 \text{ amperes of safety} \end{array}$$

The lower the amount of amperage safety, the greater the limitation in the selection of lighting sources. Therefore, an alternative method of calculation is used. It is called the "paper amp" system.

By consulting Table 15–2 and using the "paper" capacity values, the formula would be calculated as:

Two 5K's	=	100.0 amps
Three 2K's	=	60.0 amps
Two 1K's	=	20.0 amps
Five 750's	=	37.5 amps
One Gallon	=	40.0 amps
		257.5 amps or 258 amps

Table 15–2 Ratings of Most Common Fixtures

Fixture	Light Source Capacity (watts)	Wire Size	Light-Source Capacity (amperes) 120 Volts Actual	120 Volts Paper	230 Volts Actual	230 Volts Paper
Titan	Carbon Arc	00	350	350	—	—
Brute	Carbon Arc	00	225	225	—	—
150 Arc	Carbon Arc	0	150	150	—	—
Tener (10K)	10,000	4	83.3	100	43.5	50
Senior (5K)	5,000	8	41.6	50	21.7	25
Junior (2K)	2,000	12	16.7	20	8.7	10
1500 (1.5K)	1,500	12	12.5	15	6.5	7.5
1000 (1K)	1,000	16	8.3	10	4.3	5
800	800	16	—	—	3.5	4
Lite Baby	750	16	6.3	7.5	3.3	4
650	650	18	5.4	6	2.8	3
500	500	18	4.2	5	2.2	3
Midget	250	18	2.1	2.5	1.1	2
Inky	200	18	1.7	2	.9	1
Singlesoft	1,000	16	8.3	10	4.3	5
Singlesoft	750	16	6.3	7.5	3.3	4
Half-gallon	Two 1,000's	12	16.7	20	8.7	10
Gallon	Four 1,000's	8	33.2	40	17.4	20
Two-gallon	Eight 1,000's	8	66.4	80	34.8	40
Broad/Scoop	2,000	12	16.7	20	8.7	10
Broad/Scoop	1,000	16	8.3	10	4.3	5
One-lite	650	18	5.4	6	2.8	3
Two-lite	1,300	16	10.8	12	5.7	6
Four-lite	2,600	12	21.7	25	11.3	12.5
Five-lite	3,250	8	27.1	30	14.2	15
Six-lite	3,900	8	32.5	40	17.0	20
Nine-lite	5,850	8	48.8	50	25.4	30
Twelve-lite	7,800	8	65.0	70	33.9	35

Again, consulting Table 15-1, it will be seen that a single no. 00 (two-ought) cable, which is capable of carrying 265 amps, is necessary to carry a load of 258 amps safely. Subtracting the actual amperage from the no. 00 amperage:

$$\begin{array}{r} 265 \text{ amps capacity of no. 00} \\ -\underline{215} \text{ amps actual load} \\ 50 \text{ amps of safety} \end{array}$$

A safety factor of 50 actual amperes would allow the limited use of additional fixtures without overloading the lines.

In countries where lamps are constructed with filaments capable of operating on power sources of 230 volts, the amperage values are different (see Table 15-2). The method of load calculation, however, is the same.

The formula for HMI fixtures requires a slight alteration in order to account for the power factor (P.F.) of the ballast. P.F. is based on the resistance of the internal components in a ballast, which increases the unit's amperage. Power factor will vary depending on the size and materials used by the manufacturer. Therefore, it is essential to know the specific P.F. of a ballast being used on a job. Surprisingly, many electrical crews do not take P.F. into account, which could result in some serious power problems.

Some manufacturers print power-factor data on the identification labels affixed to the ballast. Others provide this information only in technical printouts pertaining to the specific ballast. Note that with the great number of ballasts in use, and the constant, almost daily, refinements in their performance, it is impossible to list the P.F.'s of all manufactured ballasts here. It is best to obtain the latest data regarding a specific ballast's power factor either from the manufacturer or the rental house when utilizing an HMI. The following formula is for computing HMI load calculations:

$$\frac{\text{Wattage of a single HMI fixture}}{\text{Power Factor} \times \text{Voltage supply}} = \text{Amperage}$$

Consider a 12K (12,000 watts) HMI that has a ballast with a power factor of 0.8 that is utilizing an input of 240 volts:

$$\frac{12,000 \text{ watts}}{0.8 \text{ power factor} \times 240 \text{ volts}} = \frac{12,000}{192} = 62.5 \text{ amps}$$

Then, like the incandescent example above, the individual lamps are added together in order to determine the total amperage. Once amperage is calculated, Table 15-1 can be consulted to learn the minimum cable size of the feeder cables that will safely carry the entire load.

Regardless of the voltage (120 or 230 volts) or lamp source (incandescent or arc) load calculations are *always* figured on a continuous-use basis. To calculate a formula on an intermittent-use basis is to risk premature burnout of lamps, overloading of the wiring and *the strong possibility of fire on the set.*

United States laws pertaining to handling electrical equipment are found in the National Electric Code.* While the Code covers almost every aspect of the electrical industry, of most importance to film and television personnel are the following Articles:

---

*Published by the National Fire Protection Association, Batterymarch Park, Quincy, MA 02169.

Article 530: Applies to electrical Standards for Motion Picture and Television sound stages, and similar places where the facilities do not include an audience.

Article 520: Applies to electrical standards for legitimate theaters, motion picture theaters, live concerts, game shows and/or sitcoms, restaurants with live entertainment (whether a full band or one piano player), or any other presentation with an audience present, in a building used exclusively for those purposes.

Article 518: Applies to places of assembly where 100 or more persons meet: sports arenas, stadiums, places of worship, museums, bowling alleys, meeting rooms (such as an awards banquet in a hotel), etc., etc.

Article 110: Applies to requirements for electrical installations in private homes and commercial buildings, which must satisfy all rules, methods, and safety practices regarding tie-in and grounding.

Depending on the type of production, and where it is to take place, familiarity with the NEC articles is of utmost importance before using electrical equipment in any location. For example, certain practices are allowed on a soundstage where the regulations of Article 530 apply, but if the same electrical practices were carried out at a live concert, where regulations of Article 520 apply, they would be in violation of the law and the production could be shut down—legally. If it happens five minutes before showtime (and it *has* happened), the ramifications of noncompliance could go on long after the event has become a memory to everyone but the litigants. It is important for all camera and electrical people working in the film or television industries to know the rules and if asked to violate them, present those who asked with a handwritten memo (while keeping a copy) of the illegality of their request.

A *final word of warning:* Electricity can be a killer if the person working with it does not recognize its potential danger. "Splitting" 220-volt loads to 110 volts, balancing the load, running cable, etc., are the responsibility of the Gaffer (Chief Set Electrician) and Electricians. On location/remote shoots it is important to remember that in most municipalities, "tying in" to bussbars or power boxes requires a certified electrician to do the "hook-up," with a member of the fire department standing by to see that it is done properly. An unlicensed electrician (and most Gaffers, regardless of their years of experience, are not licensed), as well as the Director of Photography/Lighting Director and Production Manager, can be held criminally responsible for injury, death, fire, or damage to the property caused by illegal "tying in." To save a Producer a few dollars or to risk injury or fire to satisfy one's ego is plainly foolish. Insurance companies have been known to reject claims for a catastrophe when criminal negligence was cited, and many city, county, and state governments have been known to prosecute those who were unauthorized to do the "tie-in."

chapter 16

Generators

Generators used with equipment for film and video shooting vary in size from huge truck-mounted units capable of producing hundreds of amperes to small handtruck-size types that produce only 3000 to 4000 watts. Tiny, hand-carried units of 1000 watts or less, such as the Kubota (55 pounds) and the smaller Honda, are in daily use on some exterior film sets. However, the size of a generator is always calculated in terms of its maximum power output in amperes (e.g., 750 amps, 1500 amps, etc.), not its physical size or weight.

Since a *generator* is a machine that converts mechanical or solar energy into electric energy, and since its purpose is to supply power to location/ remote areas where no means of obtaining electricity exists, the unit must be able to provide enough power to service *all* the fixtures that will light a scene and have power in reserve to handle an additional 15 to 20 percent of the total amperage required (see Powerline, Load Calculation, Ch. 15).

The mechanical component of a generator (called the *"prime mover"*) can be either a gasoline-driven engine, a diesel engine, or a propane-gas engine. Mechanical prime movers work on the principle of combustion. A solar generator's prime mover is comprised of a grid of silicon disk collectors (Fig. 16–1); trace materials in each disk produce an electrical charge that is directed to and accumulated in a number of batteries. The electromotive force (voltage) is either tapped as direct current (DC) or routed through an inverter that converts the electricity to alternating current. Unlike a mechanical prime mover, there is no atmospheric pollution from fuel vapors or engine exhaust. The unit *will* work on overcast days, although its batteries do not charge as rapidly as on sunny days.

Regardless of the type of prime mover, and depending on the type of armature, windings, and magnetic field of its electrical component, a unit can either generate alternating current (AC) or direct current (DC); sometimes both.

The electrical component of a generator works on the principle of *induction*. The production of electricity is achieved by a magnet and a rotating coil of wire that has been inserted between the magnet's two poles. When the coil of wire turns, it interrupts the magnetic field, thereby cutting the lines of force, which causes a current to be generated in the coil.

The rotating coil cuts the lines of force, producing current in one direction, then it reverses itself; thus, the generator produces alternating current (AC). Such current is usually tapped by slip rings. When the rotating coil

Figure 16–1 A solar generator with collector panels aimed at the sun. Courtesy of the Media Project.

cuts the lines of force in alternating directions but the current is directed to flow in one direction only (by a device called a *commutator*), the generator produces direct current (DC). Direct current is usually tapped by sticks of carbon called *brushes*. The tapped current is then routed to a bussbar panel (on large generators) or receptacle panel (on small units). Feeder cables fitted with lugs or plugs are connected to the panel and the cables run to the lighting area.

On most generators, a rheostat allows the operator to vary the voltage to the feeder cables. Some units are capable of providing only a fixed voltage.

Filament lamps will operate on AC or DC; HMI-type lamps operate on AC only and require a generator fitted with a *frequency regulator* that "locks on" to a desired frequency with a variation of only ± 1/4 Hz. Carbon arcs operate on DC only.

A generator should have an Operator in constant attendance to monitor the voltage and/or frequency. Generators have been known to "run away." The prime mover accelerates out of control, which in turn increases the voltage and "blows out" the filaments. They have also been known to "lug;" i.e., slowly decelerate, decrease the voltage, lower the color temperature, and/or "unlock" the frequency, causing a "flicker" effect (see The HMI Lamp, "Flicker Effect," Ch. 8). Generators are very costly and should *never* be left unattended. This is an excellent rule regarding *all* equipment, whether rented, or belonging to a studio, or personally owned. It will pay off!

Mechanical prime movers are noisy. Therefore, when dialogue or natural sound effects are to be recorded, it is essential that the generator's mechanical plant be enclosed inside a housing fitted with baffle-plates and insulation. The baffles are situated within the housing to "break up" the sound waves, and the insulation absorbs the scattered acoustical "fragments." Air vents, usually fitted with intake and outlet fans, draw in cool air and expel the heat from the prime mover. Depending on whether it is AC or DC, the pitch of the noise of the prime mover units (AC units have a tendency to "sing," DC units are inclined to "grumble"), and the "horses" (horsepower) of the engine, the space needed around the prime mover to keep it at optimum thermal efficiency will vary. It is the housing, with its requirement of air space, baffles, fans, and insulation, that give a generator its outward-appearing bulk. The unit's engine exhaust mufflers are usually oversize or in multiples.

The noise level of a generator determines its proximity to the filming/telecasting site, and that distance in turn determines the size and length of the feeder cables that carry the "juice" to the lighting area. Therefore, the type of fixtures to be used, the noise level of the generator, and the amount of cable necessary to light an area is something to be considered *before* the unit is taken on a distant location/remote.

Once the generator arrives on a location site the unit must be placed *downwind* from the action area, preferably behind a building or an equipment truck, to minimize the unit's noise. If it is a large generator and is to be run for any length of time, the unit must then be leveled so that the armature bearings will wear evenly. While some generator Operators may claim that precaution as unnecessary, the person who levels a generator will be saving the eventual rebuilding of the bearings.

chapter 17

Using the Fixture

The questions most frequently asked of a Director of Photography or Lighting Director by visitors to a film or video set are: How do you know

1. Which fixture to use?
2. Where to place it?
3. When to add a light?
4. When to take a light out?
5. How to keep track of all the units?

While there are no hard and fast rules pertaining to placement of lighting units, there *are* guidelines. Fixtures serve many purposes depending on the desired mood for the scene and, while lighting diagrams are often used to suggest the placement of lighting units, it is the conviction of the authors that referring to such diagrams to "learn how to light" is of no value unless one is duplicating that specific setup for a reshoot.

No two persons, however talented, are likely to choose identical units or place them in identical positions for a given scene. Creativity is unique to each person, and the selection is based on the individual's concept of the lighting that will best elicit an emotional response from viewers: The light and shadow within the scene must accomplish the desired result. A guide to placement of fixtures on a set follows.

17.1 SETS

There are differences in the way fixtures are placed to light a set constructed for film and one constructed for video.

17.1a Film Set

A set constructed for film has catwalks along its perimeter. The catwalks generally hang from the stage rafters. The flooring of the walks is aligned with the tops of the set walls. Fixtures are then mounted on the edges of the catwalks so that the units can be angled down into the set. Each fixture is intended to serve a specific purpose, and occasionally there is a mounted spare unit for backup. Very wide and/or deep sets are spanned by additional hanging catwalks that support lighting units at various intervals.

Each lighting unit it turned on or off, focused, and locked into position by a Lamp Operator (electrician) on the catwalks, and on occasion, fixture circuits are controlled by a switchbox from the floor.

Where there are no catwalks, fixtures are hung on ropes and lowered from high-roof rafters so as to "cover" areas unreachable by fixtures on the catwalks. A number of other fixtures on rolling stands are worked from the floor.

17.1b Video Set

In video, most sets are constructed without surrounding catwalks—they are braced by jacks. Access to the few fixtures mounted on top of set walls is by ladder.

Most of the lighting units are hung above the entire set area from an overhead grid of iron pipes, from which they can be aimed in all directions. The floor is left clear for movement of cameras and cables. It is common practice to hang extra fixtures on the grid as backup should units cease to function, in which event another fixture that has already been aimed to "cover" the area can be put into use without stopping the show for a major light change. Grid fixtures are generally focused and locked into position prior to telecasting by an electrician on the floor. He or she uses a long pole to make adjustments, unless a major rigging of the set is called for. Then, on major stages the grid is lowered to the floor so that the fixtures can be clamped to or removed from the pipes. When rigging is completed, the grid is "flown" (raised to operating height). Each lighting unit is connected to a central control board, from which it can immediately be "punched up" or "killed" (turned on or turned off).

Fixtures to be used for several shows may be mounted on the same grid, since many sets are assembled and taken down daily, depending on the number of productions scheduled for telecast. The only exception is a continuing daily show, such as a "soap," which has a given number of permanent sets. Once hung, lighting units are not taken down until the show is canceled, goes on a long hiatus—or the set is struck.

Whether the medium is film or video, the number of fixtures to be used on a set will depend on the size of the set, the physical size of the lighting units, and their individual intensities, as well as on the action that is to take place.

17.2 FUNCTION OF FIXTURES

Every lighting unit on a set fulfills a definite purpose. The terms applied to these functions are as follows:

- Key light
- Fill light
- Eye light
- Back light
- Side light
- Background light
- Miscellaneous light

17.2a Key Light

The major source of illumination on a set can appear to be the "sun," an electrical "practical" (e.g., a table lamp), or just a "tiny candle." Therefore, the first thing to establish when illuminating a set is *what* the predominating source light is presumed to be and *where* it will come from: The *key light*. Once this is determined, the source must be consistent—the light must come from the same direction to maintain a sense of "reality." For example, when a scene is to take place in the "daytime" on a set with a large window, the source is *light spilling into the room from outside,* and that will be the *key.*

Ideally, a single large carbon arc placed at the window would be used as the source light to "key" the entire set, so that the light creates one shadow. In practice, when a carbon arc is not available, more than one large incandescent fixture may "cover" the set equally well.

Additional lighting is necessary to light the interior or shadow side of the actors, and that additional light must be subservient to the "key," so that the viewer will believe that *all* the light is coming from the window, just as in real life.

When a set is illuminated for night, the major source of light must appear to be emanating from a "practical" inside the room; the actual illumination comes from units outside of camera range or on catwalks above the practical. When the practical is a bare bulb or an open flame, it must be the brightest spot in the room; an additional fixture is placed out of camera range and aimed at the practical to create a "hot spot" around it.

A set illuminated for night also can have more than one source of light. When there are a number of practicals in a scene, the key lights will come from several directions. However, the presumed source of the light *must* be established to achieve believable lighting.

In a close-up, the key light must always match the key light established in the wider shots. A certain amount of cheating is permissible. A fixture on the floor can be brought around to light the face better. Too much cheating, however, will call attention to the change and totally destroy the illusion. It is very disturbing to a viewer to see a wide or medium shot lit with a definite source followed by a cut to a close-up where no definite source is used, and then cut back to the wider shot with *its* definite source.

When there is no window or practical, or other source from which the illumination can be presumed to be coming, a plausible source must be invented — that is, arbitrarily decided on. Light is necessary in order to see a scene and get an exposure. Therefore, a key is "invented" by making a determination as to *what* the source is and/or *where* it is coming from. The side of the camera at which the invented key is placed depends on the position of the actor being favored in the scene, so that the majority of his or her actions and delivery of dialogue will be toward camera and in the most flattering angle.

The invented source is commonly used in the lighting of game and panel shows, as well as in TV film production, where fast and furious shooting schedules may demand a lesser degree of artistry and a greater degree of adherence to time schedules.

In most instances, when the invented key-light fixture is placed to the left or right of the camera, it is situated so that the light falls at a three-quarter front angle on the subject. Three-quarter front can be anywhere from 15 to 35 degrees from the axis of the camera. Less than 15 degrees will provide a very "flat" light; if more than 35 degrees, one runs the risk of projecting a nose shadow across the cheek of the actor. When the key light is placed close to or over the camera, the scene will also look flat; the light will obliterate texture and detail and at the same time eliminate form and shape. This is why flat light is often used on older actors and actresses to "smooth out wrinkles." Another method is to drop a scrim in the key light and add an A or B glass diffusion to the camera lens. The latter method retains a direction to the light while still eliminating the wrinkles. Flat light is to be avoided if possible. However, when diffusion glass and/or nets are not available and flat lighting is the *only* solution, the intensity of a back light will help take away the onus of a flat-lit closeup and provide the shot with planes of contrast.

Again, the established key light must be as large a source as possible and be elevated so that the shadow produced is cast downward. The unit cannot be so high that long shadows will form under the actor's nose or in the eye sockets. Too low an angle will cast the actor's shadow on the wall. The best height is when the nose shadow does not fall on the actor's upper lip but shades the nostrils. When there are two actors in the same shot, the scene may have to be "double-keyed" to cover both.

The quality of a key light can be *hard* or *soft*. Hard light has a "snap" and a brilliance; soft light is smooth and diffuse. The selection of quality in a key depends on the degree of "reality" required in the scene. When duplicating rays of sunlight streaming through a window, the key desired should be specular and of high intensity. When the window is covered with a lacy curtain, which in reality would diffuse the light, a soft light key of high intensity is called for.

High-intensity soft light has a tendency to bend around subjects, which conveys a roundness and requires very little fill light to offset the contrast between light and shadow. It is used extensively in film and video commercials.

Low-intensity soft light is flat and can be used to create the effect of an overcast day. It is also utilized to create gloomy daylight interiors in horror films. However, it will convey a lackluster quality if employed without highlights and modeling.

Exceptions   The exceptions to the establishment of key light as a definite source occur in the realm of fantasy, children's fairy tales, and adult horror. In fantasy, lighting is created to emphasize cuteness or grisliness. Consistency in its application is not necessarily mandatory; anything that builds unreality or fantasy will work. The key light may be altered from one shot to the next — left, right, high, low. For example, when lighting elves skipping toward Santa's workshop or a transition from handsome actor to ugly monster, there need be no concern as to where the source emanates from, provided each light change has a definite visual impact, such as gaiety or fear. The possibilities for creativity in fantasy are boundless, and most lighting persons take great delight in latching onto a project of this nature.

17.2b Fill Light

Fill light is a secondary source used to dilute shadow caused by the key light. It is often referred to as "hard fill" or "soft fill." The terms do not signify larger or smaller volumes or intensities of light, but rather its *quality*.

A *hard fill* is used to dilute shadow caused by sunlight, carbon arc, HMI, etc. on exteriors. It imparts a sharp edge to the shadow. A *soft fill* is one that has been scrimmed, diffused, bounced, or is generally very low in intensity. Its dilution of shadow is subtle and varies in degree. A soft fill imparts a fuzzy, or almost no, edge to its shadow.

Ideally fill light should *not* cast a shadow. However, actual use interferes with this premise, as can readily be seen when carbon arcs or HMIs are needed to fill areas of darkness in a sunlit scene. It is the *volume* of fill light (hard or soft) used in a scene that determines whether the scene is high-key or low-key.

17.2c High-Key/Low-Key Fill Light

In film and video, the terms *high-key* and *low-key* do not refer to the *intensity* of the key light, but rather to the *ratio* of fill to key light. A great deal of fill light that dilutes and permits the viewing of detail in a shadow is termed *high-key;* very little fill light that obscures or shows no detail in a shadow is termed *low-key.* The amount of fill light used to dilute shadow is an important aspect to consider. If a scene is high-key, then how high is high; if low-key, then how low is low?

High-key   Overall, a high-key scene shows illumination from a definite source, has a "snap" of brilliance, and imparts a feeling of well-being and safety. High-key lighting is used extensively in comedies, musicals, industrials, and many commercials, especially where product shots are concerned.

Often, in video, sit-coms are flat lit with a great deal of soft light or diffusion on the fixtures. Such lighting could be considered high-key. However, there is a difference between high-key soft light lighting with a definite source and flat lighting. In a high-key scene, shadows are "filled in;" i.e., although the shadow is discernible, there is light enough that great detail is still visible.

Fill light that *equals* the intensity of the key light should be avoided, as it will throw a second shadow with a density the same as the key shadow. Equal fill can be recognized when everything in the scene has a double-shadow, and especially in a close-up where two nose shadows appear, slanting across the upper lip.

Fill light that is *greater* in intensity than the key destroys the continuity of the established source by becoming the new key light. Direct fill light is always of less intensity than the key. Bounced fill light is created by pointing a fixture of equal or greater intensity than the key light at a white card or silver reflecting umbrella. The card (or piece of white foam) or umbrella, in turn, is aimed at the shadow side of the subject.

The degree of dilution of shadow — how light or how dark the shadow should be — depends on the visual impact desired and the limitations of the emulsion or the video camera sensitivity.

A rough rule of thumb for high-key lighting is a key-to-fill ratio varying from 1¹/₂:1 to 4:1, i.e., if the key light alone reads 300 footcandles, then the fill light alone on the shadow side of the face would read anywhere from 200 footcandles (which is a 1¹/₂:1 key-to-fill ratio) to 75 footcandles (which is a 4:1 key-to-fill ratio).

The use of a meter to check lighting ratios is recommended. Only a very experienced person is able to judge the ratio of key-to-fill by "eyeball." In video, key-to-fill ratios can always be checked immediately by consulting a studio monitor.

Low-key   *Low-key* is a term that either refers to (1) a scene of high contrast predominated by shadows rather than highlights, or (2) a scene having *dark tones* only and with little contrast. The degree to which shadows are filled in depends on the desired effect.

1. A low-key scene shows illumination from a definite source, but with little or no fill light in the shadows, and it imparts a feeling of secretiveness. High-contrast low-key lighting is used to create the illusion of night, mystery, etc. Night scenes generally have little or no detail in the shadows, conveying a possibility of someone or something lurking in the dark.
2. The shadows range in density from middle tone with moderate detail to dark tone with little detail, as well as an occasional absolute-black shadow with no detail. The soft contrast between the dark tones imparts either a somber feeling or romance; the subdued lighting is used to convey isolation from the outside world as well as the private world of lovers.

A scene lit with a variety of densities ranging from dim to barely discernible to absolute blackenss creates more emotional effect than a scene with shadows of only one density — degrees of detail provide plane of depth.

When working with color emulsion, a rough rule of thumb for determining the density of shadows in a low-key situation is a ratio varying from 6:1 on the shadow side; that is, if the key light alone reads 300 footcandles, then a 6:1 fill light alone on the shadow side would read approximately 50 footcandles (300 ÷ 50 = 6) or, with 6:0 ratio, none at all. However, when a film is intended for later transmission on video or the video is a live/tape telecast, the ratio of key to fill should not be greater than 5:1. This latter ratio will avoid an absolute black that will "ghost" when transmitted.

17.2d Eye Light

An *eye light* is a fixture containing a low-intensity lamp that is clamped at the top of a camera and is used to impart "sparkle" to an actor's eyes by highlighting the pupil (Fig. 17–1). It is not used for illumination per se. The larger the lighting unit, the larger the highlight in the eyes will be; this is why "broad-type" fixtures are generally used as eye lights.

In Hollywood studios, an eyelight is often referred to as an "Obie light." Some people erroneously believe the term *Obie* stands for "On Board." Not so. The term first came into use in the 1930s when a fixture was mounted on top of the camera to enhance actress Merle Oberon's beautiful, expres-

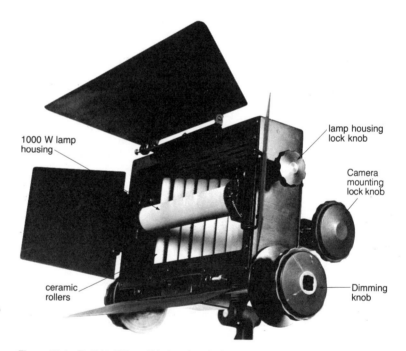

Figure 17–1 Eyelight. This eyelight is unique in that it is fitted with a number of interlinked ceramic rods. Each rod is vertically striped from full white to a flat, nonreflective black. The rods are mechanically linked to a dimming knob. The knob enables an assistant to rotate the rods synchronously from white to black and vice versa. Thus, the light reflecting from the rollers can be adjusted to any desired brightness; i.e., the reflected intensity of the 1000-watt, 3200K lamp aimed at the rods can be lowered as the camera moves toward the subject or increased as the camera moves away. Since the rollers reflect the light of the unit's lamp and the lamp within the housing is never dimmed, the lamp's color temperature remains constant. Courtesy of Panavision Inc.

sive eyes. Originally, it was called an "Oberon light," then "Obie's light" and finally, when other Directors of Photography began to utilize it to achieve the same effect with other performers, an "Obie light."

Today, an "Obie light" is the name for a particular dual-purpose tri-lamp fixture (not shown). When used on exteriors, the unit is fitted with three dichroic 650-watt lamps. It is clamped to the top of the camera, is quite intense in output, and is utilized as a general exterior fill light. Each lamp works off an independent switch, so that the intensity can be controlled through the use of one, two, or three lights at a time. On interior sets, the dichroics are often replaced with 3200K lamps and heavily scrimmed. When not used on the camera, the Obie light can always be mounted on a stand and utilized as a broad fill light.

Tiny units such as the "dinky" are also used as an eye light, particularly to fill in deep-socketed eyes. Great care must be taken when using an eye light to make sure the illumination value does not change as the camera moves toward or away from the subject.

The British call an eye light (and any other fixture that clamps to the front of a camera) a "basher." The Germans favor *"owgen-heiter"* (cheerful eye). The Mexicans refer to it poetically as a *"luz del alma"* (light of the soul). In the U.S. and Canada it's an eye light.

17.2c Back Light

A *back light* is a fixture used to separate an actor or object from the background walls. It is usually placed high and opposite the camera; its actual placement on the perimeter of the set is not determined until the movement of the actor or position of the object is known. Illumination from the back light must be consistent. When the actor moves across a high-key single-room set, he or she must be "covered," that is, separated from the background at all times. A number of backlights must be utilized, with each aimed at a given area and all beams overlapped. When the light is not overlapped and the actor walks rapidly in and out of alternating back light and "holes" of darkness, he or she will appear to "flicker." When actors walk slowly in and out of alternating back light, they appear to "bloom" and "fade." However, when the actor goes from room to room or through a doorway, the light can vary and it will be believable.

Back light that illuminates an actor also falls on furniture or other objects within the scene, giving the objects highlights and planes of light that greatly add to the illusion of depth. The intensity of a back light varies and should be determined by the strength of what a "supposed source" would normally be.

"Supposed source" A *"supposed source"* is light a viewer can see and relate to in a scene, such as sunlight or a candle. On a set, when an actor stands with a sunlit window behind him or her, the supposed source is the sun. When the rays of the fixture that is *actually* being used to back light the actor are very weak, the intensity will be wrong. Conversely, in a night scene, when the actor is back lit by a fixture that is being used to represent the light emanating from a candle behind him or her and the rays from the back light are too intense, it will not be believable. Since viewers know what real sunlight and/or real candlelight look like, the lighting person must light for believability.

"Invented source" Where there is no supposed source a viewer can relate to, a back light is invented. Its intensity is a matter of preference, but is usually very low.

A back light gives hair and fabric very appealing "sparkle." In an "invented" situation, the intensity depends on the color of the hair, skin, and clothing. Obviously, a blonde actress wearing a white dress in a coal mine with its black walls will receive less back light than a brunette actor wearing navy blue standing next to her. His hair and suit will require intense light to separate him from the anthracite background.

In cases where planes of fabric of the same texture and/or color are to be separated, considerable intensity is required and will be acceptable from back light. The term *"same on same"* (white on white, wool on wool, etc.) is used, generally in commercials, when a product of a particular color is placed on a surface of the same hue or texture, or both, such as a glass of milk on a white tablecloth or rows of one-color suits on a clothes rack. Only hard back light can separate them.

Forward-thrown shadows A back light that overpowers the front illumination key light and fill light will throw shadows forward. This usually causes a dark area under the chin of an actor when the fixture is directly above and behind. A shadow will be thrown on one shoulder when one lighting unit is placed directly above and to one side; two back lights will cast shadows forward on both shoulders. On a product shot, a single back light will cast a straight or diagonal shadow line forward (depending on its position behind the product), while two equidistant back lights will cast an inverted V forward. Forward-thrown shadows cannot always be eliminated, but they can be lessened by reducing the intensity of the back light, either by "flooding out" the unit, scrimming it down, or using stronger front light.

Back-lit exteriors On exteriors, the naturalness of daylight and the scenery imparts depth and roundness to subjects. However, there are times when the color of an actor's hair or clothing will match and blend into the far background. This blending is not easily discernible outdoors because the human eye will automatically compensate for the differences between foreground and background depths. It could be easy to forget that the lens *compresses* the scene. In truth, back lighting on an exterior is a big "cheat" (there is only one sun). When the planes of depth are nil or foreground and background scenery colors match, back lighting is necessary to separate the actor from the background. This is a condition that many lighting persons can easily overlook, especially when working under pressure (and that can be most of the time). A color contrast viewing glass is helpful.

Arcs and/or reflector boards are used to create exterior back light. Great care must be exercised to prevent stray rays of light from striking the camera lens.

Barndoors Barndoors are necessary when back lights are in use. The top door is used to prevent the emanating light from striking the camera lens, which can cause a flare on the emulsion or target area. The bottom door is used to keep the fixture rays from flooding the floor with too much illumination, especially when the floor is of a light hue and shows up shadows from the back lights or when the fixture is at such an angle that it "skips" a reflection off the floor's surface into the camera lens.

Rim light and kicker light These two types of back lights can be used interchangeably, but for clarity of a set, they are distinguished. *Rim light* is intense back light that outlines an actor's entire body—hair, shoulders, arms, legs—with no, or very little, front light. Normally, the rim-light fixture is placed at the same level as the camera lens and in back of the actor;

the actor's body keeps the rays from flaring the lens. There is very little "roundness" of light rays on the actor.

Most rim light is relegated to night scenes and, when used judiciously, it creates mystery that will "telegraph" an unknown person, an approaching monster, etc. Rim light can help create an "arty" daylight scene with the sun outlining the actor. Occasionally, it is used to liven up an otherwise dull scene.

A *kicker light* is a lighting unit used to apply a slight rim to an actor's face and is aimed at the shadowed or fill-light side of the face from an angle behind and to the side of the actor. Whether placed high or low, it is still less than an absolute side light and does not eliminate the shadow; it emphasizes the shadow.

Barndoors on a kicker light are positioned vertically to keep the light rays off the actor's nose and cheek. A "hard" kicker light depicts masculinity; yet the same light rays, scrimmed down, depict femininity. In both cases, a kicker light will outline and complete the contours of the face. Care must be taken that a person's hair, framing the face, does not prevent the light from rimming facial shadow.

17.2f Side Light

Side light is the term applied to any light that comes from a direction (left or right) 90 degrees from the axis of the camera lens. Exterior scenery photographed in side light causes the shadows formed by depressions, humps, fissures, foliage, and outcrops to add to the visual dimensions of depth and height. When photographed front lit, scenery appears on the screen as a flat plane without depth.

On a shallow-stage set, side light is used to create planes of depth by accentuating one edge of vertical pieces, such as pillars, decorative doorway beads, wrought iron, etc. Side light will also emphasize texture and fabric. A heavily pleated curtain can be accentuated greatly by "skipping" the rays from a side light along the folds, so that the fabric alternates with highly lit edges, moderately lit sides, and deeply shadowed folds. An otherwise drab room can be brightened considerably and given an added dimension.

In night interior scenes, side light can come from right or left, high or low, to add depth and variation to a scene. A good way to "extend" the length of a hallway is to open all the doors and hide the fixtures in the openings (at different heights) so that the rays emanating from the doorways will side light the passage of an actor as he or she moves away from or toward the camera. As the actor passes each doorway, one side of the body is alternately in light and the other side is in darkness.

To add an illusion of greater *depth* to the hallway, the light falling on the person needs to be stronger close to the camera and weaker farther away. To accomplish this, the fixtures hidden in the doorways need to be more heavily scrimmed the farther away from the camera they have been positioned.

On night exteriors, such as deserted roads or forests, fixtures are placed at intervals so that "puddles" of side light and/or three-quarter back light permit the action to take place in lighted areas alternating with dark areas to retain the feeling of surrounding night. The viewer will "buy" this artificiality — will subconsciously suspend reality in order to see the action.

When another source of illumination enters the scene, such as an automobile headlight, a match, or a flashlight, etc., then that new light immediately becomes the key, with just enough supplemental lighting added to prevent the action from being obscured.

In the city, overall night exterior scenes are most effective when three-quarter back lit, with an occasional building side lit, and a street lamp or lighted window showing. In night scenes, closely viewed action, such as a quick facial expression, or an action requiring special emphasis or important dialogue, etc., is about the only time a front light is used. Excessive front light can destroy the illusion of night; the illumination must be sparingly used, or "broken up" by controllers.

Cross light   When side light is directed from opposite sides at the same time (left *and* right of the lens axis), it is referred to as *cross light* and can be treated as key and fill: A strong side light from one direction is filled with a soft side light from the opposite direction, and no front light is necessary. At other times, the fill light can be as intense as the key light. The problem with cross lighting an actor who looks straight into the camera is that a ridge of shadow can appear down the middle of the actor's face. For a brief moment, viewers will accept this, but they will become annoyed if it is maintained for any length of time. Pillars, however, take on an added dimension of roundness if cross lit.

Cross light can be used to advantage to illuminate two actors who are *facing* each other. Some Directors of Photography and Lighting Directors refer to this setup as "cross-key light." The lighting unit at camera right illuminates the face of the first actor and back lights the second actor who is closest to the fixture. The lighting unit at camera left illuminates the face of the second actor and back lights the first actor, who is closest to that fixture. The amount of fill light used to dilute the shadow sides of their faces, which are toward camera, would depend on the nature of the scene.

Cross-key light is also employed when it is known that alternate over-the-shoulder shots are to be incorporated in a sequence. In a one-camera show, with its individual set-ups, light falling on a first actor's shoulder can be scrimmed or flagged to direct attention to the second actor's face, but in a multiple-camera show, where continuity cannot be interrupted, this may not be possible — an actor may not stand exactly on his or her marks. When a pre-set scrim or flag intended to reduce the light on the first actor's shoulder does not prevent a "bloom," then the shoulder gets all the viewer's attention to the detriment of the second actor's action and lines. This is an added reason why a lighting person must insist on checking the actor's wardrobe before lighting the scene, especially when working with multiple-camera lenses.

17.2g Background Light

Background light is used to illuminate the walls of a set, painted scenery representing exteriors outside windows or doors, or flats beyond an interior opening or door that mask the fact that it is a stage set. Walls are usually the first to be illuminated. Fixtures placed up high are aimed *across the set* to light the opposite wall. One should always illuminate exterior and/or interior walls so that light falling on them appears to be coming from a definite source (the key light).

On daylight interiors, the light illuminating the walls is barndoored near the top of the walls to force attention downward. On night interiors, the light is barndoored to about midwall to force attention to the foreground. Additionally, a slight lowering of the intensity of the illumination on the walls, either through scrimming or diffusion, will change the quality of an interior from "day" to "night."

Whether lighting for day or night, it is important to remember that once the intensity of the light falling on the walls is established, the same intensity should be maintained throughout the sequence. After an establishing shot, which usually includes all or most of a set, care should be taken when readjusting a foreground fixture, especially when moving in for a closer shot of the same action. The foreground fixture's rays can spill on, and be added to, the light already "covering" the background. When this happens, the color is altered. What appeared to be a subdued hue in the previous scene will suddenly, in the relit scene, become a bright reflectance, which can jar the viewer out of believability.

Evenly lit walls should be "broken up" either by using a cukaloris (see Light Modifiers, Ch. 13) or by slightly varying the intensity of the fixtures lighting the surfaces. Whenever possible, a tree branch or window frame, something with a pattern that will cast a surface shadow, should be strategically placed for better effect.

Stark walls of white or light tones can have the "chill" taken off by placing a filter (see Fixture Filters, Ch. 14) of straw, amber, or Y-1 on the units lighting the walls.

"See-through" sets   A *"see-through" set* is one with a door or window that reveals another room or an exterior. When working on location/remote, either filters (see Fixture Filters, Ch. 14) and neutral densities are used on windows and doors that reveal an exterior to convert the light, or fixtures fitted with "daylite" light sources are used to illuminate the interior so that the light is compatible with the light entering through the doors and/or windows. On a sound stage, an interior/exterior "see-through" can also be lit with either incandescent or daylight sources, but never a mixture of the two.

There are three basic approaches to lighting a sound stage interior/exterior. First, a wall through which the outside can be seen is lit anywhere from 1 to $1\frac{1}{2}$ stops lower in intensity than the other walls in the set. The exterior portion is lit at the same intensity as the foreground action. The resultant subtle difference helps the scenery being viewed through the opening appear as though it were more intense than it really is.

Second, the exterior background flat or scenic cyclorama outside a window or door is normally illuminated by skypans, and the intensity may be anywhere from the same as the foreground action to as much as 3 stops greater, which imparts a "hot" aspect to the exterior. Great care must be taken with shrubbery or trees placed between the opening and the flat (for an added dimension of depth); their shadows must not fall on the flat.

Third, when actors must walk from an interior to an exterior, or vice versa, the fixtures inside are diffused, whereas the outside fixtures are not. Inside fixtures can be of the high-intensity softlite type (see above) or nonsoftlite fixtures scrimmed down to impart softness to the scene. The units lighting the exterior portion of the scene should be as large as possible (arc, 10K, etc.) to impart a hard light to the outside. Exposure can range from the same (the quality of the light from soft to hard will add to the illusion of interior/exterior difference) to anywhere from 1 to $1\frac{1}{2}$ stops more outside than inside. In the latter case, if overexposure occurs, the laboratory or video controller can do a "go-to" light correction. For the next setup, one goes back to normal exposure.

Interior-interior "see-through"   When action is taking place simultaneously in foreground and background rooms, the room furthest from camera is lit with the same intensity as the foreground room, unless the script calls for a different lighting effect.

An interior background flat, referred to as a "partial," is a wall that represents another room (or is glimpsed briefly when a door opens). It is illuminated either with equal intensity, or at 1 stop less than the light on the set walls for daylight, and 2 or 3 stops lower in intensity for night scenes.

In night scenes, a diagonal slash of illumination on a partial wall will indicate the presence and depth of a wall beyond a door and adds even more depth to the set. The slash indicates that the space is more than just a black hole.

17.2h Miscellaneous Light

Miscellaneous units used on a set are called by the name of the function they serve, such as:

- *Clothes light.* To add highlight for texture, color.
- *Torch light.* Provides a circle of "hot spot" for burning log or stick.
- *Sign light.* Provides brighter illumination on lettered area, giving emphasis to separating letters from surrounding area.
- *Water-effect light.* Creates reflection on water. etc. etc.

Conclusion

There are an infinite number of ways to light a scene. Given the assignment to photograph a flounder on a blue platter, one thousand photographers would come up with, no doubt, one thousand similar pictures, and most would be acceptable — a few would be outstanding. The difference would be the individual's creativity. That is why there are no "lighting diagrams" in this book.

With the exception of traditional portraiture, where "balanced" lighting is the formula (key light, fill light, back light), there is no "right way" to light a scene. One must start with an innate sensitivity, a solid knowledge of the parameters of a film or tape stock, the potential of the equipment available, and a thorough understanding of the demands of the story. Then, and only then, can a Director of Photography or Lighting Director know whether to use one fixture, 20 fixtures, or 100 fixtures to illuminate, illustrate and delineate the story and point of the performance.

The objective, in the final analysis, is that the project evoke the response from its audience that is sought by the writer, director, actor, and director of photography or lighting director.

To light well one must study light: the way it depicts changes on faces, in daylight, and at night; the flatness of rainy days; the sparkle of a sunny morning; the hue of an autumn sky at dusk. The look of all things must be memorized so that in the artificial environment of a studio stage the representation of the real thing can be reproduced on demand — and, ideally, the techniques employed will be undetectable to the viewer. For all the inherent artistic leanings — or talent — one might possess, reproducing "the real thing" requires the skillful application of the tools of the art to accomplish that ideal.

Skill is learned through practice and experiment and "putting one's self on the line." From those efforts emerges the filmic or video artist.

You can be that artist.

Glossary

adaptor A short length of cable with one type of plug and a different type receptacle

admedium Half way between a medium and a mogul screw base

ampacity Amperage capacity

anode A negative electrode

arc A brilliant light formed when a break is made in an electric circuit

automatic circuit breaker (ACB) A thermal sensitive unit that extinguishes an overheated lamp

baby A fixture containing either a 500-, 750-, or 1000-watt lamp

background light Any fixture used to illuminate walls, flats, scenery

backing A scenery flat placed outside a door or window

back light Illumination that separates an actor or object from the background

ballast A combination transformer/choke coil that increases the initial current to the electrodes to create an arc and then regulates the current so that it does not burn out the lamp

barndoor A bracket with hinged, opaque panels (usually two, but sometimes four) that are used to screen light from an area on a set or from the camera lens

bayonet base A lamp base with two prongs (called bayonets) on the rim

bispost base A lamp base with two long metal contacts

blackening "Boiloff" of the tungsten from the filament that adheres to the inside of a tungsten-standard bulb

blade A small narrow flag that may either be opaque, net, or of diffuse material

blister A swelling of a small part of a bulb

"booster" A filter that raises the color temperature of a light source

broad An open-face fixture that utilizes the soft illumination of its lamp, as opposed to indirect illumination (see softlite) on a subject

Brute A 225-amp carbon arc fixture

butterfly A large scrim measuring not less than 4 × 4 feet (1.22 × 1.22 meters)

c Symbol for coiled filament

cc Symbol for coiled-coil filament

cathode A positive electrode

choke coil A device that creates an impedance and regulates the current if the current exceeds or drops below a given rate of flow

coil A straight piece of filament wire that has been wound around a round bar

coiled coil A coiled wire coiled once more to allow greater incandescence in a small space

collector A screen or grid that attracts tungsten "boiloff" and prevents it from adhering to the interior lamp wall

colorblind Incapable of distinguishing differences in color other than in gradations of gray

color deficient Incapable of distinguishing one or several colors, but sees all other colors

color-enhancement filter Any filter that is used on a light source to impart a particular hue to a given area

color temperature The temperature at which a black body emits energy whose color visually compares to a given source (such as lamp, sun, etc.)

combination A large scrim that measures a minimum of 10 × 10 feet (3.05 × 3.05 meters) and is suspended between two gobo stands

combination filter Any color filter combined with a neutral density filter

compact filament A filament staggered in such a manner as to distribute its glow to all the inside surfaces of the bulb

compact fixture A small fixture that folds up for storage

connector A fitting that joins wires without splicing (see *plug; receptacle*)

continuous spectrum A spectrum containing *all* wavelengths

controller The general reference to an opaque or near-opaque unit that intercepts a ray of light (see *fixture controller; floor controller*)

conversion filter A filter that retards certain wavelengths and permits others to pass through; a filter that changes the spectral balance of a source light

"cookie" A cukaloris

crosslight Two side lights placed at 90 degrees to the axis of the camera

cukaloris A unit made of fine-mesh hardware cloth and perforated with irregular holes to create a mottled shadow effect on a flat surface; sometimes made of plywood and perforated

current Electron flow

cutter A long narrow flag

cyc or cyclorama A curved cloth or wall that covers the back of a soundstage; large painted scenery on a stage used as a backdrop

cyc strip A type of fixture similar to a broad used to illuminate cycloramas

day-for-nite The simulation of night that is achieved during the daylight hours

daylight-to-3200K A term referring to the conversion, by filtering, of daylight (5600 + K) to a color temperature compatible to film balanced for light of 3200K

dichroic A glass coated with a thin film (measured in nanometers) that permits only selected wavelengths to pass through

diffuse A dull-finish surface that reflects soft light rays

diffusion Any material that reduces the light level and at the same time changes the character of the light

dinky A small fixture with a fresnel lens and lamp of 100 watts

discoloration Change of hue or appearance

distribution box A central unit where one source of electricity is dispersed to many other units

dot A circular flag 3 inches (76.2 millimeters) or less that may be of opaque, net, or diffuse material

double-pole switch An electrical switch having two blades with two contacts for opening or closing both sides of a circuit simultaneously

douser A unit on a follow spot that produces immediate blackout of the projected beam

effect filter A general term applied to any filter that is used to create a simulated impression, such as fire, moonlight, day-for-nite, etc.

efficiency The ratio of the amount of light emitted based on the amount of power expended to create the light

emulsion A general reference to unexposed film; silver halides and dyes mixed in gelatine

electrode A conductor used to establish electrical contact with a nonmetallic portion of a circuit, such as gas or air

electron An elementary particle of an atom

ellipsoidal A mirror with two focal points; a type of fixture fitted with such a mirror

extension cable A length of cable used to extend power from a secondary feeder to a fixture or small distribution box

eye-light A fixture of very low intensity intended only to impart a "sparkle" in the pupil of the eye

feeder cable Heavy-gauged wire that brings electricity from the power source to the distribution boxes

ferrule A male shaft on a lamp base that fits into a receptacle of the same conformation in a fixture

filament Tungsten wire that glows intensely when heated

fill light Illumination that dilutes the shadow caused by the key light

five-hundred A fixture with a 500-watt light source

five-K A fixture with a 5000-watt light source (see *Senior*)

fixture A complete lighting unit including its housing, lens, reflector light source, and accessories

fixture controller Any controller (barndoor, scrim, gooseneck, etc.) that is placed *on* a fixture and used to intercept its light rays

flag A wire frame covered with a black duvateen material

flat blade A connector with two flat prongs and a U-shaped ground on the plug and similar-shaped shafts on the receptacle

FLB filter A camera lens filter used under fluorescent lamps to correct the wavelength emissions and bring them closer to the phosphor (continuous) spectrum; used with film balanced for light of 3200K to 3400K

FLD filter Same as an FLB filter but used with film balanced for daylight (5600K +)

flood The largest, most diffuse beam obtainable in a focusable lighting unit; any lamp that produces a broad beam

floor controller Any controller (flag, net, diffusion) that is placed in a gobo stand on the stage floor and used to intercept light rays

follow spot A large fixture that projects strong light rays and can be swiveled and tilted on its base so as to follow a performer

fluoresence Light caused by radiation of a phosphor coating

fluorescent filter Any one of a family of filters used to convert light to a continuous spectrum

footcandle A measurement of incident light falling on a subject at a specific point; 10.8 lux

frame Plywood with cutout designs that throw patterns across the set (large windows, prison bars, etc.)

framing shutters Opaque panels inside an ellipsoidal fixture that intercept the light beam and produce a hard-line cutoff to a circular pattern

fresnel lens A plano-convex lens with the convex surface "flattened" into concentric rings that collect and direct scattered light into parallel rays

gelatine A thin sheet of collagen that has been dyed

glass filter Optical flat glass that is either impregnated or coated with a filter dye; a gelatine filter that is sandwiched between two pieces of optical flat glass

gobo Any opaque unit used to eliminate light from a particular area; a "go-between"

gooseneck   A flexible shaft with a clamp at one end for securing to a post, fixture stand, yoke; the other end contains a small thumbscrew in which to tighten down small flags, scrims, dots, targets, etc.

grid   A network of uniformly spaced horizontal and perpendicular pipes in a video studio from which fixtures are hung; an integral unit of a studio arc that reduces input current of 120 volts to 73 volts across the electrode gap

H   Lighting manufacturers' code for mercury

Hertz   A unit of frequency: one Hertz (Hz) per second is the same as one cycle per second (the latter term is now obsolete)

HID   High-Intensity Discharge; a type of lamp

high-key   A mode of illumination where detail is seen in all the shadows; a low contrast scene

HMI   A mercury, metal-halide, iodide lamp with a multiline spectrum

housing   The metal portion of a fixture that covers the light source, socket, and reflector

hybrid spectrum   A continuous spectrum dominated by a line spectrum

hydragryrum   the Greek word for mercury

I   Lighting manufacturers code for iodides; also the symbol for intensity

incandescence   The glowing of a body due to its higher temperature; a reference to the glow from a filament lamp

indirect   Light that is reflected from a surface before it falls on a subject

infrared   Long wavelengths invisible to the eye

inkie   A 100-watt fixture with a fresnel lens

insulation   A nonconducting material (rubber, neoprene) used to cover current-carrying wire

intensity   The light-giving power of a source

interference filter   A filter that disrupts wavelengths, causing them to cancel out

jacket   Rubber or neoprene covering on a cable; an additional glass covering that either protects the lamp from the weather or halts the lamp's ultraviolet rays

"juice"   Electricity

"junior"   A 2000-watt fixture with a fresnel lens

K   Electricity: the math symbol for 1000; Color Temperature: the symbol for Kelvin, a scale that compares the visible aspects of a light source to a heated body

Kelvin   Relating to a thermometric scale where absolute zero in degrees Kelvin equals $-273°$ Celsius

key light   The major source of illumination

kicker light   A type of back light that is used to apply a rim light to an actor's face

lampholder   A unit that accepts the base of a fluorescent lamp

leaker   A lamp in which the seal has been broken and air has entered

light center length (LCL)   The distance from the filament *center* to a certain reference point on the lamp base (the reference point varies depending on the type of lamp)

lighting ratio   The relationship of key light plus fill light to the fill light alone

light source   An emitter of light (sun, sky, lamp, arc, etc.)

linear filament   A filament that extends the length of the bulb

line spectrum   A spectrum divided sharply into defined wavelengths

low-key   A manner of illumination in which detail in the shadows is subdued or obscured completely; also high-contrast lighting predominated by shadows

lumen   An amount of light energy within an area

lumens per watt   The ratio of light output to the amount of electrical input

luminous flux   The transfer of energy in the visible wavelength range

lux   The metric measurement relating to incident light that falls on a subject (10.8 lux = 1 footcandle)

M   Lighting manufacturers' code for *metal hallide;* also symbol for *medium arc*

MacBeth   A deep blue glass filter that converts tungsten light to a color temperature compatible to daylight

maximum overall length (MOL)   The distance from the top of the bulb to the bottom of the pins, buttons, ferrules, posts, etc.; from tip to tip

mickey   A 1000-watt open-face fixture

midget   A 200-watt fixture with fresnel lens

mighty   A 2000-watt open-face fixture

mini   A 2000-watt fixture with fresnel lens, smaller than a midget

miscellaneous light   Any fixture used to illuminate a special item

mixed   A surface that reflects specular *and* diffuse rays

modifier   The general reference to a unit that has an effect on the intensity or character of a light ray

module   A fixture with a single lamp and its own switch that is clustered with other units of the same type and is worked singly or as part of a group

mogul base   A lamp base larger than standard residential size

monochromatic   Seeing in gradations of one particular color only

nanometer   One-billionth of a meter (10^{-9})

net   A cloth material with a hexagonal weave

neutral density   A filter that inhibits light transmission without affecting color

nite-for-nite   The shooting of film or the videocasting of exterior night scenes in the nighttime hours

one-and-a-half K   A 1500-watt open-face fixture

one-fifty   A 150-amp carbon arc

one-K   A 1000-watt fixture, either open-face or with fresnel lens

oxidization   An electrochemical "welding" of two different metals

"paper amps"   An amperage rating given in rounded numbers higher than actual amperage

parabolic   A mirror shaped like a parabola that directs a beam in parallel rays

phosphor   A material that glows when activated (as when struck by electrons)

pin connector   A connector that is fitted with slender rods of copper on the plug and slender matching shafts on the receptacle

pitting   The forming of tiny holes on the surface of a base or socket

planar filament   A group of filaments arranged in such a manner that they are in one plane (lined up evenly)

plano-convex   A lens with one flat surface (plano) and one spherical surface (convex)

plastic filter   An acetate, polyester, vinyl, or Mylar impregnated with a color

plug   The male end of a connector

power   The rate at which electrons move through a wire

prefocus base   A lamp base that fits only one way into a socket so the filament is in correct relationship to the reflector

prime   An open-face fixture whose basic use is a key, kicker, or back light

receptacle   The female end of a connector

reflectance factor   The ratio of light reflected by a surface to the amount of light falling on it

"rifle"   A reflector board with a mirrored surface that has an intense beam

rim light   A type of back light that outlines an actor from head to toe

S   Lighting manufacturers' code for *sodium vapor;* also symbol for *straight filament*

SB   Self-ballasted

scattered   A surface that is crinkled, stippled, or creased and reflects light in all directions

scoop A bowl- or bell-shaped, open-face housing that utilizes the soft illumination of its lamp (as opposed to indirect) on a subject

screw base A lamp base spiral-grooved to fit a matching spiral-grooved socket

scrim A mesh material of metal that reduces the level of light

secondary feeder A length of cable that clamps to a distribution box and terminates with a number of fused receptacles

SED graph A spectral energy distribution diagram that illustrates how light is divided into its many wavelengths

senior A 5000-watt fixture, either with fresnel lens or open face

seven-fifty A 750-watt fixture, either with fresnel lens or open face

"shower curtain" A vinyl material hung in front of a fixture to diffuse the light

shutter A moveable cover or screen that can shut out either all the light of a fixture of a portion of it

side light Any light that illuminates a subject at 90 degrees from the axis of the camera, either left or right

signal-to-noise ratio The fixed or approximate relation of the image transmitted through a piece of video equipment to an unwanted interference generated within the equipment itself

silk Any material that has a bright translucence to it and is used as a diffuser

single-pole switch An electrical switch having only one blade and one contact for opening or closing one side of a circuit

six-fifty A 650-watt open-face fixture

skypan A circular unit with a bare bulb at its center used to illuminate backings

slip rings Continuous circles of metal from which the brushes on a motor take or deliver current

snoot A bracket with a solid face except for an opening (sizes vary) that has a long tube that forms a circle of light when placed on the front of a fixture

socket A device that receives and grips the base of a lamp

softlite Any fixture that utilizes the principle of indirect illumination

solid A large opaque flag used on a butterfly frame

spectral energy distribution The relationship of wavelengths to each other

spectroradiometer An instrument capable of separating and measuring light waves

specular Mirror-like surface that reflects hard rays

spherical A mirror that directs a beam in all directions

spike A singular wavelength that stands alone or predominates a continuous-spectrum curve

splicer A single piece of cable that has one plug at one end and two (called a Y) or three (called a W) receptacles at the other end.

spot The smallest, most intense beam obtainable in a focusable fixture; also any lamp that produces a very narrow, intense beam

spud A short metal projection at the center of a fixture's yoke that fits into a recess on a light stand, or into a pipe clamp

step lens A plano-convex lens similar to a fresnel lens but with the concentric rings cut into the plano side

studio arc A fixture with carbon electrodes that does not contain a mirror or aperture; it relies only on the electrode flame for intensity

switch A device for making or breaking a contact in an electrical circuit

target A circular flag 3 inches (76.2 millimeters) or larger that may be of opaque, net, or diffuse material and used to intercept light rays

target area Also called image plate; the area in a video camera where light rays are focused and registered

teenie A 650-watt open-face fixture

ten-K A 10,000-watt fixture with fresnel lens

Titan A 350-amp carbon arc

transformer A device that increases or decreases the flow of current

transverse wave A wave in which the electric field moves perpendicular to the line of light travel

tungsten-halogen An incandescent lamp containing a regenerative element

tungsten-to-daylight A term referring to the conversion by filtering of tungsten light to a color temperature compatible to daylight

twistlock A connector that is engaged by a turning motion so it cannot be pulled loose and is disengaged by an opposite motion

two-K A 2000-watt fixture with a fresnel lens, or open-face

ultraviolet Short wavelengths invisible to the eye

video A reference to visual electronics

voltage Electromotive force

watts A measurement of power

Index